CRIME AND JUSTICE
IN THE YEAR 2010

CONTEMPORARY ISSUES IN CRIME AND JUSTICE SERIES
Roy Roberg, Consulting Editor

The Myth of a Racist Criminal Justice System (1987)
William Wilbanks, Florida International University

Gambling Without Guilt: The Legimation of an American Pastime (1988)
John Rosecrance, University of Nevada at Reno

Death Work: A Study of the Modern Execution Process (1990)
Robert Johnson, The American University

Lawlessness and Reform: The FBI in Transition (1990)
Tony G. Poveda, State University of New York at Plattsburgh

Women, Prison, and Crime (1990)
Jocelyn M. Pollock-Byrne, University of Houston—Downtown

Perspectives on Terrorism (1991)
Harold J. Vetter, Portland State University
Gary R. Perlstein, Portland State University

Serial Murderers and Their Victims (1991)
Eric W. Hickey, California State University, Fresno

Girls, Delinquency, and the Juvenile Justice System (1992)
Meda Chesney-Lind, University of Hawaii, Manoa
Randall G. Sheldon, University of Nevada at Las Vegas

Juries and Politics (1992)
James P. Levine, Brooklyn College

Media, Crime, and Criminal Justice: Images and Realities (1992)
Ray Surrette, Florida International University

Street Kids, Street Drugs, Street Crime: An Examination of Drug Use and Serious Delinquency in Miami (1993)
James A. Inciardi, University of Delaware
Ruth Horowitz, University of Delaware
Anne E. Pottieger, University of Delaware

Ethics in Crime and Justice: Dilemmas and Decisions, Second Edition (1994)
Jocelyn M. Pollock, Southwest Texas State University

It's About Time: America's Imprisonment Binge (1994)
John Irwin, Professor Emeritus, San Francisco State University
James Austin, National Council on Crime and Delinquency

Sense and Nonsense About Crime and Drugs: A Policy Guide, Third Edition (1994)
Samuel Walker, University of Nebraska at Omaha

Crime Victims: An Introduction to Victimology, Third Edition (1995)
Andrew Karmen, John Jay College of Criminal Justice

Hard Time: Understanding and Reforming the Prison, Second Edition (1995)
Robert Johnson, The American University

Morality in Criminal Justice: An Introduction to Ethics (1995)
Daryl Close, Tiffin University
Nicholas Meier, Kalamazoo Valley Community College

Renegade Kids: Suburban Outlaws (1995)
Wayne S. Wooden, California State Polytechnic University, Pomona

A World of Violence: Corrections in America (1995)
Matthew Silberman, Bucknell University

Crime and Justice in the Year 2010 (1995)
John Klofas, Rochester Institute of Technology
Stan Stojkovic, University of Wisconsin—Milwaukee

☆

Crime and Justice in the Year 2010

Edited by

JOHN KLOFAS
Rochester Institute of Technology

STAN STOJKOVIC
University of Wisconsin—Milwaukee

I(T)P™   Wadsworth Publishing Company
An International Thomson Publishing Company

Belmont • Albany • Bonn • Boston • Cincinnati • Detroit • London • Madrid • Melbourne
Mexico City • New York • Paris • San Francisco • Singapore • Tokyo • Toronto • Washington

Assistant Editor: Jason Moore
Editorial Assistant: Jessica Monday
Designer: Andrew H. Ogus
Print Buyer: Barbara Britton
Permission Editor: Jeanne Bosschart
Copy Editor: Gail Elber
Illustration, Production, & Composition: Summerlight Creative
Cover: William Reuter
Printer: Malloy Lithographing, Inc.

Printed in the United States of America
1 2 3 4 5 6 7 8 9 10—99 98 97 96 95

For more information, contact Wadsworth Publishing Company:

Wadsworth Publishing Company
10 Davis Drive
Belmont, California 94002, USA

International Thomson Editores
Campos Eliseos 385, Piso 7
Col. Polanco
11560 México D.F. México

International Thomson Publishing Europe
Berkshire House 168-173
High Holborn
London, WC1V 7AA, England

International Thomson Publishing GmbH
Königswinterer Strasse 418
53227 Bonn, Germany

Thomas Nelson Australia
102 Dodds Street,
South Melbourne 3205
Victoria, Australia

International Thomson Publishing Asia
221 Henderson Road
#05-10 Henderson Building
Singapore 0315

Nelson Canada
1120 Birchmount Road
Scarborough, Ontario
Canada M1K 5G4

International Thomson Publishing Japan
Hirakawacho Kyowa Building, 3F
2-2-1 Hirakawacho
Chiyoda-ku, Tokyo 102, Japan

Library of Congress Cataloging-in-Publication Data
Crime and justice in the year 2010 / edited by John Klofas and Stan
    Stojkovic
        p.   cm.
    Includes bibliographical references and index.
    ISBN 0-534-17502-3 (acid-free paper)
        1. Criminal justice, Administration of--United States.
    I. Klofas, John.   II. Stojkovic, Stan.
HV9950.C72   1995
364.973'01--dc20   94-25019

This book is printed on acid-free recycled paper.

Dedication

To Walter Byron (Casey) Groves,
whose spirit and intellect
energized this field
during his far too brief career.

Contents

Preface   *xiii*

PART I   **THE NATURE OF CRIME AND**   **1**
              JUSTICE IN THE YEAR 2010

    1   *Criminal Justice in the Twenty-First*   *4*
              Century: The Role of Futures Research
              GEORGE F. COLE

              In this article, the author examines the future of
              crime and justice and describes the relevance of
              various methodologies in studying the future.

    2   *Criminal Justice in 2010:*   *18*
              The Past as Prologue
              JOHN A. CONLEY

              This article examines the effects of the past on
              both the present and the future. In addition, the
              author explores the relevance of examining the
              future by understanding the past.

    3   *Explaining Crime in the Year 2010*   *36*
              L. EDWARD WELLS

              The author of this article suggests that any
              comprehensive perspective on the future of
              crime must explore theoretical explanations and
              examine the various criminological models and
              their contributions to understanding crime in
              the future.

4   *The Law of the Future*   *62*

JAMES R. ACKER

In this article, the author argues that the courts
directly influenced the law during the 1980s and
that concerns for due-process protections have
been overshadowed by a crime-control ideology.

5   *The Nature of Common Crime in*   *86*
     the Year 2010

CHESTER L. BRITT, III

The author explores the nature of common
crime in the future and shows the possible
effects of the crime-prone age group's changing
size. He also proposes that crime will not be
much different from that of the late 1980s.

PART II   **CRIMINAL JUSTICE SYSTEM**   **103**
          RESPONSE IN THE YEAR 2010

6   *The Community-Policing Movement of the*   *107*
     Twenty-First Century: What We Learned

JOHN CRANK

The author examines the importance of the
community-policing movement within police
circles and speculates on the future of policing
within the context of what police have always
done and the viability of the community-
policing philosophy.

7   *The Future of Criminal Court: Due*   *127*
     Process, Crime Control, Optimism,
     and Pessimism

CANDACE McCOY

In this article, the author makes both optimistic
and pessimistic predictions for the future of
criminal courts. She suggests that many factors
will direct courts of the future, and an important
consideration will be the role of ideological
variables on their future functioning.

8   *The Trials of Tamika Watson: The Future of*   *146*
     Criminal Sentencing
     LYNNE GOODSTEIN and JOHN R. HEPBURN

     In this article, the authors explore the future of
     criminal sentencing through the eyes a fictitious
     judge. They examine the influence of changing
     social expectations on criminal sentencing and
     how new alternatives to prosecution will alter
     sentencing procedures.

9   *Grim Tales of the Future: American Jails in*   *166*
     the Year 2010
     DAVID KALINICH and PAUL EMBERT

     The authors of this article show the importance
     of economic, political, and social factors on local
     jails. They describe the jail system of the future
     as bifurcated, with wealthier communities
     providing their own jail services and poorer
     inner cities rely on diminishing finances to
     operate their jail facilities.

10   *The "Pen" and the Pendulum: Finding*   *185*
     Our Way to the Future of Incarceration
     LUCIEN X. LOMBARDO

     In this article, the author examines the many
     contexts that shape the correctional landscape
     and suggests the importance of consciously and
     deliberately creating the imprisonment of the
     future. He also offers several approaches for
     viewing the future of imprisonment.

11   *Ophelia the CCW: May 11, 2010*   *205*
     TODD R. CLEAR

     The author of this article explores the changing
     nature of probation and parole and uses a
     scenario approach to describe the future and
     how technology will direct affect the delivery of
     probation and parole services.

PART III   OTHER CRIME AND JUSTICE   **225**
               ISSUES IN THE YEAR 2010

     12   *Drugs and Crime: What If . . .*   **228**
            RALPH A. WEISHEIT

            In this article, the author offers two scenarios of
            the future: with and without drugs legalized. He
            also discusses the many social, economic, and
            technological factors that affect the drug context
            and their relationship to crime.

     13   *The Penalty of Death in the Next Century*   **251**
            GENNARO F. VITO

            The author of this article shows the many
            factors related to the death penalty and reviews
            relevant case law. He also argues that the death
            penalty will be used in the next century despite
            uncertainty about its deterrent effects.

     14   *Juvenile Justice in the Next Millennium*   **267**
            CARL E. POPE

            In this article, the author surveys the relevant
            aspects of juvenile justice's future and suggests
            that the system will be both similar and
            dissimilar to the existing system, with a greater
            proportion of minority youths represented. He
            also ties this overrepresentation of minorities to
            larger social and economic factors.

PART IV   **CRIMINAL JUSTICE IN 2010:**   **279**
             A FINAL LOOK

    15   *Preparing for the Year 2010*   *281*
            STAN STOJKOVIC and JOHN KLOFAS

            In this concluding article, the editors review the
            volume's important and recurrent themes and
            highlight the significance of learning from the
            past in preparing for the future of the criminal
            justice system. They also discuss the skills that
            will be needed by those working in the system
            of the future.

            About the Contributors   *297*

Preface

For decades the symbol of the future has been the coming of the new millennium: the arrival of the twenty-first century. Whether the field is medicine, space exploration, or criminal justice, that turn of the calendar has held a unique fascination. Now, as we approach the end of the century, a new reality is forming from that fascination. Still distant enough to pique our curiosity but close enough that our expectations and analyses can be guided by reality, life in the next millennium can be the focus of productive and practical inquiry.

Such inquiry can be useful to academics, planners, students, and others for whom the future of crime and justice is no abstraction but an important stage in their careers and in their contributions. Past the year 2000, today's students will be tomorrow's experts and have the education and experience to carry them into positions of leadership. Education today not only can describe crime and justice as they are, but also help to prepare students by prompting them to consider what their futures might be like.

This book began as the product of a discussion at a recent meeting of the American Society of Criminology. Interest was focused on the importance of providing a framework for understanding the future of crime and justice. Included in those discussions was the need for examining the education and skills that today's students require to be effective scholars and professionals over the course of their careers. Such interests guided the timeframe considered in this book. By focusing on the relatively near-term future—the year 2010—reasonable and realistic perspectives on the future could be generated. Those perspectives and the thinking and discussions they foster can help us plan for the future and understand the present.

This book is a collection of original essays in which accomplished scholars and researchers in the field of criminal justice describe their vision of the future in the areas of their expertise. The authors presented here are among the most accomplished scholars working in their fields. They are not, however, scholars whose work is associated with any specialized theory or perspective. They were drawn together because of their broad-based knowledge of their areas rather than their advocacy of particular perspectives. That knowledge, firmly grounded in the present and the past, has guided their efforts to look into the future. Most of these authors do not consider themselves futurists, that is, specialists in speculating about the future. Instead, their efforts here are best appreciated as attempts to extend today's knowledge base modestly forward for a decade and a half and perhaps to influence those who are willing to make more daring leaps.

No matter how qualified experts may be, the risk remains that their musings about the future may, at best, ignore significant issues or, at worst, be little more than fantasies. Careful selection of the authors and attention to detail can help avoid such problems, but additional safeguards also have been included. In preparing this book, the authors engaged in a modified form of Delphi analysis (see Chapter 1 for an extended discussion of this method). They began their efforts with general instructions on the intent and direction of the book. We expected that each essay would take one or the other of two forms. They would either describe the author's expectations (for example, what policing may be like in 2010) or describe an alternative future that would depend on policy decisions (for example, what crime may be like if we do or do not legalize drugs). The intent of this first round was to provide enough direction to help set the course without limiting the expert's approach. With drafts completed and shared among authors, the group members met for a lively discussion and defense of their works. The issues that were debated ranged from the extent to which the near future was best viewed as a direct extension of the present or as likely to molded by other influences to the authors' moral responsibilities for helping to shape the future.

After opportunities to rethink their work in light of that discussion, the authors also received comment from other scholars in the field. All of the chapters were reviewed in a series of presentations at the Annual Meeting of the Academy of Criminal Justice Sciences. Again, some of the authors chose to make significant revisions based on those discussions. In their current form, then, the chapters in this book represent the best efforts of respected scholars, critiqued and revised, first through comments within the group of experts and then by others in their field.

The completed chapters attempt to synthesize and extend in time information on the workings of the criminal justice system, the nature of law, explanations of criminal behavior, and other issues that are central to the question of social order early in the next century. They should not, however, be viewed merely as predictions or prognostications. The authors' roles have been to promote thought and discussion, not simply to defend some vision of the future. Their quest is not so much for accuracy as it is to stimulate. Students will be asked to question the purposes of the criminal justice system and how it functions within a larger political, social, and economic context. They will be forced to grapple with the philosophical questions concerning what constitutes a "just" system of criminal justice and how it might look in the future.

The student also will be asked to address pragmatic issues of criminal justice management. Many of the chapters highlight the importance of taking an active posture in regard to the functioning of the criminal justice system. Instead of being passive actors within the criminal justice system, students will be forced to examine what roles they play in the criminal justice system's construction.

As a coursebook, this volume may be used in conjunction with more descriptive texts in first or second classes in criminal justice, or it may be used in more specialized classes dealing with the future of the field. It is, we think, not material that should be left only to upper-division students to consider. As an accompaniment to an introductory criminal justice text, this book will complement the emphasis on descriptive material. The idea is that students can be immersed in detail on case law or policing and then personalize the material by ending with a discussion of where those issues may be as they mature in their own careers. Combining study of the present with discussions of the future can improve thinking about both periods. With the coming of the new millennium and with the sense of expectation that implies, now is the perfect time to use the future to contribute to education in the present.

This effort to stimulate thinking about the future in criminal justice begins by focusing on the discipline needed to undertake the task. The tools and methods of thinking about the future are discussed, as is the significance of understanding the past. The body of the text is composed of the authors' efforts to describe the future in specific areas ranging from the nature and distribution of crime to the death penalty and the war on drugs. The approaches differ. Some authors chose to develop scenarios, while other relied on more formal reviews of literature and analysis of trends. The authors also differ in the degree of optimism with which they face the future. The variety should help to stimulate thinking and raise questions about the reader's own outlook. The last chapter attempts to identify the major themes that emerge from the collected efforts of the experts and to suggest both the values and the skills that can aid students in creating their own futures in this field. Finally, the authors also hoped to make their writing accessible to students and to those readers who have not specialized in criminal justice. Although their arguments are of high quality and well substantiated, they knew that fellow academics were not their ultimate audience. To assist readers, they have avoided detailed references and opted instead for listing additional works that interested readers are encouraged to examine.

The production of this book was made possible through the efforts of many dedicated people. To begin, we would like to acknowledge the efforts of Ms. Cynthia Stormer. The initial inspiration for the book grew out of discussions with her. With Cindy's support we were able to start and finish this project. In addition, we would like to extend our appreciation to Ms. Cat Collins and Ms. Peggy Adams for their commitment to the book in both its initial and later stages. To the authors who agreed to complete the chapters in a timely fashion, we extend our gratitude and appreciation for putting up with the long delay between their initial drafts of their chapters and the final production of the book. Thanks, too, to Roland Dart, California State University at Sacramento; Nella Lee, Washington State University; Dennis Hoffman, University of Nebraska; and Tom Winfree, New Mexico State University, who reviewed the manuscript and made helpful suggestions. Finally, we would like to thank our students, who inspired us to think about the future in an imaginative and creative way. This book is for them. Without the ever-critical eye of the student, the ideas for this book would have never had the opportunity to be heard. We hope this book meets with their approval.

John Klofas
Stan Stojkovic
Rochester, New York

☆

PART I

The Nature of Crime and Justice in the Year 2010

What will crime be like in the future? How will we understand and explain it, and how will we respond to it? These are important questions if we are to begin to plan and prepare for the future in criminal justice. In this section, five authors provide the tools necessary to help us take such a look. In Chapter 1, George F. Cole examines the importance of using systematic methods to explore the future. In Chapter 2, John A. Conley uses a hearing into a fictional incident to discuss the importance of considering how historical developments will affect the future. L. Edward Wells focuses our attention in Chapter 3 on the need to consider theoretical explanations of the origins of crime. James R. Acker, in Chapter 4, examines the forces of ideological change and stability on the criminal justice process in general and the courts in particular. Finally, in Chapter 5, Chester L. Britt calls our attention to the data on crime and the importance of carrying statistical trends from the past into the future.

Uncertainty about the future both fascinates and frightens us. Until recently, exploring this uncertainty has been the exclusive province of mystics and soothsayers. But skepticism about fortune-tellers does not

mean that we are left helpless pawns of unforeseeable events. George
Cole makes the case for planning through disciplined thinking about
the future. Although all uncertainty cannot be removed, he argues that
we can still plan and prepare for the future by systematically examining
a range of possibilities using established methodologies. The very idea
of "futures research" may strike the reader as odd. That there may be
scientific methodologies to explore events that have not yet occurred
would seem inconsistent with the notion of science as analyzing established facts. But science is disciplined, and organized thinking and the
methods of science can contribute greatly to thinking about the future.
The data to guide forecasting can be found through examining experts
and literature to identify converging expectations of the future or
through constructing and assessing possible scenarios—that is, chro-
nologies of changes that take us out of the present and into the future.
Cole also offers suggestions on the influences that should be considered
in constructing possible futures in the field of criminal justice.

One source of information that can help us understand the future is
the past. That is a point illustrated in Conley's fictionalized hearing after
a fatal shooting incident in an undercover drug operation. In this
example of the importance of historical developments, the origins of
the incident are found in changing patterns of urban development and
the accompanying trend toward privatization. In the examination of the
incident or even some of the testimony, these root causes may seem a
distant influence. But, as Conley points out, the impact of history will
be revealed in seemingly disconnected events.

Historical influences also extend beyond the events themselves. The
very way we think about crime is a product of developments in the
history of ideas. Ed Wells traces the growth of criminological theories
to the development of major intellectual traditions. Enlightenment
philosophers brought with them rational views of crime. The growth of
the natural sciences was reflected in biological explanations of deviance.
Today, skepticism about empirical explanations and political conservatism have influenced explanations of crime. We thus look again toward
individualistic explanations that emphasize deliberate conduct. Wells
calls our attention to the way in which theoretical explanations change
over time. Evolutionary atavism and skull shape are currently out of
vogue, but the same fundamental processes that attracted Lombroso to
them in the late 1800s will continue to shape criminology. Explanations

of crime and thus our response to crime will reflect changes in technology, research, intellectual developments, and ideology. Wells shows how these and other factors may influence crime explanations in the future.

If you find yourself falling into the view that everything is changing in the world of crime and justice, Chapter 4 should give you reason to reconsider. James Acker provides a different view of change and stability. He presents the law as a generally conservative institution in which change may be thought of as a shifting equilibrium of competing forces. The struggle is between the interests of protecting citizens from crime and the need to preserve individual liberties. Although previous chapters may have focused on forces driving change, Acker highlights the forces that restrain it. Constitutional restrictions, precedent, and judicial temperament have all been stabilizing forces. At the same time, Acker looks at ongoing change. Restrictions on access to the courts and a weakening support for precedent suggest a continuing movement back toward concern with public protection. What emerges is a legal system that now emphasizes a crime-control ideology while it continually changes and seeks a balance of fundamental interests.

The chapters of this section have explored the factors that will influence the direction of change in criminal justice through the early part of the next century. Against this background of historical change and theoretical and ideological shifts, the statistical facts of crime also must be considered. In the final chapter of the section, Britt offers a foundation, or a context, in which to examine other changes. His is a statistical projection of crime from the present into the future, based on changes in the population of the United States. It is a reminder that, along with the ideological shifts and philosophical dilemmas that will continue to influence crime and justice, our predictions of the future also must take into account the empirical realities we cannot escape.

The goal of this section of reading is to highlight the tools needed to make sense of the future of crime and justice. They are the tools of the disciplined futurist: sound methodology, a sense of history and theory, an appreciation for the importance of ideology, and a knowledge of key factual data. Using these tools, we may not all arrive at the same expectations of the future, but they should help us to think clearly and systematically about the future and to evaluate the ideas of others. Keep these concepts in mind so that you can evaluate the visions of the future of the criminal justice that are described in the next section.

1

☆

Criminal Justice in the Twenty-First Century:

The Role of Futures Research

GEORGE F. COLE

University of Connecticut

How likely is it that the beginning of the twenty-first century will find the United States in a crime wave as dramatic as the one that so aroused the country during the late 1960s? Can we expect that drug use will continue to occupy the attention of the criminal justice system? Is it possible that crime and concern about it will taper off during the next decade so that resources can be reallocated to other pressing social problems, such as acid rain, homelessness, and poverty among children? What *will* be the crime and justice environment in the United States in the year 2010? This is an important question that requires serious thought by government officials, criminal justice researchers, planners, and concerned citizens. Students planning criminal justice careers should also be concerned about the future nature of the law enforcement, adjudication, and correctional systems within which they will be working during the early period of the twenty-first century.

Issues having to do with crime and justice impinge on all of our lives as citizens, taxpayers, practitioners, and potential victims. The new century will soon be here. Will we as a nation be ready to deal with the crime problem in the very different social environment that can be expected when the milestone is passed? How can lawmakers, police, courts, and corrections begin to plan for the eventualities that lie ahead?

It is essential that policy makers be given the best evidence as to prospects for future developments pertaining to the justice system and the broader socioeconomic and political context within which it will operate. Not all uncertainties about the future can be removed, but systematic and insightful exploration of the range of possibilities can provide a sounder basis for planning and a useful perspective on priorities for innovation. This is a task with which futures research can help.

DEVELOPMENT OF
THE FUTURES FIELD

Effectively discussing and planning for the future is a challenging enterprise that, in the least, must grapple with the complexities of numerous interrelated, uncertain, and potentially unprecedented developments. Systematic and sustained considerations of the prospects, issues, and opportunities associated with the future are invariably required to ensure adequate discussion and assessment.

For most of history, people generally left the depiction of coming events and conditions to fortune-tellers and science fiction writers. During the past several decades, however, futures research has emerged as a field whose concepts and methods are designed to help planners and policy makers better understand conditions that might prevail in the longer term.

A volume of essays by British biologist H. G. Wells published in 1901 is often cited as one of the earliest works of futures analysis. Most such research, however, began after World War II. The nation's first "think tank," the RAND Corporation, was created in 1944. Development of the Delphi technique in 1953 furthered the emerging field. In 1966 the founding of the World Future Society in Washington, D.C., helped to institutionalize the discipline. Publication of Alvin Toffler's *Future Shock* in 1970 brought the approach to the attention of the general public. Additional publications such as the magazine *The Futurist* have informed a small but growing public about the potential of futures research.

Futures research is now a well developed discipline that uses various methodologies and concepts to help policy makers better understand the conditions that might prevail over the long term. The field is an amalgam of individuals with professional interests in forecasting (e.g., technology, economics, demographics, social conditions), those involved in management-related activities (strategic planning, policy analysis, etc.), and other specialists with interests in ongoing developments in one or more realms of society—from political activists to utopians.

THINKING ABOUT THE FUTURE

A good deal of futures research is directed toward examining the long-range prospects for the external environment in which an organization operates. Expected trends, forces for change, and uncertain or emergent developments are all important aspects of this inquiry—whether in regard to social factors, new technology, economic conditions, legal considerations, the political setting, and so on. Information yielded by this process provides both a means of alerting planners and policy makers about alternative future possibilities and a basis for developing futures-responsive organizational strategies and plans.

How do futures researchers proceed with this endeavor? The methodologies employed by futurists emphasize systematic questioning and synthesis of information across a number of fields. Much of the field's research activity involves assembling well-informed insights about future prospects from projections of possible developments, based on expert inputs and a variety of supporting analyses.

Futures research is about forecasting the future. The field has come to recognize, however, that predicting the most likely set of future societal conditions can be quite challenging. The underlying dynamics of human systems are extraordinarily complex, with the processes of change—particularly over the long run—only imperfectly understood.

History shows that the path along which human systems progress does involve gradual, evolutionary development—for which present and emerging trends are often valuable markers for the future. But unprecedented events and conditions also play significant roles, often yielding "discontinuous" changes that interrupt and perhaps redirect the dominant trends in progress. The chronological history of any system or subsystem is partially written in terms of unprecedented events (the Great Depression, the end of the Soviet Union, the outbreak of AIDS)—indeed, they often are the essence of an era. Futures research needs to bring an appreciation of both of these dimensions of change to focus in its assessment.

A wide variety of theoretically and statistically based methods are available for forecasting—in demography, economics, technology, and the like. These tools often play valuable roles in the work of futures researchers. It is not possible, however, to rely entirely upon them in probing the future's possibilities. This is due partly to the limited understanding of social change that they (unavoidably) embody and partly to the uncertain relevance of their historical calculations to future unprecedented conditions.

Good analysis, well-based on what science understands about the behavior of human systems, is a key aspect of the futures inquiry process. But probing for discontinuities or fundamental changes in prevailing conditions and trends is also important. Disciplined *speculation* about events and conditions that might come to pass must play a role here.

Thus, several different kinds of thinking are needed for futures research. A broad overall approach has evolved from practical applications to guide this inquiry. Environmental scanning, scenario writing, and strategic assessment are the major elements. Each deserves further comment.

Environmental Scanning

Environmental scanning is a systematic effort to identify in an elemental way future developments (trends or events) that could plausibly occur over the time horizon of interest and whose occurrence could alter an organization's environment in important ways. Such developments could possibly come from a number of domains—economic conditions, demographic shifts, government policies, international developments, social attitudes, technological advances, resource availability, and so on.

In essence, the scanning process is concerned with answering questions such as, "What is going on out there?" and "What future conditions could emerge that would affect us?" Futures researchers are particularly interested in identifying those developments—whether of low or high likelihood—that are capable of producing the most significant changes in the character of the environment.

A number of approaches are useful in undertaking the scanning process. Two methods are most frequently applied: (1) systematically reviewing and synthesizing the professional literatures in disciplines relevant to the futures problem at hand and (2) gathering the opinions of panels of experts through techniques such as the Delphi process.

Published resources can be particularly helpful. An extensive amount of useful commentary on current trends and possible future developments in many domains exists in business publications, government reports, and the technical literatures of various professional disciplines. Targeted review and a focused synthesis of these materials can typically yield a great deal of insight on future prospects in specific areas of interest.

A considerable portion of this source material is already available in computer-retrievable format. With proper focusing and design of an appropriate search strategy, pertinent citations from a wide range of fields can be identified and accessed in a quite timely and expeditious way.

Original research in collecting the opinions and judgments of experts about future developments can also be an important element of the scanning activity. Various techniques—questionnaires, telephone conferences, and face-to-face group meeting—have been utilized to capture expert opinion and to encourage discussion and consensus. The Delphi process is a frequently used approach for this purpose.

Delphi takes its name from the ancient Greek oracle. It is a technique by which a panel of experts can be convened to examine and debate the likelihoods and probable impacts of a series of possible future developments. The process is designed to obtain the most reliable consensus of opinion among a group of experts through a series of intensive questionnaires interspersed with controlled opinion feedback. Unlike opinion polling in which respondents do not have an opportunity to change or modify their opinion, the Delphi technique encourages respondents to benefit from the views of fellow participants and to revise their own views so as to build a consensus.

As originally conceived, Delphi was conducted completely through a series of written questionnaires. Recent applications, however, have used facilitated task groups, supported by electronic voting and other computer software, to achieve the same goals. With proper leadership and creation of an atmosphere that lends itself to free and open discussion, a panel of experts can be particularly productive, and results can be achieved in a timely way. Through the give-and-take of the discussion, various points of view can be expressed, debated, and restated, and a consensus can be reached.

The "PC Voter," a personal computer-based tool that facilitates voting in task group settings, has been used effectively in the Delphi process. Handheld communications hardware provides each member of the panel with an individual channel by which to cast an anonymous vote weighted by a self-estimated level of confidence. All of the votes are rapidly collated by the computer, with the results subsequently presented on a video monitor for group discussion. Illustratively, each member of a panel might contribute his or her view on the prospects of increased computer crime by the year 2010. An electronic switch on each participant's handheld communications unit provides a way to register an opinion on a scale of zero to ten, for example, on the likelihood of computer crime greatly increasing by the year 2010. Each participant can also select a weighting value (running from zero to ten) on a second switch to record his or her degree of confidence in this opinion. The computer then displays the group's weighted opinion with the extent of agreement and disagreement graphically visible.

Based on this information, the task group facilitator can then expeditiously direct the next stage of the group's discussion—whether to further consider an item for which disagreement is high or move on to another item.

Scenario Writing

Scenario writing is an effort to describe how current conditions may evolve systematically in the future. It is a mechanism through which the influences of the possible future developments identified by the scanning process—their timing, impact, and interdependence—on the system of interest can be examined. Many different outcomes are usually feasible, and good scenario writing strives to identify the range of possible conditions that might emerge, given the variety of forces and events deemed feasible.

Scenarios are not forecasts per se, though they can be characterized as more or less likely (based on current understanding). They are plausible descriptions of what might come about, portrayals of events and trends as they could evolve. A scenario can be designed to provide either a snapshot of the future that describes conditions at a particular future time or a future history that describes how the state of various variables of interest move from the present into the future. Although their purposes were literary, one can point to such authors as Jules Verne (*20,000 Leagues Under the Sea* and *A Voyage to the Moon*), Aldous Huxley (*Brave New World*), and George Orwell (*1984*) as writers of particularly powerful scenarios.

Methodologically, an analyst has to make several crucial choices in preparing a set of scenarios that will be useful for planning and policy applications. Primary among these are questions such as, "What variables should be included?" "How many scenarios should be depicted?" "What condition or issues should be studied?" and "How can internal consistency be ensured within each scenario?"

Families of scenarios are often developed to illustrate the consequences of varying assumptions about just which trends and events will occur, what their timing and impacts will be, what policies are employed, and so on. A study of the crime and justice environment, for example, might involve constructing several scenarios that differ in their assumptions about birthrates, population, economic conditions, levels of disorder, and public attitudes. When a set of scenarios is prepared, each treats the same variables, but the resulting outcomes will vary according to the dynamic interactions that occur.

Sets of scenarios can be generated by changing one or several key assumptions in turn. With regard to the criminal justice system, for example, economic growth (a factor that affects funding) might be assumed low in one scenario, moderate in another, and high in a third. In addition, it might be important to gain an understanding of conditions that result not only from demographic and arrest-rate variations but also other conditions, such as innovations in technologies available to assist or complicate the work of the police, courts, and corrections. The dimensions usually are chosen to represent the leading or most influential variables from which other conditions will evolve.

When scenarios are constructed, it is important to search for future developments that are plausible and particularly relevant to the subject at hand. Often, a good approach to a set of scenarios is to represent the range of challenges an organization might have to face in the future. Sometimes, interesting and instructive scenarios can be constructed by including low-probability, high-impact developments. Such developments can be used in "what if" situations. For example, what if the federal judiciary rules that all prisoner litigation must originate and end in the state courts? What if a drug is developed to prevent substance addiction? Or what if handheld minicomputers become standard equipment for all patrol officers?

Strategic Assessment

Futures research is rarely able to dispel all uncertainty about what conditions will prevail in the future. A range of possibilities, each with varying implications for an organization, is the more typical result. Thoughtful analysis of scanning and scenario writing, however, can usefully sketch out the structure of the uncertainty—for example, sources of opportunities and downside risks and factors of most influence. This kind of *strategic assessment* of the possible future terrain provides an essential input for organizational planning and strategy formation.

The modern approach to strategic management—whether applied in business or public organization settings—gives considerable importance to understanding the future form of the external environment. Any organization's planning, in essence, must reflect certain expectations about the shape of the external world beyond its control. Changes in these expectations create the prospect that current objectives and action plans may become less able to cope with the new challenges and requirements. Adjustments in strategy may be needed, depending on the nature of the environmental changes expected—although these expected changes can rarely be known with certainty, and explicitly hedging uncertainty is frequently an important aspect of the strategy formation process.

Environmental scanning and an initial set of scenarios based on the scanning findings can provide useful information for critically assessing the value of a system's current plans and strategic commitments in meeting the operational challenges that may be confronted in the future. Subsequent rounds of scenario preparation, using revised strategy or policy initiatives, provide a way to examine the value of alternative plans in meeting these possible new challenges and identifying the dimensions of flexibility that the system will need to hedge the most important uncertainties.

Thus, the environmental scanning and scenario-writing processes fit well with the requirements of strategic management. Taken together, these provide a particularly powerful framework from which to address long-range planning issues.

FUTURES RESEARCH
AND CRIMINAL JUSTICE

Let us apply the futures methodologies of environmental scanning, scenario writing, and strategic assessment to the criminal justice system of the United States in the year 2010. We will first want to scan the literature of the social and behavior sciences to develop a list of drivers that may have an impact on the future crime and justice environment. This information should be supplemented by the opinions of experts as to the probability of these changes occurring and the extent of their impact on the criminal justice system. From the data thus assembled, scenarios can be developed that depict alternative future conditions. Having sketched possible conditions in the year 2010, criminal justice managers and planners can assess the results and develop alternative strategies to deal with the expected new environment.

For the purposes of our discussion, let us assume that scanning of the literature reveals four categories of drivers that identify possible trends and events affecting the criminal justice system by the year 2010. Demographic shifts in the size and composition of the population, changes in the U.S. and world economies, technological advances, and trends in criminality can each be used to organize our thinking about likely impacts on the future crime and justice environment.

Table 1.1 presents a sample list of such drivers. As each is considered, we must reflect on the probability of its occurring by 2010 and its potential impact on the crime and justice environment.

Researchers apply the findings from the environmental scanning to scenarios describing the future state of affairs. Suppose the environmental scanning indicates that four major forces are particularly important in accounting for the various outcomes represented by possible future developments in Table 1.1. One of these forces might be the rate of future economic growth, with analysis showing that slow, moderate, and high growth are equally likely over the next quarter century. Second, analysis might show that the levels of disorder in society could be either high or low. Third, the public's level of tolerance of disorder also may be either high or low. Finally, a fourth factor, the institutional capacity of the criminal justice system (levels of resources, capabilities, public support), might be high or low. A scenario space and alternative world morphology based on these major forces can then be constructed as shown in Figure 1.1.

As the figure shows, multiple scenarios could be written, each describing alternative worlds characterized by the four major forces discussed above. Not all of these worlds are logically probable and not all will be helpful in developing planning strategies. With the idea of characterizing the range of future challenges to the criminal justice system, the following subset of scenarios might be selected for more detailed attention:

Scenario 1: a strained and turbulent nation in which criminal justice resources are short but the need for them is acute, given high levels of disorder and an aroused public.

Table 1.1 Sample List of Drivers Likely to Impact the Crime and Justice Environment by the Year 2010

Demography

1. Overall U.S. population increases to 300,000,000.
2. Proportion of Americans older than 40 grows from 37% to 45%.
3. Minorities increase to 26% of the population.
4. The flow of legal immigrants, increasingly from Latin America and Asia, continues at a rate of about 750,000 per year.
5. Advancing technology and a changing economy result in a disproportionate impact on less skilled, lower socioeconomic groups.

Economics

1. Restructuring of the economy continues with disruptions in some mature industrial sectors, rapid growth in the high technology and service fields, and some outflow of jobs and capital to other nations.
2. The federal budget deficit improves, but only slowly, so funding for domestic programs remains tight.
3. Economies of the nations of the former Soviet Union remain unstable.
4. Checks and credit cards assume a larger portion of consumer monetary transactions.
5. Real growth in output and income generally is slow but steady.

Technology

1. Copying technologies advance rapidly.
2. Automation of financial transactions increase.
3. Miniaturization of computers gives patrol officers instant access to crime information files.
4. Scientists discover a chemical that has the ability to break the physical dependence on drugs from which addicts suffer.
5. Gains in laser and fiber-optic technologies revolutionize organizations.

Crime Factors

1. The war on drugs of the 1990s has been cut back as cocaine use declines and law enforcement proves costly.
2. Participation of women in criminal activity increases as their societal role is redefined.
3. Handguns continue to be owned by a significant portion of the population.
4. Incarceration rates stabilize as construction of costly new prisons declines. There is an expansion of the use of probation and intermediate sanctions.
5. Disposal of nuclear and toxic wastes becomes a major organized crime activity.

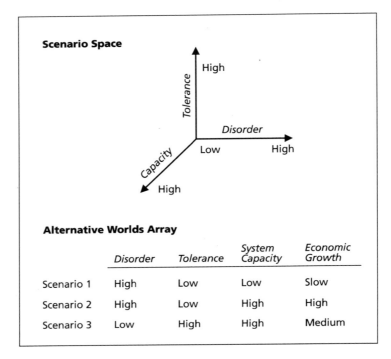

Scenario Space

Alternative Worlds Array

	Disorder	Tolerance	System Capacity	Economic Growth
Scenario 1	High	Low	Low	Slow
Scenario 2	High	Low	High	High
Scenario 3	Low	High	High	Medium

FIGURE 1.1

Scenario 2: similar to scenario 1, but the economy is growing rapidly so that system resources have expanded to meet the needs.

Scenario 3: a United States in which crime has declined to low levels, the public has come to accept the existing levels of crime, and yet the capacity of the system is high given moderate growth in the economy.

More detailed projections of the conditions to be expected in each of these worlds might then be described by focusing on some of the following: demographic characteristics, technologies available to the system, shifts in the nature of criminality, operational problems faced by criminal justice organizations, and so on. Scenarios describing these worlds and the likelihood of the impact of the drivers can then be used to discuss the needs of criminal justice in the future.

The futures research approaches discussed in this chapter can help to characterize the nature of the long-term developments and to assist administrators and planners in understanding their implications for the criminal justice system. The tools of futures research promise to be an important addition to criminal justice officials as they face the challenges of the decades ahead.

FOR FURTHER READING

Marvin Cetron and Owen Davis. *American Renaissance: Our Life at the Turn of the 21st Century.* New York: St. Martin's Press, 1989.

This work is an excellent example of the application of futures research to contemporary American society.

Joseph F. Coates, Jennifer Jarratt, and John B. Mahaffie. *Future Work: Seven Critical Forces Reshaping Work and the Workforce in North America.* San Francisco: Jossey-Bass, 1990.

This reference tool identifies seven groups of trends that will dominate workforce planning in the next decade.

Edward Cornish. *The Study of the Future.* Washington: World Future Society, 1977.

This work describes the development of futures research and its methodologies.

Handbook of Futures Research, Jib Fowles, Ed. Westport, CT: Greenwood Press, 1978.

This is an essential collection of essays that describe various approaches to futures research.

Olaf Helmer. *Looking Forward: A Guide to Futures Research.* Beverly Hills, CA: Sage Publications, 1983.

This work explores and discusses futures methodologies.

Alvin Toffler. *Future Shock.* New York: Random House, 1970.

In this work, Toffler argues that stress and disorientation is induced in the individual subjected to too much change in too short a time. This work provided much of the public with its first exposure to futures thinking.

DISCUSSION QUESTIONS

1. Fortune-tellers and science-fiction writers have long speculated about the future. How can planning for the future of criminal justice be systematic and scientific rather than simply speculative?

2. What specific methods and approaches are available to help planners think about the future in systematic ways?

3. The future of criminal justice will not occur in a vacuum. What major trends in society will influence criminal justice between now and the year 2010?

4. What kind of career do you think you will have by 2010? How will your job be affected by some of the "drivers" discussed in this chapter?

5. Are there factors that are not mentioned in this chapter that will help shape criminal justice in 2010? How can you prepare yourself for these possibilities?

2

Criminal Justice in 2010:

The Past as Prologue

JOHN A. CONLEY

State University of New York at Buffalo

THE INCIDENT AS CATALYST

As Carol O'Connell, chief of police, sat in the boardroom of the Federated Bank Investments (FBI) corporate headquarters on January 22 waiting for the first session of the Governor's Panel of Inquiry (they don't call them "task forces" or "commissions" anymore) to begin, she flashed back to the headline two weeks earlier on January 5, 2010: "Bungled Police Arrest Results in One Dead and Four Wounded." The governor had moved fast this time and within forty-eight hours established the panel of Charles Brown, FBI's chief legal counsel, Deputy State Attorney General Anthony Piccolo, and the Reverend Francis Twining, Episcopalian bishop.

The news media had not dropped the story since it began. Coverage was universal, if repetitive, across all news outlets and had even made network news on two occasions. The repeated story, based on police reports, was that two undercover city police officers arranged to meet two individuals at 10:30 P.M. in an underground public parking garage downtown for the purpose of a drug buy. Two nonuniformed officers from Public Protective Services had observed the four individuals on the closed-circuit television monitors and watched them walk into the garage in pairs about fifteen minutes apart. The PPS officers investigated and came upon the four individuals just as the city police officers made the drug buy and were drawing their guns to make the arrest. Not knowing they were city police officers, the PPS officers drew their weapons, as did the drug sellers, and the subsequent shootout resulted in the death of one city police officer and the wounding of one PPS officer, one couple who lived in the suburbs, and one drug seller. Apparently, the bystanders had just exited an elevator and were in the line of fire.

The news media focused on the tragic result of the police activity and questioned why the city police officers did not identify themselves to the PPS officers. The media also wanted to know why the city police and PPS did not cooperate more fully on these types of operations, and commentators called on the city police to establish mechanisms for improving communication between the two organizations. Although the media avoided a deeper analysis of the issues surrounding private and public policing and the underlying social problems that have driven the demands on private and public services in general, they did mention the possible link between the incident and two previous disturbances: public protests at the building site of the newest condominium development and at the opening of the new rapid transit station downtown. The implication left by the media was that the level of unrest was out of control.

The panel, on the other hand, was interested in determining why the incident happened and what changes could be made quickly to assure suburbanites, commercial property owners, and downtown condominium owners of the safety of the downtown area. The governor established the panel quickly because the county executive and the downtown business interests requested a formal inquiry. They did not miss the potential damage that this incident could wreak on the public's perception of safety and on investor confidence, nor did they miss the cumulative effect of the previous protests and this incident of violence. The panel would serve to forestall any decrease in public confidence in the area, and by formally gathering information as a government panel, it would serve as a symbolic reminder to investors that the state would protect their investments.

PRIVATIZATION OF PUBLIC POLICY

Although the panel was an official government body, it would function more as a corporate task force. There would not be opportunities for input from a wide segment of the area's population or its elected representatives. The panel members were handpicked by the governor and the county executive for their knowledge of and direct involvement in the area's economic revitalization. These panel members, in turn, determined who would testify before the panel. This was a controlled performance, and holding the hearings in the corporate boardroom simply gave another measure of control. It also, of course, illustrated the panel's link to investment interests.

All this was not lost on Chief O'Connell. She had been in this boardroom many times since she became chief. The FBI's corporate board constantly took the pulse of the community, at least on those aspects of community order that affect perceptions of safety. In fact, it had become commonplace, in the first decade of the twenty-first century, for government officials to appear before corporate executives to report on existing social conditions and potential problems as city governments lost their central place in the political structure of the state.

The panel members had direct links to the community's economic interests. FBI legal counsel Charles Brown represented the corporation's interests. FBI was a major investor in the downtown area through real estate, the rapid transit system, and government bonds. In addition, Brown was vice president of the City Center District, a privately run municipal authority comprising more than 2,000 commercial property owners, real estate developers, and financial institutions in the downtown area. Deputy Attorney General Anthony Piccolo had been corporate counsel for a national security firm located in the city before the governor had appointed him to the state office. Piccolo was the primary architect of state legislation that created special private municipal districts and expanded the authority of private safety services. Bishop Francis Twining was president of Citizens for a Safer Community, a nonprofit group interested in issues related to safety in the downtown area. Bishop Twining was also treasurer of the City Center District.

Chief O'Connell, however, focused on a larger question. How did this city reach this stage of confrontation and divisiveness and could her police department have prevented it? She remembered when she first joined the Emerald City Police Department twenty-five years ago after her graduation from college with a criminal justice degree. Were there signs then indicating the potential for the chaos that took place two week ago? She remembered that her teachers discussed the trends that took root in the 1970s and 1980s. There was the shift to the political right and the ascension of a conservative ideology that emphasized a lowering of federal involvement in many phases of the economy and a dismantling of federal social services. The stated objective was to return that responsibility to the states, which were closer to the problems. There was also a strong law-and-order mood in the country in reaction to rising crime and violence, which resulted in more arrests and prosecutions and longer prison sentences. She remembered how she and her fellow students believed that there would be an expansion of the criminal justice system and career opportunities would be good for them.

THE TRAPPED POPULATIONS

Her thoughts were interrupted by the words of the sociologist from the state university who was testifying before the panel. He was a specialist in urban development. The city of Emerald had experienced a mixed pattern of population movement over the past twenty years, he said, which was a result of the redistribution of the economic base of the city. As many of the older manufacturing firms closed, moved their plants to the outlying sectors of the county, or moved to other states, the urban center began to decay. The loss of unskilled factory jobs steadily increased unemployment until it reached its current general level of 29 percent in the city compared to 8 percent countywide. More significant was the 45 percent unemployment rate in the 18-to-30-year-old category within the racial groups of African-Americans, Hispanics, and the newer immigrants from Southeast Asia. Most of the employed worked in the service industries of food, commercial retail stores, and entertainment for the minimum wage of $6.25 an hour. Most of these jobs are part-time with no job guarantee, medical insurance, or retirement benefits.

The sociologist presented a variety of tables that coldly illustrated and supported his conclusions. The loss of jobs had sapped the economic vitality of the working-class neighborhoods, and small, family-owned stores had closed, housing stock had deteriorated, people had lost their homes to foreclosure, and absentee landlords had bought these properties by the thousands over the past twenty years. The physical deterioration was reflected in the loss of cohesiveness of the neighborhoods, and a large portion of the population had become transient, adding to further instability. Social disorder increased and resulted in severe strain on the government's social and safety services. Residents in these neighborhoods became fearful of victimization, and their lifestyles changed dramatically from open participation in neighborhood activities to an almost reclusive model.

For four decades the suburbs had been a magnet for those people who could move, but with the economic downturn of the 1980s, the recession of the 1990s, and the subsequent sluggish growth of the economy, many people could no longer move out of the city. The population flow outward slowed, leaving the city's population today at 400,000, down 100,000 from the 1990 census. If not for the inflow of 80,000 upper-middle-class and young professionals into the apartments and condominiums of the downtown area, the city's population would be that much lower. The impact of that shift in population was not anticipated by policy makers of the 1990s and beyond, he argued, because we were trapped by our vision of the past. When the population began moving to the suburbs in the post–World War II era through the 1960s, jobs were generally plentiful in a growing manufacturing sector, the economy was growing, and the low tax bases could absorb the necessary increases for governmental services. As the manufacturing sector shrank, the world economy became more complex and competitive, and the tax burden increased in the 1980s, the lower economic classes had little room to maneuver and remained within the city boundaries. They experienced a real loss of equity in their homes and were hit hard by the socioeconomic changes in their neighborhoods, which were mentioned earlier. We did not anticipate the impact of these demographic shifts and ended up with a two-tier population in the city: the poor in the outer rings and the middle and upper classes in the center.

In contrast, however, he showed how the closing of factories in and around the city center drove property values down and made that land attractive to real estate developers. A number of new office buildings changed the skyline of the downtown area and attracted corporate offices as well as government agencies; the result was that more than 100,000 people commuted daily into the downtown. Developers also constructed many beautiful new condominium buildings and renovated many of the old factories as condominiums in and around the central core of the downtown area. These developments attracted the young professionals who worked in the city and the middle-aged couples from the suburbs who no longer had children living at home. There was a consistent rise, as a result, in economic development in the service and entertainment industries. Such small businesses as grocery stores, laundries, taverns, and restaurants opened around these condominiums. The newly renovated theater district included live theater, movie houses, the new symphony hall, and the ballet center for the performing arts. The sociologist concluded that the central city area is populated by two very distinct groups: the upper middle class and the poor. These groups, over the years, placed very different demands on the city government.

Chief O'Connell agreed with that statement. When she was a lieutenant in the 1990s, her department experienced heavy pressure to address the fears of the new urban residents while at the same time responding to the ever-increasing level of disorder and victimization in the poorer sections of the city. The reform model for policing during that period had been "problem-oriented policing," in which departments attempted to identify and address underlying causes of the problems to which the police responded. The objective was to address the cause (taverns catering to minors) rather than simply responding to the results (fights or driving-while-intoxicated accidents involving minors). The police and the neighborhoods were to work hand-in-hand in identifying and addressing community problems. At the same time the Citizens for a Safer Community, a coalition of citizens and downtown businesses, pressured the police to keep the downtown streets safe. The result was a severe strain on police resources with neither area receiving the level of service it needed.

PRIVATE PRISONS
AND PUBLIC PRISONERS

The regional director of the state department of corrections had begun his testimony before the panel, and his words brought Chief O'Connell's attention back to the moment. The current prison population reached 110,000 inmates last week, he said, double what it had been in 1990. The state had built a few new prisons in the 1970s and 1980s, but these new institutions went above their intended capacity by 20 percent within a few months of opening. The county jails in this region, as is true in other counties throughout the state, had tripled their bed space in the past twenty years through the construction of new and larger facilities in the 1980s and through a growing reliance on the issuance of contracts to private prison firms to house county inmates.

He pointed out that the practice, begun in the 1980s, of contracting with private firms to build prisons and house inmates for the state also continued. The long-term economic recession of the 1990s, which resulted in recurring billion-dollar deficits in the state budgets, forced the state to stop building new prisons and increased the attractiveness of contracting with private firms to handle the continuously increasing inmate population.

Assistant Attorney General Piccolo, a strong proponent of private entrepreneurship and expansion in the government service area, interrupted and pointed out that these contracts saved the county more than $2 million a year, and the combined savings to the state, when all county and state contracts for prisoners were calculated, reached well above $40 million a year. He suggested to the director that the state may need to expand that contract model to provide more space for prisoners.

Unfortunately, responded the director, the state's fiscal stability and the loss of its triple-A bond rating did not make the prison contracts an attractive investment for the few respected private prison firms. As a result, weaker firms sought and won the contracts, but, unlike the 1980s, these firms did not invest private capital in the projects. These firms rented warehouses, old unused factories, abandoned schoolhouses, and hospitals to house their prisoners. Currently, 52 percent of the state's inmates are housed in state prison facilities, half of which use double and triple bunking of prisoners to hand the load; 38 percent are housed in the private firms' makeshift facilities; and 10 percent are held in county jails.

The impact of these developments over the past twenty years, he continued, is that the state's prisons are filled with hardened and violent inmates because the minimum and medium security risks are sent to the private prisons. The continuous pressure of increasing numbers of prisoners entering the corrections department combined with frozen state budgets and decreased funding for corrections has resulted in a continuous decrease in treatment programs for inmates, a de facto custodial mission for the prisons, and biannual purges of the prison population to make room for new prisoners. The private prisons also release large numbers of prisoners, and the combined load has overwhelmed the state and local parole systems.

The budgets of the parole systems have not kept pace with the increased demands, he said, and administrators had to concentrate their limited personnel on a very small percentage of the most violent ex-inmates. Electronic bracelets and computer monitoring of home-bound parolees have not worked effectively because there simply are not enough personnel to investigate violations. Finally, there is no incentive for the private prisons to develop accurate information systems to identify and track the prisoners they release. The private firms are paid on a per-capita-plus-overhead funding formula only for the prisoners in their custody. The overall impact is that too many ex-inmates are not under state control and, unless they are arrested again, criminal justice officials do not know where they are.

In a summary statement that showed the director's frustration with the current state of affairs in corrections, he flatly informed the committee that all of these so-called reforms of private contracts, electronic bracelets, computer monitoring, and other state-mandated solutions for the plight of corrections in the 1980s and 1990s were nothing more than bandaids. These highly publicized policy initiatives were symbolic images of reform that temporarily assuaged the public's fears but did little to address the fundamental problems in corrections. In fact, these symbolic reforms camouflaged the countermeasures taken by the legislature that shifted funds from corrections and the probation and parole systems to other state agencies. The result was a steady decrease in staffing and frozen budgets that had stifled any creative initiatives from the corrections field for the past twenty years.

In response to a question from Chairman Brown, who wanted to know why there was such a large growth of inmates and why the state's corrections department had not made plans to address the growth, the corrections director claimed that the state budget process simply did not allocate enough funds to the corrections department to handle the chronic problem of overcrowded prisons. In addition, he said, crime had been rising steadily since the drug wave of the 1980s and it was a natural outcome that prison populations would increase. Finally, he said, corrections has little control over the number of inmates it receives because the police are the gatekeepers of the criminal justice system, and they activate the flow into the system with their arrests. The prosecutor and courts, in turn, filter the flow by their respective decisions and processes. Corrections is at the tail end of the justice process and has no influence over the decisions made earlier in the process. As a result, corrections does not have the capability of planning for or adjusting quickly to shifts in the flow of inmates.

Chief O'Connell winced at the simplicity of the director's response but felt compassion and a deep kinship for the director's dilemma. Yes, crime has increased, she thought, but not across all categories. In fact, the national crime data showed that property and some violent crimes had tapered to a flat trend. Crimes of interpersonal violence, however, had increased, and crimes using guns had run ahead of all violent crimes. But the largest increase occurred in those crimes collectively labeled "disorder crimes," such as tavern brawls, street muggings, and public disturbances. The media focused on the gun-related violence and the disorder crimes. This news coverage increased the levels of fear among the population but with little context. There was no lasting perspective that recognized the distinction between different types of crime, that crimes tend to be localized by type to specific areas of the city, or that most crimes are intraracial and intraclass. These distinctions got lost in the news coverage and the subsequent hysteria.

Chief O'Connell knew that the director knew all of this, but she also knew that panel members were not interested. They had a more direct concern that focused on how to avoid and control (not necessarily prevent) the type of violence symbolized by the so-called bungled arrest. It probably would do no good to remind the panel that the sheer numbers of individuals processed through the criminal justice system had been affected significantly by a combination of the law-and-order mood of the 1990s, a criminal law reform package of state legislation that lengthened prison sentences and widened police and prosecutor powers while also limiting the court's sentencing discretion, and the massive growth of private security. Nevertheless, she wished she had taken the opportunity to expand on some of the complex social, political, and economic reasons why the criminal justice system was strained beyond capacity. She smiled to herself as she wondered what her college professors would think about such radical thoughts coming from her.

LOCAL GOVERNMENT, PRIVATE INTERESTS, AND THE SHIFTING LOCUS OF POWER

Testimony from a political scientist from the university followed the corrections director, and she wasted no time in confronting the panel. The recent violence and public protests, she said, emerged from the underclass's chronic mistrust of and frustration with the political system. Its members had no political clout as a group because of the redistribution of political power that occurred over the preceding thirty years. Traditionally, she said, the poor and working class had their most effective political influence in the cities. In the early 1900s, the urban political machines responded to their needs and provided the kind of government support services necessary to maintain order in their communities and neighborhoods. These machines also gave them political clout in state and national arenas.

This influence and involvement in the political process was weakened slightly during the good-government movement of the Progressive period. This reform movement placed strong elected mayors with professional city managers and weakened political wards—the power bastions of the poor—by instituting the election of at-large candidates. The effect of this reform on the poor and working class was blunted because this movement was most successful in medium and small cities that had homogenous populations; it was less successful in large cities that were multiculturally and multiracially diverse.

She went on to say, however, that the reforms of the 1980s through the 1990s that emphasized deregulation, limited government, and lower taxes shifted the local political center up to the county and the entitlement responsibility down to the states. The result of this shift and the concomitant shrinking and slowing down of the economy was that the locus of political power shifted away from the cities. This left the growing poor and marginal working class with little influence in governmental policy development. More and more they saw government as unresponsive to their needs, which, in turn, resulted in a constantly increasing loss of legitimacy for the government among this population.

In addition, because of the powerful effect on the tax base of the states, she said, corporations experienced an unprecedented increase in influence at the state and county levels. Corporate leaders began to have a wider and more public role in policy development across spheres other than business issues. The involvement of corporations in government matters increased and became more open. Corporate executives surfaced regularly as critical members of government fact-gathering committees. The situation in Emerald was a good example of what had happened and was continuing to happen nationwide. The private sector was expanding its influence and involvement in public arenas to control and manage public areas for the benefit of private economic and social interests. The expansion of the privatization of public services is an example of the profit model and the involvement of corporate executives in analyzing social problems and developing policy initiatives, she said—as you are doing with this panel, which is an example of private-sector control and direction of public policy.

Brown interrupted the political scientist and challenged the implication of her testimony that this increased private-sector involvement
in public policy had negative results. He pointed out that public policy
initiatives developed and supported by the private sector resulted from
better planning, were quickly passed by the legislature, increased the
level and quality of public services, and were more efficient than
previous policy initiatives developed by public bodies. The direct involvement of the public sector, he said, is more openly acknowledged
now than in the past. He concluded that the people are better served.

The political scientist countered that argument by first agreeing
with the general thrust of Brown's argument. Then she methodically
countered each of his points by arguing that the better planning resulted from a narrow focus on the problems and an overemphasis on
programmatic efficiency at the expense of broad services. She also said
that the closer link between the private sector and legislators developed
because the weakening of local political power resulted in a drastic loss
of checks and balances in the state legislature. Finally, she agreed that
the level and quality of many of the services had improved, but noted
that only a narrow segment of the population benefited from these
improvements. These services addressed the needs of the middle and
upper classes and diverted funds away from direct services to the
shrinking working class and the expanding underclass. She concluded
by saying that the recent protests were graphic examples of the frustration and fear of the urban poor, who are increasingly forced out of the
mainstream of American society because of the shrinking opportunities
available to them.

ORDER, CONTROL, AND THE NEW POLICE

The next person to testify before the panel was a tall, distinguished-look-
ing man who could pass for a bank executive. He was the director of
Public Protective Services (PPS), the private 250-employee police agency
funded by the City Center District. Before accepting this position, he had
retired after serving twenty-five years with the U.S. Treasury Department
as chief of the Fraud Investigations Unit. He wasted no time in protecting
his agency from any potential blame for any of the recent violent incidents
in the downtown area. He immediately charged the city police with
violating agreed-upon procedures in not notifying his agency about the
undercover investigation taking place in the downtown area.

He also said that the recent protests could have been avoided if his agency had been given primary responsibility for public order. The shared responsibility with the city police caused confusion and conflicting goals. For example, he said, the city police allowed the protest groups to march near the sites with a police-cordoned barrier between the site and the protesters. This allowed the protesters to taunt the construction workers and dignitaries. If the state legislature would expand the authority of the City Center District, giving the PPS sole jurisdiction for law enforcement throughout the district, his agency would have banned any protest and arrested violators. He reminded the panel that PPS did have sole jurisdiction over all private housing and parking facilities and some specified commercial buildings, such as the FBI building and some specified streets in the center city, but shared jurisdictional authority with the city police on other public streets, public parking lots, and structures and the fringe of the downtown area. This arrangement contributed to confusion and competition between the agencies.

He reminded the panel that twenty years ago, when the PPS was created, the agency performed only a security function. His personnel were unarmed, had no arrest powers, and served as roving uniformed security guards for office buildings, the downtown mall, and hotels. Within a few years, at the request of the City Center District, the state passed legislation that expanded the authority of this agency through the expansion of the powers and responsibility of the City Center District municipal authority. PPS received police powers of arrest, authorization to carry firearms, and a widening of its jurisdiction throughout the two-square-mile downtown area. He claimed that this expansion of jurisdiction allowed PPS to provide comprehensive police coverage to all commercial sites and residents of the district, but that it also duplicated the services of the city police. This duplication contributed to tension and conflict between the two agencies. He concluded with the suggestion that the panel recommend legislation that would make PPS the sole police authority for the district.

Chief O'Connell was next, and she had to regain her composure after her initial anger at the charges leveled against her agency by the PPS director. She began her testimony by reminding the panel that one police officer had died and other people had been seriously wounded in the incident that generated the call for this panel of inquiry. As tragic as that incident was, she said, it only served as a symbolic reminder of the larger problems that were crippling this community and the criminal justice system. The impact of the long-term economic recession on the working poor resulted in chronic unemployment, increased levels of competition for scarce part-time employment, and severe competition for these jobs among the poor. Added to these conditions was the deterioration of the neighborhoods caused by the replacement of homeowners with absentee landlords. The level of social disorganization increased and spread rapidly through the neighborhoods lying just outside the center of the city. Governmental services, including the police, were severely strained to keep abreast of the people's needs over this twenty-year period. Service demands increased while government resources decreased.

At the same time, she said, we experienced rapid economic growth and a dramatic shift in population in the center of the city. The real-estate development boom in condominiums coinciding with the growth of corporate office buildings not only changed the physical skyline of the downtown, but also brought thousands of middle- and upper-class people into the downtown area as permanent residents while displacing the former poor residents. These social and economic changes painted a stark contrast between the richness of the center city and the poverty of its outlying areas, which resulted in heightened levels of frustration and anger among the poor. They were more willing to confront through protest the examples of that wealth such as the construction sites and the new commuter train station. The middle- and upper-class residents also saw the contrast and the protests and began to view the poor as criminals or the dangerous class, much as they did in the late nineteenth century. The conditions for political conflict were in place by the year 2000, and, with the decreasing political importance of city government where the poor traditionally had influence, the poor took their demands to the street. "I remind the panel of these conditions, which were described in detail by previous testimony," she said, "because the issues before the panel are not solely law-enforcement issues or issues of crime and criminals. They are larger social issues that did not begin with a drug arrest or a public protest. We must remember that as we discuss the current state of criminal justice."

As a result of these social, political, and economic changes, she went on to say, the delivery of criminal justice services also changed. She claimed that there were dual or parallel systems of justice operating in the community and throughout the state. The private and public prisons were examples of that duality. In law enforcement, there existed public and private police forces that originally were supposed to have separate responsibilities. But as time moved on, she said, the two agencies began to have overlapping responsibilities, which resulted in bifurcated law enforcement.

This development did not occur in a vacuum, she said, because the crime problems of the 1980s generated widespread fear in the community, and the public demanded a response by government. At the same time and well into the turn of the century, the economy had slowed and governments began to search for alternatives to tax-supported public services. The irony, Chief O'Connell said, was that at the very time that more and more people needed the support and protection of the government, public services were being curtailed or shifted to the private sector.

Law enforcement is a good case in point, she explained, because the impact of these social and economic pressures on police services resulted in a restructuring of the law-enforcement system. Our city police department, she said, decreased in fifteen years from 700 to 400 sworn personnel. This occurred at the same time that crime and social disorder levels increased because of the deterioration of the center city as outlined by previous testimony. Yet the jurisdiction and responsibilities of the city police were not altered. The decreasing tax base and the subsequent impact it had on local government, she said, forced budget cutbacks to the point that all city services, including police, were sharply reduced.

The PPS, on the other hand, grew from 30 to 250 personnel. The state expanded its authority and gave it general police powers but limited its powers to a specific geographical area, the City Center District. Its budget is generated by contributions made to the district authority by the developers, commercial shop owners, and financial institutions. This contribution is a private "tax," and the government is not involved in the collection, budgeting, or distribution of these funds.

The result of these developments, Chief O'Connell said, is that the city has a bifurcated system of law enforcement. The PPS has police powers, jurisdiction over a wide variety of criminal behavior in a specified geographic area, and limited government control. PPS serves the security needs of a tiny but wealthy population. The public police serve the security needs of the poor, who live on the fringe of the center city, are constantly fighting against the decreasing ability to police the larger community, and are taking on the role of a reactive army to the crime and disorder problems of the poor. PPS has a system of closed-circuit television cameras with zoom lenses strategically but inconspicuously mounted on top of buildings and light poles in the downtown area. Twenty years ago, this type of closed-circuit system was used only in isolated parking garages and walking ramps. Now these cameras allowed PPS to monitor all downtown streets to protect pedestrians from criminal activity. No such system of cameras exists in the poor neighborhoods to protect pedestrians there. The city, she said, is sitting on a tinderbox and. . . .

The explosion brought Carol upright with a jerk. A few seconds went by before she realized that the explosion was the radio alarm and that she must have been dreaming. She got out of bed, walked to the bathroom, looked at herself in the mirror, and said, "Well, Lt. O'Connell, it's 1995, not 2010, and you must have a little anxiety about your final interview today for promotion to captain to have generated that dream."

Then she began to wonder if 2010 would be anything like her dream. What has occurred in the late 1980s and 1990s that might have wide-ranging implications twenty years from now? What impact will the economic restructuring have on criminal justice over the next two decades? On the level and types of criminal activity? What do we know about social, economic, and political changes going on now? How would we measure patterns and trends to project ahead twenty years? Can we? These are heavy and important questions, she thought. Questions that need answers; nay, questions that need to be asked. Damn, she said to herself, I wish the department would support this type of long-range planning activity. She remembered how her professors twenty years ago lamented the lack of research and planning in police agencies and other criminal justice agencies. Maybe when it's "Chief O'Connell" I can institute such planning, she thought, or will it be too late?

EPILOGUE

This essay was written as a scenario, a potential of what could happen based on an interpretation of current history projected twenty years ahead. Although the analysis is written in a fictional style and does not represent real facts about a real place, the factual points (e.g., economic shifts, privatization, overcrowding, weakening of local government, etc.) and the anecdotal incidents have occurred recently. Some reflect patterns; some are isolated incidents. Whether they develop into trends and long-term changes in American society in general and criminal justice in particular remains to be seen.

If you were a historian in 2010 trying to understand current developments then and were conducting research over the previous twenty or forty years, you might well come across transcripts of such testimony before official bodies. Obviously, this testimony would not give you all the answers. That is the nature of research in history. Indeed it might only raise more questions, but it would give you leads to follow in your research. Those leads would draw you to the kinds of data and analyses found in the remaining chapters of this book.

If you were a planner or policy analyst today, you would also need to study the data and analyses found in the remaining chapters. In short, you cannot understand the present without the past, and you cannot predict the future from the present. But you can project into the future from the past because the past can serve as prologue if you respect the data available to you.

FOR FURTHER READING

Bernard Bailyn et al. *The Great Republic—A History of the American People*, 4th ed. Lexington, MA: D.C. Heath, 1992.

This text is a comprehensive history of American society.

Charles Brace. *The Dangerous Classes of New York and Twenty Years Work Among Them.* Montclair, NJ: Patterson-Smith, 1967.

This is a classic study of the underclass of the late nineteenth century. The parallels between then and now are striking.

Robert M. Fogelson. *Big-City Police.* Cambridge, MA: Harvard University Press, 1977.

This detailed study examines the police from the late nineteenth century through 1970. Police reform has been slow to develop and has been limited in its scope.

Herbert A. Johnson. *History of Criminal Justice.* Cincinnati, OH: Anderson, 1988.

This broad survey of the evolution of criminal justice from ancient times to the present places American developments in the context of our English heritage.

David J. Rothman. *Conscience and Convenience: The Asylum and its Alternatives in Progressive America.* Boston: Little, Brown, 1980.

This book explores the intellectual underpinnings that shaped the development of criminal and juvenile justice and mental health programs in the twentieth century. The discussion of the successes and failures of reform movements outline the legacy behind current issues of incarceration, punishment, and social control.

Samuel Walker. *Popular Justice: A History of American Criminal Justice.* New York: Oxford University Press, 1980.

This is a broad survey of criminal justice in America. The author discusses the close relationship between the popular will and developments in criminal justice.

DISCUSSION QUESTIONS

1. Major incidents such as prison riots or notorious crimes have often changed criminal justice policy. What incidents can you recall that have shaped or influenced criminal justice operations during your lifetime?

2. Increasingly, citizens are turning to the private sector for services once provided only by the government. What are the strengths and weaknesses of such movements as private policing or privately owned and operated jails and prisons?

3. How do changes in population characteristics or composition and changes in economic conditions in cities affect the crime problem and our response to it?

4. The scenario presented in this chapter suggests that increasing gaps between the wealthy and the poor in our society will have implications for crime policy. Has the criminal justice system in your community already begun to show this pattern?

5. The author of this chapter is a historian. How important is having a sense of history to examining the future in a field such as criminal justice?

3

☆

Explaining Crime in the Year 2010

L. EDWARD WELLS

Illinois State University

Crime presents a problem for us in many ways, especially in understanding and explaining it. Why does crime occur? Why do people hurt—even kill—one another and steal from each other? What causes some people to do it, perhaps repeatedly, while others do not? Why does crime happen much more frequently in some situations, neighborhoods, or groups? What social conditions cause crime to increase or decrease? Such questions imply that there must be explanations, that things happen for reasons we can know if we only look hard enough. And, in turn, these explanations imply that there must be some effective means to deal with or control crime, if only we find the right explanation and apply it wisely.

When it comes to explaining crime, we seem to have an embarrassment of riches but a poverty of results. Theories about crime have always been plentiful, providing various answers to such puzzles as why crime occurs, what prompts people to do it, what kinds of people do it, and how it can be controlled. However, the amount of useful explanation they provide is not very satisfying. None of the available theories provides a complete or precise explanation, none demonstrably better than any of the others. We may prefer some theories on ideological

36

grounds, because they are more consistent with our values, but none has proven noticeably more effective in explaining, predicting, or controlling crime.

LOOKING FORWARD
AND LOOKING BACKWARD

Will criminological theory in 2010 be different? Will our efforts to develop a comprehensive and really effective explanation of crime succeed? How will we explain crime in the year 2010, and will this be very different from the explanations we have now? Will they work any better in 2010 than the ones we now have?

Predicting the future, especially the future of ideas, is an uncertain business. However, there are two strategies that we might use to improve our forecasts. One is to heed the old adage that "the best predictor of the future is the past." This does not mean that the future simply repeats the past verbatim. It suggests that by looking at past ways of explaining crime, at how they have changed and evolved to the present, and at other changes that seem to be occurring, we might reasonably extrapolate to future directions in crime theory. The other strategy is to identify the social, political, and economic factors that shape our ideas about things such as crime and punishment. Then, by making reasonable guesses about social, economic, and political trends over the next decade or so, we can estimate how these will affect future thinking about crime.

THE DEVELOPMENT OF
CRIME EXPLANATIONS

Our ideas about crime—what it means and why it happens—have varied considerably over the past several hundred years. We have changed from (1) viewing crime as the work of the devil to (2) describing it as the rational choice of free-willed economic calculators to (3) explaining it as the involuntary causal effects of biological, mental, and environmental conditions, and then back to (2). In the process, our ideas about how we ought to deal with or punish criminal offenders have also changed dramatically. We have moved between torturing and mutilating offenders in order to drive out the devil, to imprisoning them for purposes of social protection, to educating and counseling offenders for the purpose of rehabilitating them, and then back to social protection.

In considering the changes in theories of crime, we notice that "change" does not necessarily mean "progress," at least in an obvious and direct way. The flow of ideas about crime has not been characterized by a simple progression upward from ignorance toward truth, in which old ideas are gradually modified, adjusted, or updated by new and better, more sophisticated, and more accurate versions of those ideas. Unlike idealized elementary descriptions of scientific progress, the real growth of knowledge is much more irregular and nonlinear. It often changes in fits and starts; changes may be made in any direction, including backward or sideways leaps onto tangents that provide explanations for a different set of questions.

Two features of the way that crime theories have changed and developed are notable. One is the regular use of theoretical *recycling* in which we rediscover older ideas that have been pushed aside and forgotten, but which look new when reexamined from a new vantage point. The centuries of thinking about crime have actually produced a small number of basic ideas that have been reworked and presented in a variety of different ways. We hope for a breakthrough that will revolutionize how we can explain and control crime. Yet, in a basic sense, there is little "new under the sun" in our thinking about crime. Because we generally assume that "old" means "obsolete," we tend to overlook the kinds of ideas used in the past to explain crime and to forget what has already been tried. As a result, we spend a lot of our efforts reinventing the wheel, a situation that may explain the common feeling that we are not getting very far very fast in our efforts to deal with crime.

The other notable feature of criminological theory is the use of theoretical *rivalry* as a way of developing and presenting new explanations. Rather than being accumulative, theory development has mostly been an oppositional or reactive process in which new explanations are developed in contradiction of or as reactions to the already existing theories. New theories are not simply presented as additional and better ways of thinking, rather their introductions also seek to discredit and reject the theories that they replace. While the oppositional method is useful for clarifying the basic features of our explanations, it has some weaknesses. First, it usually results in oversimplification of important ideas or concerns by overstating and overemphasizing the ways in which a particular theory differs from its predecessors and competitors. Second, by accentuating the differences between theories, it exaggerates the incompatibilities between them and makes potentially useful integrations of theories much more difficult.

PAST EXPLANATIONS OF CRIME

Historically our attempts to explain crime have reflected three distinctive themes or ways of thinking about crime that are labeled the *supernatural,* the *classical,* and the *positivistic.* The oldest and most traditional approach is a supernatural perspective that depicts crime as the product of evil forces or spirits. Supernatural explanations provided the dominant way of thinking about crime through the Middle Ages and into the eighteenth century. To some degree we still rely on such explanations, particularly as we base our policies for punishing criminals on concerns about retribution. We have not completely rejected supernatural accounts, but they have been largely supplanted by more modern and scientific explanations.

The supernatural perspective reflects a view that the ordinary events of everyday human behavior are shaped and prompted by powerful forces of good and evil that exist beyond the mundane reality. Crime is defined in moralistic and absolute terms as the violation of universal laws rather than as just the violation of legislated rules or codes. In supernatural terms, a criminal act is fundamentally an evil deed that disturbs the moral balance of the world, which can only be repaired by inflicting retribution on the offender. In this view, people are morally weak, carnal, or sinful by nature; they are irrational and subject to manipulation by outside spirits who prompt them to do things beyond their ordinary nature. Invariably, the supernatural perspective prompted harsh, retributive punishment aimed at driving the devil out of the offender and at the offender atoning for sinful deeds through suffering.

The second perspective entails a rationalistic view of moral behavior. Emerging during the eighteenth century in the period known as the Enlightenment, the classical model of crime developed in opposition to the supernatural model. It resulted from social developments that dramatically changed how people thought about human nature, human knowledge, government, legal control, and criminal behavior. Political conflict, changes in economic systems (from feudal agriculture to mercantilism), the spread of literacy, and the development of new ideas in philosophy and literature all combined to make a separation between the content of human experience and religious dogma or orthodoxy. A critical change was the development of the physical sciences—principally physics, chemistry, astronomy, and mathematics. Together these depicted the world as more mechanical, predictable, and understandable without need for demons or capricious deities to explain worldly events. The world could be known and explained through scientific laws that relied on logic and mathematical calculation rather than secret rituals and ordeals.

The classical perspective viewed human nature in materialistic and individualistic terms. People have autonomous free will, are able to calculate the consequences of their actions, are able to make choices based on whether they will gain or lose, and are morally accountable for the actions they choose. Outside forces or spirits were irrelevant to explaining crime, since individuals had free will and caused their own behavior. At the same time, crime was defined not by divine law, but by materialistic terms for the social and political harm it caused the community. The law's purpose in prohibiting and punishing crime was to protect society and its members rather than to maintain a supernatural order or appease the gods. Thus, the goal of punishment was the deterrence or prevention of future crimes rather than retribution for past crimes.

The classical view postulated that people are universally hedonistic. That is, they are motivated to seek out pleasure, comfort, and wealth while avoiding discomfort and loss. They act—and commit crimes—when they calculate that the gains from such actions outweigh the costs or risks. Everyone is potentially capable of committing crime, depending on their calculations and perceptions that it pays. There are no essential differences between criminals and noncriminals, since everyone has free will and follows the same pleasure-seeking, gain-calculating logic. The classical view of crime was a philosophical theory based on simple, idealized assumptions about human nature and social order. As such, it was more a philosophical argument for social control than a specific theory of criminal behavior. Yet it constituted one of the most influential and enduring explanations of crime we have.

The third theme in explaining crime, termed *positivism,* developed in the nineteenth century but continued to develop on through the twentieth. This involved the application of scientific methods of empirical research and theory testing to the problem of crime. Positivism sought to extend scientific logic and method to cover all aspects of human experience—not just inert physical phenomena covered by physics or chemistry but also animate phenomena involving living, actively changing systems. The nineteenth century heralded the emergence of the natural sciences—e.g., zoology, botany, physiology, medicine, geology—as full-fledged scientific fields and carried the promise (in the developing fields of psychology, sociology, economics, anthropology) that even uniquely human aspects of behavior would be explained and understood in scientific terms.

A basic element of this positivism and of the scientific method was its empiricism. In contrast to the abstract philosophical analysis of the classical model, the positivistic view emphasized the rigorous collection and analysis of empirical data. Note that the "positive" in "positivism" refers not to logical certainty, but to the basis of scientific knowledge in observation, measurement, and "positive" facts (rather than abstract hypothetical principles or supernatural forces). In positivism, it was not enough to apply common sense or logical deduction; all ideas about crime must be based inductively on precise empirical measurements and ultimately verified by careful experimental tests. Equally important, positivism stressed the objectivity of scientific research, where issues of scientific fact were clearly separated from matters of value and moral judgment.

One central element of the positivist model for explaining the occurrence of crime was its reliance on causal determinism. To explain some event was to identify what led to it and caused it to happen. In traditional form, the idea of causality was deterministic. In explaining human acts such as crime, this meant that notions such as free will and personal choice were meaningless or illusory. From this perspective, everything a person did, legally or illegally, was the consequence of a set of prior causes (which were themselves the effects of another set of prior causes and so on). People only appeared to have free will or choice, because the analysis never managed to identify all of the causal factors that controlled a person's acts. Thus, while the unexplained part of behavior might be interpreted as free and willful behavior, it merely represented an incomplete analysis.

Since the scientific model of crime described it as caused by factors outside the person's control or choice, what particular kinds of things are causes of crime? The earliest scientific explanations of crime mainly emphasized biological factors. This emphasis reflected developments in the nineteenth century that gave scientific credence to biological or physical accounts. One was the impressive progress made in medical science where human suffering, long taken to be an inevitable result of human sinfulness or mortality, was increasingly explained and reduced by use of scientific methods. Crime was readily incorporated into the medical model by extending the notion of "disease" as a pathological condition of the physical body to include "crime" as a pathological condition of the social and moral body. The other important development was the Darwinian theory of evolution, which emphasized the physical nature of human beings as evolved from animals and the natural biological foundations of human society (including its political, social, and moral structures).

Biological positivism tended to explain crime as a result of physical inferiorities or aberrations; these were presumed to be mostly hereditary, although a few might result from disease or injury. Criminal offenders were viewed as physically distinctive people who could be identified through careful measurement and diagnosis. Where the physical causes of crime were hereditary, a policy of social prophylaxis was advocated. This meant physical removal of defective persons from society, prevention of defective or inferior persons from reproducing (either by institutionalization or surgical sterilization), and restricting immigration quotas to minimize the influx of persons from inferior groups or races. Where the crime-producing conditions were acquired rather than hereditary, some sort of medical intervention such as surgery, drugs, or therapy might be advised to treat or cure the person.

Biomedical explanations predominated into the early twentieth century, at which time they fell into disfavor. This decline resulted partly from their association with controversial and overtly racist political policies. It also resulted from their weak ability to explain empirical patterns of crime. In particular, biological explanations could not account for the large, readily observed variations in crime over time and across different social conditions where biological factors seemed to be mostly constant. For this reason, biological explanations became the negative reference point from which most of our modern criminological theory developed initially as a negative reaction to biological determinism.

In the twentieth century, explanations of crime moved in two different directions, each an opposing response to the early biological theories. Psychiatric theory developed as an extension of medical science. It continued the theme of differentiating between criminals and noncriminals and of locating the causes of crime within the individual person. However, psychiatric explanations depicted the causes of crime as learned or acquired through experience (rather than being inborn) and as mental (rather than physical). They emphasized the effects of early experiences and childhood development of personality in determining adult thought and social adjustment. Specifically, psychiatric theory explained crime as a result of personality traits or defects that either directly caused antisocial behavior (as in neurotic or psychotic disorders) or indirectly caused it by hindering the normal development of prosocial behavior (as in psychopathic personalities). Psychiatric theories became the dominant form of explanation within correctional work in criminal justice, since they provided the rationale for the rehabilitation model and the conceptual basis of devising individual treatment of offenders. However, they did not dominate criminological theory in general, because criminology as an academic and scientific field became primarily identified with sociology. This shifted the focus of crime theory from individual criminality to crime rates and group variations.

The other prong of modern positivism involved sociological explanations whose basic premise was that crime is a *social fact* that is neither reducible to a collection of individual facts nor explainable by individual traits or aberrations. Such accounts opposed the idea that the crime was a result of inborn physical conditions. In addition, they rejected the premise that the effective causes of crime were located within the individual person (as either mental or physical traits) as well as the assumption that criminal and noncriminals were two distinctive types of persons who could be clearly differentiated by personality measurements or character diagnoses. For sociological explanations, the real causes of crime were located outside the individual in the social environment. While individual differences occur and may be substantial, they do not account for the regular variations in crime patterns or rates that are a result of changing social conditions.

Sociological positivism gave rise to a variety of different and competing explanations of crime, each focusing on a different aspect of social life to locate the efficient causes of crime as well as making different assumptions about human nature and normal social structure. *Strain* or "anomie" theories argued that crime was the inevitable result of the tensions and disjunctions that occur in modern society between different areas of social life. Human beings were seen as social animals who naturally conform and seek social ties or obligations. They were led to commit crime when the social structure placed conflicting demands on them that could not be realized without breaking the law. *Subcultural* theories argued that people conform to the norms and values of the social groups in which they are embedded as members. However, in modern heterogeneous societies, groups often have competing interests and conflicting definitions of right and wrong. Where a subgroup has norms and values that disagree with the predominant law of the land, it will cause subcultural crime. People will commit crime not because they are motivated to deviate, but because they are motivated to conform in this case to the deviant subculture of their group.

Social control theory argued that everyone was motivated to commit crime, since is was often rewarding or fun; however, the theory maintained that most people did not act on their selfish impulses due to the mechanisms of external social control built into society. Such things as attachments to groups or other persons, commitments to valued roles, involvement in noncriminal activities, and shared beliefs in the validity of legal norms normally held people in check. Crime occurred when social control mechanisms weakened and failed to restrain individual impulses. In contrast, what was termed *labeling* theory argued that strong social control made things worse, paradoxically causing more, rather than less, crime. It posited that everyone engaged in incidental deviate (nominally illegal) behavior but that in some cases the deviance was identified and formally labeled as crime. The process of labeling and stigmatizing persons as criminals caused them to systematically commit crime as a consequence of being socially cast in a criminal role and acquiring a criminal identity.

Such sociological theories provided little basis for treating individual offenders in correctional settings; however, they carried clear implications for setting broader social policies and programs. Much of the social welfare policy in the United States during the 1960s and 1970s was shaped by some version of either strain theory or subcultural theory. The policies of minimizing official prosecution for minor non-predatory offenders (e.g., diversion into treatment programs, decriminalization of victimless crimes, and deinstitutionalization of persons who do not need to be incapacitated) were directly shaped by labeling theory explanations. Many of the programs to reduce juvenile crime by involving youth in recreational programs and extracurricular groups were explicitly shaped by social control theory. Thus the practical effects of these explanations were substantial, particularly through the 1970s.

The positivist approach provided the dominant framework for thinking about crime and how to control it through the 1960s and into the 1970s. Criminologists did not seriously question the assumption that with the continued evolution of social science, we would accumulate more precise knowledge about crime and its causes, and we would develop more effective technologies for controlling it. We would progress toward the good life and the good society through the accumulated advances of science. However, by the mid–1970s, faith in that positivist vision was beginning to weaken and doubts about the criminal justice policies based on it were growing. Increasing criticisms appeared of the rehabilitation model for corrections (psychological positivism) and the social welfare or social engineering model for public policy (sociological positivism). Accumulated crime data suggested that such policies based on this approach did not really reduce crime, and in fact crime rates and criminal disorder seemed to be getting worse under such policies. Political attitudes were shifting in a more conservative direction that favored thinking about crime in more moralistic, less scientific terms and taking a stronger, more punitive stance toward criminal offenders. The dominance of the positivist framework for explaining crime was greatly reduced, and the search was open for alternative approaches, including reconsideration of earlier frameworks. For instance, in the late 1970s, the *justice* model emerged as a major rival to positivist explanations and policies. Interestingly, the alternative provided by the justice model was essentially a return to the classical model that had preceded it.

CONTEMPORARY

EXPLANATIONS OF CRIME

After the past decades and centuries of changes in crime theory, where are we now? What kinds of explanations of crime are most plausible and appealing in the mid–1990s? More than in prior decades, no single theoretical view dominates thinking or controls the research agenda in criminology. If anything, the reverse is true: Research and policy seem to control the development of limited theories chosen to suit practical contingencies. Thus, a notable feature of current crime explanation is its theoretical ambivalence, reflecting uncertainty about which theories actually have been tested and which are empirically disconfirmed or supported. It suggests a situation of theoretical pluralism in which all theories seem equally valid scientifically and so must be distinguished on other grounds.

In that case, theoretical explanations are favored because of their intuitive or ideological appeal. For example, *rational choice* explanations provide one of the currently popular ways of describing crime. These represent a very broad category of explanations that draw upon a variety of different theoretical sources but which are not neatly contained within any specific theoretical model. Rational choice explanations provide individualistic explanations of crime as pleasure-seeking or profit-calculating behavior; they combine elements of the classical school, psychological learning (reinforcement) theory, cognitive psychology, microeconomic theory, and sometimes neurobiology. They may generate elegant, equation-like accounts of human choices that appeal both to our intuitions and our intellectual sense of logic. However, the research base for such explanations is tentative at best, since it depends heavily on untestable assumptions about human rationality and unmeasurable perceptions or calculations of utility. Its appeal seems based as much on its aesthetic and political qualities as on its scientific validity.

A second noticeable feature of current explanations of crime is a subtle skepticism about the received scientific wisdom regarding criminals and their causes. While most criminologists retain an enduring commitment to scientific methods, most current explanations of crime have backed away from the whole-hearted positivism that prevailed through the 1960s. This includes first a rejection of the assumption of *determinism,* which holds that events are completely explained by a set of prior causes external to a person's will or choice. Current explanations adopt a pointedly nondeterministic or voluntaristic approach to crime in which the immediate causes of behavior are the individual choices. A second change has been a downplaying of the importance of *universal theory,* referring to the positivist search for general laws of behavior that hold for all time, places, persons, and types of crime. Contemporary analyses deal more in limited, concrete practical explanations that fit the facts and the situation at hand than in general abstract theory. There also seems to be a softening of the *empiricism* assumption that careful measurement and experimental tests are always more valid or correct than common sense and logic. And, finally, there is increasing resistance to the positivist assumption of moral *neutrality*— that scientific knowledge must be value-free, uncolored by ideological preconceptions or moral preferences. Current explanations seem to acknowledge and espouse more directly the role of values in scientific explanation.

The 1990s witnessed the emergence of criminology or "criminal justice science" as a separate academic discipline. No longer viewed just as a subfield of sociology or as an ad hoc amalgam of several disciplines, criminology increasingly appeared in separate departments with separate and independent doctorate-granting programs and with substantial research funding support from the federal government. Criminology as "criminal justice science" has carved out its own distinctive place as a multidisciplinary policy science.

Consistent with this development, contemporary explanation of crime is generally more eclectic and pragmatic. Not constrained by traditional separations between academic disciplines and focused on practical answers to policy questions, current explanations commonly draw ideas from several different theoretical traditions or sources without worrying about maintaining disciplinary loyalty or theoretical purity. Quite recently, a strong interest has developed in the process of theory integration, through which ideas, concepts, and hypotheses may be borrowed from several different theories and combined to form a fuller, more detailed, or more comprehensive explanation for crime. Such integrations are an appealing departure from the traditional oppositional mode of theory development in criminology which has emphasized divergence rather than synthesis. Integration seems like an obvious step toward better explanations of crime. However, the validity and methodology of theory integration is still open to debate, since the theories being combined may not be fully compatible with one another. Thus, theory integration emerges as a promising but unfulfilled and untested theme in current crime explanations.

An additional emergent feature of current crime explanations is its theoretical *conservatism,* referring by that term to the reliance on earlier ideas, assumptions, and values. In theoretical terms, this conservatism appears as a preference for certain kinds of explanations and congruence to certain political beliefs. One is the current prevalence of individualistic explanations that focus analysis on the personal attributes and actions of criminal offenders as the efficient causes of crime. These effectively phrase the reality of crime in individual-level terms and depict criminals as distinctive kinds of people. Another trend is the rationalistic–voluntaristic conceptualization of crime used in many current explanations. This view of crime depicts it, by assumption, as a calculated act chosen by a conscious deliberate offender according to its expected payoffs. Offenders know what they are doing and why they are doing it, and they choose to do it. The latter explains crime as the outcome of moral choices made by persons who act willfully and know what they are doing, who are morally and legally accountable for their actions, and who deserve to be punished if they break the law.

WHERE ARE WE GOING?

Having reviewed a variety of past approaches to explaining crime, how do we estimate future directions in crime theory? A cautious prediction would be that the next twenty years of thinking about crime will mostly bring more of the same—that is, our ideas generally will be a continuation of current modes of explanation. Over a twenty-year span, major changes in theoretical substance are highly unlikely, as is the introduction of any radically new ideas about crime. Large major theoretical shifts or substitutions invariably have a longer term of development. They also require a social context that is itself undergoing major upheavals, which seems unlikely at this point. In that sense, the safest prediction might be that differences in crime explanations in the year 2010 will be small alterations in emphasis, tone, or orientation rather than new ideas.

However, what kinds of things might prompt noticeable changes in the way we explain and understand crime? Are there likely developments that would modify the conservative trends of maintaining our present ideas? These changes might result from (1) ideological shifts in dominant political attitudes or moral values, (2) technological advances that produce new kinds of criminal acts as well as new ways to detect or measure the occurrence of crime, and (3) social structural changes in the economy, political systems or organizations, and basic social activities (such as work, school, family, and leisure).

One consideration might be changes in the very thing we are trying to explain—that is, the content of crime itself or in the patterns by which it occurs. When this happens, the kinds of explanation at hand may not serve well for the new conditions. Overall, we might expect the amount of violence, and perhaps street crime generally, to remain fairly stable by 2010. National victimization data have shown rather stable levels over the past two decades, with a slight downward trend in some crimes, with no indications that the next two decades would bring a reversal. However, other kinds of crime may increase as a result of social political changes.

New forms of crime may appear as a result of legal changes that criminalize activities that are now considered deviant, immoral, or undesirable but not necessarily criminal. Social debates about the morality of controversial activities such as pornography, gambling, or recreational drug use may transform criminal laws to extend or restrict the definition of what is illegal (and what is therefore counted as a "crime"). Legal events in the 1960s and 1970s changed abortion from a criminal act to a routine medical procedure; legal events in the early 1990s pointed toward a reversal of that change. Definitions of what counts as criminal violence between intimates are also in the process of changing, including both child abuse and sexual violence. What counts as a violent act in 2010, and the explanations needed to understand these newer forms of violence, are likely to be (at least subtly) different from current definitions of criminal violence, and possibly substantially different.

Technological changes will also produce new forms of crime, making possible activities and kinds of victimizations that did not occur before. Drug crime may be enhanced by technological advances that create new drugs with new effects or new ways to manufacture and distribute existing drugs. A familiar example would be the development of crack as a more potent, more readily distributed, and more easily administered form of cocaine. The development of computer technology and the spread of electronic services throughout the economy mean new opportunities for new crimes (e.g., new forms of theft, vandalism, extortion, and even violence) being carried out by new kinds of offenders who do not closely resemble street crime offenders. Evolving computer technology may also serve to redefine what crime means as a legal concept through the production of *virtual reality,* experiences that are psychologically real but physically imaginary. This offers the possibility for people to experience psychedelic sensations traditionally produced by illegal drugs but which do not require chemical substances or their harmful physical effects—that is, the possibility of "drugless drugs." Virtual reality also could be used to produce simulated thrill experiences that would be criminal if actually carried out, such as sexual assaults or assassinations, but which have no real victim—that is, the possibility of "victimless victimizations." Such developments may force a dramatic redefinition in the essential meaning of "criminal" acts.

Changes in the social structure of society may also affect the types and patterns of crime that we need to explain. Shifts in the age distribution of society can dramatically alter the overall amount of crime occurring as well as the dominant patterns of crime, since age is strongly related to the levels and types of crime found in a population. Economic changes will influence the patterns of crime, but usually in complex ways. For instance, some kinds of crime increase in periods of economic prosperity, while others increase during periods of economic decline. The continuation of racial and economic inequality will also affect the amount and nature of crime that is taking place in 2010. Many observers have commented on the growing permanent underclass in American society, which seems to be growing larger, more permanent, and more socially dispossessed with each passing decade. Rather than declining, the gap between the top and bottom classes of society has increased and become more distinct.

The occurrence of social disorder or racial or economic conflict can dramatically influence the crime situation that we wish to understand—as the late 1960s and early 1970s demonstrated. Such events may change the nature of criminal activity and motivation, prompting much more politically motivated crime than otherwise would occur—for example, the extensive terrorism that emerged in the 1970s. Thus, the occurrence of new crimes associated with noticeable social disorder and structural conflict will make us much more receptive to sociological explanations and will stimulate a boom in social structural theory. In contrast, during periods of relative order and stability, crime explanation will favor individualistic accounts, since the social environment seems more benign or nonproblematic and less relevant at such times.

A second reason for finding theoretical shifts in explanation of crime would be the development of new forms of knowledge that alter what we know about the world (even if the world itself has not changed much). Advances in scientific theory or method outside of criminology may have this effect, since they modify what we consider to be good scientific explanations. The recent elaboration of so-called *chaos theory* is an example of this possibility. While the theory does not directly bear on the issue of crime, having been developed to explain phenomena in physical or biological systems, it does subtly affect the criteria by which crime explanations are measured. The analysis of what appears to be chaos in physical systems has demonstrated that randomness or indeterminacy at an individual micro level may nonetheless lead to determinate patterns and predictability at a larger macro level of the system. That finding lends scientific approval to explanations of crime that posit causal determination of crime rates or patterns at a social level while arguing for free will and impulsive choice at the individual level. Thus, it helps resolve a traditional contradiction between the classical model of crime (in terms of individual rationality and free moral choice) and scientific models of behavior (in terms of cause-and-effect determinations).

Even developments in abstract mathematics may affect how we explain crime by providing powerful new statistical methods to analyze and quantify crime data. Such methodological advances invariably prompt the adaptation or development of new theories to conform to the format or requirements of the new methods. The persistent drive to accomplish more scientifically sophisticated analyses means that theoretical development often follows technological change, rather than the reverse.

Developments in other scientific fields seemingly unrelated to crime often have "carryover" effects into criminological theory. Developments in behavioral genetics linking particular genetic conditions to schizophrenia, alcoholism, drug addiction, or homosexuality may be extrapolated to apply to other forms of deviance and, by implication, to criminality. Thus, physical explanations of criminality may be inspired by advances in biological theory that have no direct connection to the study of crime. Theoretical developments in human geography are another source of outside theoretical influence by providing new, environmentally based models of human social organization. Such explanations of the spatial dimensions of behavior may be readily adapted to the task of explaining crime through ecological or even architectural theories of crime.

Since scientific knowledge consists of data as well as theories, crime explanations may be influenced by the accumulation of empirical facts. The existing body of collected scientific facts about something serves to define what specifically we need to explain. As these facts accumulate, they may force a theoretical modification when our current explanations do not fit or predict them very well. A classic example of this process is the sixteenth-century Copernican revolution in which the continued collection of empirical data—thousands of recorded measurements of the position and movements of the planets—forced a theoretical upheaval in astronomy that changed the face of modern science. The traditional theory, sanctioned by religious dogma, asserted that the sun and the planets revolved around the earth, since the earth was ordained to be the fixed center of the whole universe. However, the collected measurements on planetary motion did not fit the theory very well, even with unusual adjustments added to the mathematical equations. Copernicus suggested that the empirical data were much better predicted (and explained) if we presumed that the earth revolved around the sun, rather than the reverse, and that the sun was the center of the planetary system. That kind of theoretical modification revolutionized how scientific theories explained the physical world, and it prompted a shift away from theories based on religious dogma to theories derived from scientific research.

In parallel fashion, the accumulation of data about crime may prompt a change in our theories to achieve a better fit with what is empirically found to be true. The well-documented patterns of variation in crime by age, sex, and race are basic empirical data that any explanation (new or old) must be able to fit to be taken seriously. But as the new data and patterns of crime appear, they will modify and extend those requirements. For instance, the rehabilitation model dominated correctional thinking for most of the twentieth century. It posited that crime was caused by offenders' learned attitudes and social experiences, neither of which resulted from deliberate choices and both of which could be corrected by rehabilitative treatment. As the empirical evidence accumulated regarding the effect on crime rates of correctional treatments based on this model, the rehabilitation model was challenged and substantially replaced as the dominant way of thinking about crime control and punishment. As data continue to accumulate regarding the effects of programs (favoring punishment to deter and incapacitate offenders) that replaced rehabilitation, we may be led to question whether these explanations work any better.

The collection of additional crime data also tends to prompt elaboration of explanations, often yielding more complex accounts of crime that are limited in scope to particular kinds of people or situations. The accumulation of data regarding crime committed by women has forced a reconsideration of whether traditional explanations, developed to explain crime in young males, really apply to females or whether separate explanations are needed for male and female crimes. The accumulating data on sexual abuse have gradually forced a theoretical reevaluation of that type of crime, since empirical patterns that have been found are not readily predicted or explained by conventional theories. As a cross-cultural body of international data on crime has become available, they have prompted new comparative analysis of crime to develop less ethnocentric explanations that will apply across societies. That becomes necessary since the cross-cultural data often are inconsistent with crime theories developed to fit U.S. crime patterns. Thus, the development of more and better data on crime often drives theoretical changes, in order to be able to explain the factual evidence available at that moment.

A third and very important issue in how theoretical explanations change is the effect of ideological frameworks—involving the systems of moral, political, and religious values with which people regard the world. Such values will invariably define our sense of what really matters and of what ultimately must be true and good. The impact of ideological factors is obvious in the case of supernatural explanations of crime, since these reflected on ideology that dictated particular views of universal law, human nature, morality, and crime as sin. But in other periods as well, the impact of prevailing ideology on crime theory has been just as large. The dominance of biological theories around the turn of the century partly reflects their strong distinction between criminals and noncriminals as two distinct categories of human beings—one inferior and one superior—and its convergence with the then prevalent belief in social Darwinism as a justification for gross economic exploitation and inequality, as well as overtly racist policies. In contrast, the Progressive Era of the early twentieth century featured an ideology of social progress, social reform, and social welfare that minimized innate individual differences and promoted the rise of less individualistic sociological theories of crime. Such explanations began with the premise that people are basically good, morally equal, and perfectible social beings. They may be corrupted by faulty socialization or misled by social circumstances, but the effective cause of their misfortune was to be found in the larger structures of the social environment rather than in their own personal defects or willful choices.

A more recent example of ideological effects on crime explanation would be the conservative shift of political attitudes that the United States underwent in the 1970s and 1980s, which generated active skepticism and criticism toward the rehabilitation model of corrections and its positivism. This ideological change prompted a new look at how to explain crime, one that rejected much of the sociological and psychiatric explanations that had prevailed up to then. In place of external or unconscious causation, the new look favored crime explanations that (1) were premised on willful individual choice and moral accountability for wrongful actions, (2) made a clear differentiation (both morally and scientifically) between criminals and noncriminals, and (3) supported the use of punitive (over rehabilitative) methods of controlling and sanctioning criminal offenders. Although the positivist–rehabilitative model was widely reported to have been disproven, the model was abandoned in large part because it was no longer consistent with prevailing moral and political attitudes. The "new" models that replaced it—namely, of deterrence and incapacitation—have not been better supported by empirical research, but they are closer to current political sensibilities and more consistent with what people feel *should* be true.

The impact of feminism provides another example of recent ideological influences on our thinking about crime, in particular our ideas about domestic violence and sexual violence. As a result of feminist critiques articulating sexual biases in traditional conceptualization of crime, we have substantially altered our sense of what the term "criminal violence" means and what is most problematic about it. By looking at violence in these new terms, we have found patterns of child abuse and sexual assault very different from those predicted by traditional theories, so different that we must generate new explanations to account for them.

SOME SPECIFIC PREDICTIONS AND EXTRAPOLATIONS

No one can say exactly what the predominant ideological values and arguments will be and how they will be different twenty years from now, but some developments from our ongoing efforts to explain crime seem plausible. We can cautiously suggest several likely features of criminological explanation in the year 2010. In all instances, these do not represent brand new or substantially different ideas about crime, rather they are extensions, exaggerations, or elaborations of current forms of explanation that seem likely to continue and to intensify in the coming two decades.

One prediction is that explanations of crime in 2010 will be more eclectic than past theories, less tied to a single theoretical tradition or discipline. With the continued development of criminology as an independent multidisciplinary science, efforts at explaining crime will also be less concerned with maintaining traditional disciplinary separations and more concerned with looking for good ideas wherever they may be found—without regard for disciplinary divisions or identifications. The traditional academic distinctions between biology, psychology, and sociology will be much less salient or sacred. Theoretical pedigrees will be less important than how well an explanation enables us to predict and deal with crime. Correspondingly, we expect that crime theories will be more synthetic, combining ideas from several different fields and disciplines. Three of the most popular current frameworks for explaining crime are good examples of such eclectic, integrative efforts. One is the current development of biosocial and psychobiological theories that express the reemergence of biological factors in criminology as they are combined with psychological and sociological concepts. That synthesis is quite likely to expand over the next several decades, given the strong contemporary support for biological and medical research. A second is the strong interest in *social control* theory as a common framework that comfortably mixes psychological and sociological explanations and which has been developing for three decades or so. Given that persistence and its compatibility with both liberal and conservative ideologies, it seems likely to continue as a dominant theoretical framework for at least another thirty years. The third is the *rational choice* theory, which draws from a variety of different theoretical sources including classical legal philosophy, behavioral learning (reinforcement) theory, cognitive psychology, microeconomic theory, and sometimes even neurobiology.

A second prediction is that explanations of crime in 2010 will be more comparative and less confined to a single society or single dominant group within society. By tradition, crime theory has developed with a strongly ethnocentric orientation, focused almost exclusively on the United States—as if it were the whole world—and limited to specific high-crime groups—namely, young, urban, minority, poor males—as if crime were a problem confined to such groups. Recent crime data from sources other than official crime statistics have documented as empirical facts that crime is not restricted to one place or one group of persons. They show that a much greater variety of crime data must be used for a complete picture. In addition, recently available international data on crime point out the folly of looking only at crime in the United States. Many explanations developed to explain variation in crime rates in U.S. cities do not hold up when applied to other cities and countries around the world and do not explain crossnational differences in crime. As greater standardization and information sharing of crime data occur, such international comparison will provide increasingly available and important empirical tests of our explanations. At the same time, recent studies of drug crime, organized crime, and white-collar crime suggest that crime must be viewed in an international context, as a social process extended across national boundaries, if we want to develop more comprehensive and general explanations of why and how it occurs.

A third prediction is that explanations of crime will be predominantly *individualistic* rather than collective and *voluntaristic* rather than deterministic, a complete reversal of the sociological positivism or determinism that prevailed through the 1960s and a return to classical eighteenth-century ideas about crime. Current explanations of crime increasingly locate the efficient cause in individual choice rather than in objective conditions outside the individual's control, such as unconscious personality mechanisms, biological events, environmental conditions, or social structures that cause crime to happen. The latter are viewed as predisposing factors that may constrain or encourage certain behaviors (both law-abiding and criminal), but they are not causal determinants of the outcome. That is a matter of choice by the individual actor who is willfully pursuing his or her own personal interests in a conscious, calculating, rational, goal-seeking fashion. Given recent political developments—for example, the gradual capitalization of communist countries and the disaggregation of large political collectives—we would expect a continuation of the current theoretical conservatism for some time into the future, quite plausibly extending to 2010.

A fourth prediction is that crime explanation in 2010 will be distinctively more applied and pragmatic in orientation. It will be oriented more to the solution of immediate practical or political problems than to the evolutionary development of general abstract theory. That pragmatic turn is partly a function of the economic and political circumstances within which criminology has been developing as a separate academic field. It has gained influence and autonomy as a result of the availability of substantial funding (federal and otherwise) for research on crime, criminals, and crime control. But funding for research on crime has a practical, policy-limited focus, being offered to efforts to find answers to current problems. Thus, as theory development tends to follow research efforts, theory is subtly but powerfully guided toward short-term, limited-focus issues rather than toward broader scientific knowledge.

A fifth prediction is that the study of crime will pay increasing attention to white-collar crime. This category of criminal acts traditionally has been treated as not really crime, at least in the same sense as ordinary street crime, and has received considerably less criminological attention. The predicted change in attention reflects the growing prominence of white-collar crime and the growing awareness of its costs and consequences. A major concern is that white-collar crime is the area of crime with the greatest potential for expansion and growth in the next twenty years. With continued development of computers and their application into almost all aspects of our lives, new forms of crime will be created that involve illegal uses of computer for personal gain or personal thrills—what has colorfully been dubbed "hacking" and "cyberpunk." As economic change becomes increasingly a matter of electronic transfer and possession of wealth merely a matter of electronic credits in a computer account (rather than actual physical possession and exchange), forms of theft now accomplished as ordinary property crimes will be transformed into white-collar crimes. In addition, as more empirical data on white-collar crime have accumulated, they have documented how serious the loss and harm from white-collar crimes are and how extensively they may occur.

The expansion of white-collar crime and the accumulation of data to measure its effects and the extensiveness are likely to generate new, or at least greatly modified, explanations for crime. To date, most explanations of crime have been focused on physical street crime. It is not clear that such explanations work well in understanding white-collar crime, since the physical activities are different, as are the social meaning of these activities and the social contexts in which they occur.

A sixth prediction is that crime explanation in 2010 will show a renewed appreciation of the *biological foundations* of human behavior, assigning more theoretical substance to biological and medical factors. Complete integration of biological with psychological and sociological theories is not likely—not in the short span of twenty years. However, they will be viewed as less incompatible than criminology has argued during most of the twentieth century. This prediction is based on several conditions that are likely to continue through 2010. For one thing, we have continued to maintain faith in the natural sciences, including medical science, even while our confidence in the social sciences has faded considerably. We continue to believe that if only we do enough research and look hard enough, we will find a medical cure for almost any disease. Moreover, medicine is the place where real scientific or technological breakthroughs are likely to occur, rather than in behavioral or social science (where breakthroughs are rare and infrequent). And last, biological explanations are quite consistent with contemporary ideological frameworks. They allow and even encourage us to presume a clear dichotomous distinction between criminals and noncriminals. They also are consistent with our ongoing preference for individualistic accounts of behavior, where the important and immediate causes of crime are located in the person rather than in the larger social structures or groups. Biological explanations also turn out in modern versions to be fully compatible with our preference for voluntaristic, nondeterministic models of human behavior. Thus, contemporary biological models are much more congenial to the dominant theory of justice, which depicts persons making willful behavioral choices (within some natural limits) for which they are morally accountable.

SECOND THOUGHTS
ABOUT PREDICTING THE FUTURE

If predicting the future generally is an uncertain venture with faint hope of success, then predicting the future of what our thoughts and ideas will be in twenty years must seem downright silly. Our chances of predicting correctly—admittedly not very high—are also unknowable. We cannot know how well or poorly we have predicted until 2010 arrives. At that point we will have no use at all for our old predictions (except perhaps a little curiosity value). Thus, we have no way of assessing how good our predictions are and little practical use of them.

We might argue that the real value of such predictions is what they contribute to present understanding of crime, rather than how well they actually foretell the future. The utility of trying to think about future developments is not a function of their accuracy in 2010. It would still be a useful effort even if future events occurred such that our predictions turned out to be mostly wrong. Such predictions are useful because they prompt us to analyze more critically the contents and conditions of our current ideas and explanations. They push us to see what changes have already occurred and how they have been influenced by social and historical factors. We will be forced to look at our explanations and descriptions of crime from a different standpoint, one that we hope is less embedded within the contingencies and the hidden assumptions of the present context.

Ideally, if we do this carefully and thoughtfully, it will provide us with new, enhanced appreciation of the changes going on at this moment, as well as some understanding of where they might take us later on and the choices we will have to make. Thus, our paradox is that thinking about crime and criminal justice in the year 2010 is a "bootless task" but one that seems well worth the effort.

FOR FURTHER READING

New Theoretical Developments

John P. Briggs and F. David Peat. *The Turbulent Mirror.* New York: Harper & Row, 1989.

James P. Crutchfield, J. Doyne Farmer, Norman H. Packard, and Robert Shaw. "Chaos," *Scientific American, 255* (December), 46–57 (1986).

These two sources provide accessible, nontechnical introductions to the recent development of chaos theory, an emerging perspective that promises to revolutionize scientific thinking and explanation. Initially developed for scientific analysis of physical and biological systems, it has been extended to the explanation of such psychological phenomena as cognition, decision making, and risk taking, as well as to social phenomena such as economic systems and marketing. It is likely to dramatically alter how we think about crime in the future, at least within a scientific framework.

Historical Developments in the Theory of Crime

Don C. Gibbons. *The Criminological Enterprise: Theories and Perspectives.* Englewood Cliffs, NJ: Prentice-Hall, 1979.

C. Ronald Huff. "Historical Explanations of Crime: From Demons to Politics." In James A. Inciardi and Kenneth F. Haas (eds.). *Crime and the Criminal Justice System.* 1978. [Reprinted in Delos Kelly (ed.). (1980) *Criminal Behavior.* New York: St. Martin's Press.]

Ysabel Rennie. *The Search for Criminal Man: A Conceptual History of the Dangerous Offender.* Lexington, MA: Lexington Books, 1978.

These three sources provide comprehensive yet readable overviews of the development of modern ideas about crime; they provide a good sense of the historical context within which crime explanations have evolved. The coverage ranges from the earliest unscientific ideas about crime, across the past several centuries, and up through the past decade or so.

The Social Contexts of Crime Theory

Robert J. Lilly, Francis T. Cullen, and Richard A. Ball. *Criminological Theory: Context and Consequences.* Newbury Park: CA: Sage, 1989.

George Vold and Thomas J. Bernard. *Theoretical Criminology* (3rd ed.). New York: Oxford University Press, 1986.

These two books look at crime theory as a reflection of the social contexts within which it is developed. They stress that explanations of crime are not isolated or disembodied bits of abstract truth but always embedded within the practical and political settings in which they are developed and used. The first source (Lilly, Cullen, and Ball) focuses mainly on sociological explanations. The second source (Vold and Bernard) provides a more advanced and comprehensive coverage of biological, psychological, as well as sociological theories; it is widely regarded as probably *the* best single summary of theorizing about crime.

Integrated Theories of Crime

James Q. Wilson and Richard Herrnstein. *Crime and Human Nature.* New York: Basic Books, 1985.

Lee Ellis and Harry Hoffman (eds.). *Crime in Biological, Social, and Moral Contexts.* New York: Praeger, 1990.

These two sources represent two current trends in crime theory that will affect the content of future explanations. One is an explicit, unapologetic reliance on biological and physiological factors to describe the foundations of human behavior. The other is the development of integrated theories of crime that bridge the usual divisions between biological, psychological, and sociological theories. Such efforts aim at providing a more comprehensive explanation of crime that avoids the disciplinary debates of the past.

DISCUSSION QUESTIONS

1. We have always tried to explain why some people commit crime while others do not. How have our explanations influenced how we treat criminals?

2. How are classical and positivist explanations of crime relevant or useful in explaining crime now and in the future? How have these perspectives affected the operation of the criminal justice system?

3. Our understanding of crime can be influenced by many things. What factors in contemporary society influence the way in which we understand crime? Discuss the role of technology, social factors, and other influences in explaining crime.

4. How have ideologies or political beliefs affected crime research and crime policy?

5. After having read this chapter, to what degree do you think that explanations of crime have been and are currently based on scientific principles?

4

☆

The Law of the Future

JAMES R. ACKER
State University of New York at Albany

The library at Harvard Law School contains almost 1.5 million books, including more than 500 volumes of United States Supreme Court decisions, close to 1,300 volumes of federal courts of appeals opinions, and nearly 800 volumes of federal district court decisions. Law libraries also house 50 separate "titles" of the *United States Code,* which contain thousands of federal statutes, and 50 titles of the *Code of Federal Regulations,* with the massive proliferation of federal administrative rules. Hundreds upon hundreds of case reporters, statute books, and administrative publications report thousands upon thousands of judicial decisions, legislative enactments, and regulatory codes of the 50 states. Two separate computer systems make daily and even hourly updates in these references.

In light of the multiplicity of sources, the diversity and the perpetually changing nature of "the law," ours would be a daunting task if we had only to describe the law as it exists in 1995. Our mission becomes

I am indebted to my colleagues Fred Cohen and Stephen Wasby for commenting on an earlier draft of this chapter.

even more difficult as we enter the realm of prediction, of forecasting the law in the year 2010. If we are not to become hopelessly enmeshed in "the seamless web" of the law, we must narrow our inquiry considerably. We initially focus on the past, present, and likely future of criminal procedure law and then briefly examine issues that may be important to the substantive criminal law twenty years hence.

CRIMINAL PROCEDURE LAW: PAST, PRESENT, AND FUTURE

For roughly thirty years, in both the state and federal justice systems, issues of criminal procedure law have been framed and analyzed under the dominant influence of the Bill of Rights and due process guarantees of the United States Constitution. It was not always that way in the past, and it is not likely to remain that way in the future.

The Ghosts of Supreme Courts Past and Present

The laws and governments of the thirteen original states were in existence well before the ratification of the U.S. Constitution in 1789. The Constitution established a system of dual sovereignty between the states and the federal government, a system in which it was unquestioned that the states would have the exclusive province to administer their criminal laws free from federal control or oversight. The Bill of Rights was added to the Constitution in 1791 for the specific purpose of preventing the newly created federal government from encroaching upon individual liberties and the states' traditional spheres of autonomy. The design decidedly was not to require the states to adhere to the provisions of the first ten amendments, many of which merely duplicated rights already recognized under state laws and constitutions (*Barron v. City of Baltimore,* 1833). State statutes and the decisions of state courts exclusively determined the rights of those suspected, accused, and convicted of violating state criminal laws during this country's formative years.

Two legal innovations at the conclusion of the Civil War were destined to have a profound impact on federal–state relations in the administration of the criminal law. One was the ratification of the Fourteenth Amendment, with its requirement that "nor shall any state deprive any person of life, liberty, or property, without due process of law." Unlike the specific provisions of the Bill of Rights, the Fourteenth Amendment's due process clause expressly applied against *state* governments and, by direct implications, to state criminal proceedings. The second development was Congress's passage of habeas corpus legislation that empowered federal courts to determine whether a state prisoner was being restrained of his or her liberty in violation of the U.S. Constitution. Initially, neither the Fourteenth Amendment's due process clause nor the federal habeas corpus legislation dramatically affected state criminal procedures. Today it seems quite odd that it was only a generation ago in state criminal courts that

> poor people could be tried and imprisoned without a lawyer and also could be denied trial transcripts needed to appeal their convictions, unless they could pay for them;
>
> prosecutors who did not secure a conviction at a first trial could again bring a defendant to trial on the same charges;
>
> evidence seized by police without a warrant, without probable cause, or pursuant to some other illegality could nevertheless be admitted in trials;
>
> defendants could be tried and convicted without a jury, even for serious felonies; and
>
> criminal suspects could be held incommunicado by the police and subjected to prolonged interrogation without counsel, and their confessions were nevertheless deemed admissible.

Such practices were perfectly lawful under Supreme Court rulings that constrained the states only to observe "fundamental fairness" in their criminal proceedings under the due process clause (*Powell* v. *Alabama,* 1932:67) and to recognize only such rights as were "implicit in the concept of ordered liberty" (*Palko* v. *Connecticut,* 1937:325).

Then came the "due process revolution" of the 1960s. Under the leadership of Chief Justice Earl Warren, the Supreme Court held that the fundamental protections of the Bill of Rights were specifically enforceable in state criminal proceedings. Invoking the Fourteenth Amendment's due process clause, the Warren Court "selectively incorporated" an impressive roster of constitutional guarantees that previously had been binding only in federal criminal trials: the Fourth Amendment's search-and-seizure provisions (*Ker* v. *California,* 1963) and its corollary exclusionary rule (*Mapp* v. *Ohio,* 1961); the Fifth Amendment's guarantees against compelled self-incrimination (*Malloy*

v. *Hogan*, 1964) and double jeopardy (*Benton* v. *Maryland*, 1969); the Sixth Amendment's rights to counsel (*Gideon* v. *Wainwright*, 1963), to confront opposing witnesses (*Pointer* v. *Texas*, 1965), to compulsory process (*Washington* v. *Texas*, 1967), and to trial by jury (*Duncan* v. *Louisiana*, 1968); and the Eighth Amendment's prohibition against cruel and unusual punishment (*Robinson* v. *California*, 1962). Simultaneously, the Court relaxed long-standing restrictions on federal habeas corpus by expanding the scope of federal court review of state convictions (*Brown* v. *Allen*, 1953) and by liberalizing the procedures that governed the filing of federal habeas corpus petitions (*Fay* v. *Noia*, 1963). State inmates thus were provided ready access to the federal courts if the state courts proved reluctant to recognize their newfound federal constitutional rights, and the justices established an effective means of ensuring that the state courts would enforce the constitutional rights announced in their recent decisions.

Ideologically, the Warren Court was firmly committed to a due process model of criminal justice. This model emphasized equal justice, widespread access to the courts, procedural fairness, and a respect for basic human dignity, even if those values conflicted with the truth-finding function of the criminal process. Warren Court criminal procedure decisions typically were cast in sweeping language and were announced as broad rules, the better to command compliance in the lower courts. Of course, not all Supreme Court rulings during this era recognized or expanded the rights of criminal defendants. For example, states were permitted to exclude women from juries (*Hoyt* v. *Florida*, 1961), non-testimonial evidence was deemed to be outside of Fifth Amendment protection against compelled self-incrimination (*Schmerber* v. *California*, 1966), prosecutors were allowed to make racially motivated peremptory challenges in individual trials (*Swain* v. *Alabama*, 1968), and the police were granted "stop and frisk" powers absent probable cause of criminal wrongdoing (*Terry* v. *Ohio*, 1968). Nevertheless, the Warren Court is widely considered to have been the "moral conscience" of the American justice system.

Warren Burger replaced Earl Warren as Chief Justice in 1969. By 1972, President Richard Nixon, who had campaigned under a tough "law and order" platform, had named three additional justices to the Court, and the beginnings of a judicial "counterrevolution" appeared to be in the making. Early Burger Court decisions produced much "crime control" rhetoric and often chipped away at rights recognized under Warren Court rulings. Through the 1970s, these decisions worked few fundamental changes in and occasionally even extended Warren Court doctrine. However, by the time of Burger's retirement in 1986 and the ascendance of William Rehnquist to Chief Justice, there was no doubt that the Court was steamrolling in a very different direction in its criminal procedure decisions. Current trends in Rehnquist Court rulings are certain to have important implications for criminal procedure law of the future.

Back to the Future: Criminal Procedure Law in 2010

General Themes By 1993, two-thirds of the entire federal judiciary, including a majority of U.S. Supreme Court justices, had been appointed by Presidents Ronald Reagan and George Bush. These judges, many of whom are young, have been carefully screened so that their judicial philosophies bear the conservative imprint of the Reagan–Bush administrations. Their influence on the law will easily persist into the twenty-first century. Future law will owe a heavy debt to the present and the past; ironically, criminal procedure law in 2010 will have many hallmarks of law prior to the Warren Court era. We consider the causes and consequences of these predicted legal trends below.

Judicial Ideology Criminal procedure law often presents agonizingly difficult issues, owing to the multiple masters that it must serve simultaneously: promoting enforcement of the criminal law through procedures that help determine guilt reliably and efficiently, yet ensuring that state officials observe individual liberties and basic fairness while exercising their coercive powers in criminal investigations and trials. The "truth-finding" and "due process" strands of criminal procedure law are often in tension, as when reliable evidence—fingerprints on a murder weapon, a kilogram of cocaine, a detailed confession—is withheld from trial because a suspect's search-and-seizure or Miranda rights were violated. The objective of fact-finding reliability and efficiency is sometimes quite inconsistent with the goal of preserving individual liberties and fairness. Judgments about the relative importance of the law's different objectives may be crucial to the ultimate shape and implementation of specific rules of criminal procedure.

Truth has consistently trumped due process as the dominant value in criminal procedure law in Supreme Court cases decided in recent years. In addition, an invigorated respect for federalism has resulted in the

Court's reluctance to enforce constitutional rules that are not suffi-
ciently tolerant of diversity in the states' administration of criminal
justice, and its renewed interest in preserving the finality of state court
judgments. The justices have also deferred increasingly to legislative and
executive rule making, exhibiting special concern about unwarranted
"judicial activism" and about using constitutional interpretation to
assert their personal views over the will of elected representatives
(*Bowers* v. *Hardwick,* 1986, upholding Georgia's homosexual sodomy law
against due process challenge; *Stanford* v. *Kentucky,* 1989, finding no
cruel and unusual punishment prohibition against executing 16- and
17-year-old murderers). In combination, these judicial preferences for
truth, the finality of convictions, federalism, majoritarian decision making over due process values, and an active role for the federal judiciary
in policing possible constitutional violations will strongly influence the
criminal procedure law of the future.

The Erosion of Precedent The doctrine of *stare decisis,* or a respect
for precedent, is a great stabilizing influence in law, and one reason why
constitutional rules do not normally fluctuate erratically with changes
in judicial personnel. Nevertheless, the present foundation of legal rules
may not last into 2010 without substantial reworking. Much precedent
in criminal procedure law is in jeopardy of being dismantled by subsequent decisions through outright overruling or through more gradual
erosion.

The Rehnquist Court has expressly devalued the role of precedent
in constitutional criminal procedure cases, particularly when the prior
cases invoked as precedent "were decided by the narrowest of margins,
over spirited dissents" (*Payne* v. *Tennessee,* 1991:2611, overruling *Booth* v.
Maryland, 1987; and *South Carolina* v. *Gathers,* 1989, approving the
admissability of "victim impact" evidence at capital sentencing hearings). During its 1990–91 term alone, the Court overruled or repudi-
ated portions of three other cases significant to criminal procedure. In
so doing, it held that the erroneous admission of a coerced confession
at trial can be harmless error (*Arizona* v. *Fulminate,* 1991, departing from
Chapman v. *California,* 1967); authorized warrantless searches of con-
tainers placed in cars (*California* v. *Acevedo,* 1991, overruling *Arkansas* v.
Sanders, 1979); and enforced the procedural forfeiture of habeas corpus
claims without a deliberate bypass of state appeal remedies (*Coleman* v.
Thompson, 1991, overruling *Fay* v. *Noia,* 1963). Former Justice Marshall,
who took strong exception to the court's attitude about stare decisis,

charged that "the continued vitality of literally scores of decisions [decided by a vote of 5–4 over "spirited dissent"] must be understood to depend on nothing more than the proclivities of the individuals who *now* comprise a majority of the court" (*Payne* v. *Tennessee,* 1991:2623). If he is correct, such landmark rulings as *Map* v. *Ohio* (1961, exclusionary rule), *Miranda* v. *Arizona* (1966, rules governing custodial interrogation), *Furman* v. *Georgia* (1972, standardless death penalty) and many other closely decided cases could be in jeopardy of being overruled.

Overruling of precedent sometimes threatens the perceived legitimacy of constitutional decisions by conveying the impression that the law is little more than whatever five Supreme Court Justices say it is at any particular time. It is far more common for precedent to be circumvented in other ways. For instance, the Burger and Rehnquist Courts have pulled back from important Warren Court rulings by holding that neither the exclusionary rule (*United States* v. *Janis,* 1976; *United States* v. *Calandra,* 1974) nor Miranda warnings (*Michigan* v. *Tucker,* 1974; *Oregon* v. *Elstad,* 1985) are personal rights guaranteed under the Constitution. Rather, these are just judicially created devices for promoting or protecting Fourth and Fifth Amendment rights, respectively. By "deconstitutionalizing" the exclusionary rule and Miranda, the justices have freed themselves to narrow the scope of these protections significantly and even to dispense with them altogether to serve other policy objectives (*United States* v. *Leon,* 1984, "good faith exception" to the exclusionary rule; *New York* v. *Quarles,* 1984, "public safety" exception to Miranda). The Court has further limited the scope of constitutional rules of criminal procedure by selectively applying those rules based on factual distinctions between cases that have little to do with the reason for the rule; this technique allows the later-decided case to swallow the right recognized in an earlier decision (for example, limiting right to counsel at lineups [recognized in *United States* v. *Wade,* 1967] only to postindictment identifications [*Kirby* v. *Illinois,* 1972]).

Restricted Access to the Federal Courts The Warren Court significantly expanded the federal court review of state criminal convictions by broadening the scope of federal habeas corpus and relaxing related procedural requirements. The Burger and Rehnquist Courts have marched resolutely in the opposite direction. Championing values such as the finality of criminal convictions, federalism, and respect for the state courts (*Coleman* v. *Thompson,* 1991; *Stone* v. *Powell,* 1976; *Teague* v. *Lane,* 1989), more recent Supreme Court decisions have dramatically insulated state prisoners' federal constitutional claims from federal habeas corpus review. Such action increasingly has left the Supreme Court as the only federal forum available to prisoners who complain that state courts have not honored their federal constitutional rights. The Supreme Court cannot possibly review more than a handful of state criminal convictions in a year. During its 1989–90 term, for example, the Supreme Court was asked to hear 4,906 cases by appeal or petition for writ of certiorari, yet it rendered decisions on the merits in just 201 cases (4.1 percent), the great majority of which were not criminal.

Cutbacks on federal habeas corpus review of state criminal convictions have taken different form. Alleged Fourth Amendment (search and seizure) violations may no longer be reviewed at all by writ of habeas corpus, as long as the convicted offender had a "full and fair opportunity" to have such claims decided in state court (*Stone* v. *Powell,* 1976). Procedural requirements have made federal habeas litigation a trap for the unwary. Under Warren Court precedent, unless state prisoners had "deliberately bypassed" state court review of their claims, they were free to seek federal habeas corpus relief on all federal constitutional issues (*Fay* v. *Noia,* 1963). More recently, however, constitutional claims not raised at state trial (*Wainwright* v. *Sykes,* 1977) or on appeal (*Coleman* v. *Thompson,* 1991) have been barred from federal court review unless the prisoner can meet a demanding "cause and prejudice" test to excuse the bypass of state court review of the issues. Under a rigorous new standard for "abuse of the writ," which is subject only to narrow exception, prisoners who do not join all possible claims in their initial habeas corpus petition will lose altogether the opportunity to have subsequent claims reviewed (*McCleskey* v. *Zant,* 1991). Absent unusual circumstances, substantive claims that manage to survive procedural default will no longer be reviewed upon habeas corpus if the petitioner seeks to benefit from a "new rule" of law—that is, one not clearly "dictated by precedent" when the state conviction became final (*Butler* v. *McKellar,* 1990; *Teague* v. *Lane,* 1989).

While promoting interests such as the finality of state court convictions, the Court's recent federal habeas corpus decisions have effectively shielded even potentially meritorious constitutional claims from federal review and have substantially reduced federal habeas corpus jurisdiction as an instrument for constitutional law. Congress is not likely to countermand these judicial innovations by revising the federal habeas corpus statute and has shown its willingness to legislate restrictions on habeas corpus in state death penalty cases. It remains to be seen whether the Supreme Court, with Congress' acquiescence, will further limit habeas corpus relief, such as by refusing to reconsider claims fully litigated in the state courts, or by conditioning relief on a colorable showing of innocence, thus ignoring alleged rights violations that do not call guilt into question.

Diversity of Criminal Procedure Law and the Importance of State Courts and Nonjudicial Authorities Something of a vacuum will be created for the recognition and enforcement of individual rights as the Supreme Court continues to give narrow construction to federal constitutional safeguards and to restrict access to the federal courts for the presentation of federal constitutional claims. Pressure will mount on state courts, legislatures, and administrative officials to confer legal protections beyond the threshold established under the United States Constitution. A phenomenal revitalization of state constitutions as a source of individual rights began during the Burger Court era, and there is every reason to expect that state constitutional law will be even more important to criminal procedure law of the future. As a result, search-and-seizure protections in Oregon may exceed those in Mississippi, death penalty cases will be governed by different constitutional rules in New Jersey than in California, and there will be increased balkanization of criminal procedure laws throughout the country.

Diversity will be the watchword of constitutional criminal procedure law in 2010. Legal discourse will center on whether—and how significantly—state protections should exceed the federal constitutional minima announced in Supreme Court decisions. The state courts will not be alone in being pressed to fill the legal breach created by restrictive interpretations of the federal Constitution. State and federal legislatures, prison officials, and other administrators will awaken to the realization that it may make good sense to confer rights beyond those required by the U.S. Constitution.

Specific Issues

We may expect that future criminal procedure law will be shaped consistently with the general principles that we have just reviewed. Making specific predictions about criminal procedure law in 2010 is complicated, however, because one of these general principles is that there will be fewer general principles: Criminal procedure laws of the future will vary substantially from jurisdiction to jurisdiction. We limit our present focus to the baseline of rights likely to be established under the federal Constitution by 2010.

Search and Seizure Fourth Amendment claims will not be favored by the Court because search-and-seizure protections and the exclusionary rule remedy are inimical to truth finding in criminal investigations and trials (*United States* v. *Leon,* 1984). Search-and-seizure protections will be relaxed at a time when technological developments from sophisticated surveillance capabilities (Power 1989; Westin 1966) to DNA information banks (*Jones* v. *Murray,* 1991) will present unparalleled threats to individual privacy. Fourth Amendment rights will be circumscribed through different techniques.

The Fourth Amendment does not come into play at all absent governmental action amounting to a "search" (the violation of a legitimate expectation of privacy; *Katz* v. *United States,* 1967) or a "seizure," that is, a show of authority sufficient to constrain a reasonable person from feeling free to leave or the significant impairment of a person's possessory interest in an object (*California* v. *Hodari D.,* 1991; *Michigan* v. *Chesternut,* 1988). Thus, if a legitimate expectation of privacy has not been infringed by governmental action such as securing telephone records of outgoing phone numbers dialed from a home (*Smith* v. *Maryland,* 1979), conducting aerial surveillance of a private residence (*California* v. *Ciraolo,* 1986), inspecting a homeowner's garbage (*California* v. *Greenwood,* 1988), or causing a trained dog to sniff a suitcase to detect illicit drugs (*United States* v. *Place,* 1983), there has been no "search" and the police do not need either probable cause or the prior authorization of a search warrant to carry out such activities. We can expect that the warrant and probable cause requirements of the Fourth Amendment frequently will be nullified in the future by the Court's readiness to conclude that neither a "search" nor a "seizure" has taken place in circumstances analogous to the above.

The Fourth Amendment has two separate clauses, the first prohibiting "unreasonable searches and seizures," and the second requiring that "no Warrants shall issue, but upon probable cause." Increasingly, the Fourth Amendment's warrant and probable cause requirements can be expected to give way to the much less structured judicial determination of "reasonableness" of governmental activity. The reasonableness of a search or a seizure is determined by an imprecise balancing that involves the nature and extent of the intrusions on individual privacy and the benefits likely to be derived from the intrusive governmental action. This calculus, which seems invariably to be stacked against individual privacy interests, has resulted in the Court condoning government conduct ranging from police "stop and frisks" without probable cause (*Terry* v. *Ohio,* 1968) to employee drug testing (*Skinner* v. *Railway Labor*

Executives' Association, 1989) and the use of police roadblocks to stop vehicles at sobriety checkpoints (*Michigan State Police* v. *Sitz,* 1990) without any suspicion whatsoever that the target individuals have engaged in wrongdoing. Application of a balancing analysis to Fourth Amendment claims may become the norm, and probable cause and warrant "requirements" the exception, in many search-and-seizure contexts in the future.

The exclusionary rule will not survive until 2010 if alternative legislative remedies, such as administrative punishments or damage awards, are implemented to sanction Fourth Amendment violations (cf. *Bivens* v. *Six Unknown Named Agents of Federal Bureau of Narcotics,* 1971:411–424, Burger, C.J., dissenting). Barring such legislative initiative, the Court is not likely to abandon the rule outright. However, the justices are likely to extend the "good faith exception" beyond its present scope—allowing evidence to be admitted following a police officer's reasonable reliance on the authority of an invalid warrant (*United States* v. *Leon,* 1984)—and admit evidence seized in violation of the Fourth Amendment in other situations in which the deterrent value of the rule is deemed minimal, such as when the police make an arrest based on a reasonable mistake of fact (*United States* v. *DeLeon-Reyna,* 1991). Supreme Court cases have repeatedly lamented the perceived costs of the exclusionary rule to the truth-finding process, and they have resolved that the rule is not a personal Fourth Amendment right but a judge-made rule designed exclusively to deter police misconduct (*United States* v. *Leon,* 1984; *United States* v. *Calandra,* 1974). Conditions could not be better for legislative abandonment of the exclusionary rule or for the judiciary to recognize further exceptions to it.

Confessions The Miranda doctrine (*Miranda* v. *Arizona,* 1966) is likely to remain substantially unchanged through 2010. For all of its nuances, Miranda greatly simplified self-incrimination law. It did so by announcing relatively straightforward rules that the police must follow (reading a suspect his or her rights and securing a waiver) before statements obtained through custodial interrogation are admissible to prove guilt at criminal trials. Abandoning these rules not only would reintroduce confusion to the law but also could impede police work. Notwithstanding the hue and cry that erupted when Miranda was decided, the Miranda requirements neither appear to have handcuffed the police from solving crimes nor have had much impact on confession rates.

Moreover, the full potential of Miranda's safeguards has been blunted by rulings that have restrictively interpreted "custody" (*Berkemer* v. *McCarty,* 1984), relaxed requirements for both the "warnings" (*Duckworth* v. *Eagan,* 1989) and "waiver" of rights (*Colorado* v. *Spring,* 1987; *Moran* v. *Burbine,* 1986; *Oregon* v. *Elstad,* 1985), approved police trickery (*Illinois* v. *Perkins,* 1990) and the use of unlawfully obtained statements for impeachment (*Harris* v. *New York,* 1971; *Oregon* v. *Hass,* 1975), and created a "public safety exception" to Miranda (*New York* v. *Quarles,* 1984). Miranda thus has proven to be workable and a judicially acceptable compromise between law enforcement's interests and individual's self-incrimination rights. Although some justices have urged further restrictions on Miranda rights (*Duckworth* v. *Eagan,* 1989; O'Connor, J., concurring in judgment that Miranda violations should not be cognizable on federal habeas corpus; *New York* v. *Quarles,* 1984; O'Connor, J., concurring in judgment that Miranda violation should not require suppression of derivative physical evidence), and some groups have lobbied for its overruling, Miranda and its familiar warnings should be clearly recognizable in the future.

Nor should we expect major revisions in the coming years in the Court's treatment of coerced or involuntary confessions, as opposed to "simple" Miranda violations. The Court has settled that only *official* acts that overbear a suspect's will—for example, police threats or violence— must ground a claim that a confession was produced involuntarily, and that neither private conduct nor maladies such as psychosis will do so (*Colorado* v. *Connelly,* 1986). Even when it is established that a suspect's will was overborne through governmental action, which may be rare, the admission of a coerced confession at trial will be tolerated if, in hindsight, such error is considered harmless because the accused nevertheless would have been convicted on evidence that was properly admitted (*Arizona* v. *Fulminante,* 1991). The involuntary confession doctrine, which will not come into play in the vast majority of cases in any event, thus can readily be nullified, and this should help ease its passage into the next century.

The Sixth Amendment's right to counsel has proven remarkably robust in protecting confessions at a time when other exclusionary doctrines have met with judicial disfavor (*Maine* v. *Moulton,* 1985; *Massiah* v. *United States,* 1964; *United States* v. *Henry,* 1980). After the initiation of formal judicial proceedings, such as an arraignment or the return of an indictment, and absent an effective waiver (*Patterson* v. *Illinois,* 1988), the Court has prohibited government agents from resorting to deception or otherwise deliberately eliciting incriminating statements from suspects in the absence of counsel. Statements obtained in violation of the right to counsel must be suppressed, notwithstanding their reliability. The Sixth Amendment's relatively exalted stature in the confession contexts is probably attributable to the close relationship between the right to counsel and the preservation of trial rights, which is at the core of the adversarial fact-finding process (cf. *United States* v. *Wade,* 1967; right to counsel at postindictment lineups). Nevertheless, it would not be surprising to see Sixth Amendment doctrine begin to go the way of Miranda, with the Court chipping away at pretrial safeguards and more narrowly confining counsel's role to protecting the accused at the trial proper (*Brewer* v. *Williams,* 1977, Burger, C.J., dissenting; *Kuhlmann* v. *Wilson,* 1986).

Confrontation and Cross-Examination States have been allowed to dispense with literal, face-to-face confrontation between the accused and his or her accusers in sexual abuse prosecutions. When necessary to protect children from the trauma of testifying in the presence of their alleged abusers and to facilitate their communication with a jury, closed-circuit television may be used to beam children's testimony outside of the courtroom in which the defendant is being tried (*Maryland* v. *Craig,* 1990). In rape cases, even when consent is at issue, the accused may be denied the opportunity to cross-examine the complaining witness (or present other evidence) about the couple's prior consensual sexual relations if he does not file formal notice of his intent to do so several days before trial. Such a policy is defended because it promotes the state's interests in protecting alleged rape victims' privacy and in preventing surprise to the prosecution (*Michigan* v. *Lucas,* 1991).

The Sixth Amendment rights of confrontation and cross-examination directly promote the truth-finding function of criminal trials (*Pointer* v. *Texas,* 1965). Confrontation rights have roots that go back to ancient Roman law (*Coy* v. *Iowa,* 1988). As we enter the next century, important issues may arise concerning whether and how far criminal defendants' rights to cross-examine their accusers must yield in the face of countervailing state interests. Given the centrality of these rights to the actual and perceived fairness of the criminal trial—the "main event" (*Wainwright* v. *Sykes,* 1977:90) in the entire criminal process—the Court is likely to proceed cautiously.

For instance, it is doubtful that the need for face-to-face confrontation will be sidestepped in adult rape cases or in other circumstances where there are no uniquely vulnerable victims such as children. On the other hand, rape-shield laws, which normally operate to prohibit cross-examination about an alleged rape victim's prior sexual conduct with persons other than the accused, will probably receive the formal blessing of the Supreme Court. Such laws have been upheld in federal courts and in nearly all states in the union. In other contexts, we should not expect cross-examination rights to be relaxed beyond their present scope.

Juries The minimum size (six) (*Ballew* v. *Georgia,* 1978) and decisional rule requirements (9–3 verdicts are constitutionally permissible, but nonunanimous six-member jury verdicts are not) (*Burch* v. *Louisiana,* 1979; *Johnson* v. *Louisiana,* 1972) for state criminal trial juries are firmly established and should not change by 2010. At present, all death penalty states require that capital juries comprise twelve members who must decide cases unanimously, but the Supreme Court would probably approve deviations from these norms in the interest of federalism (cf. *Schad* v. *Arizona,* 1991; *Spaziano* v. *Florida,* 1984). Notwithstanding Supreme Court disclaimers, there is little doubt that diluting size and unanimity standards jeopardizes certain values promoted by the traditional twelve-member unanimous jury, including the effective participation of racial and other minorities in jury deliberations. Future developments in jury law may well focus on procedures for selecting and impaneling trial jurors, including actions that threaten minority group representation on juries of six or twelve.

Trial jurors, of course, find facts—who did what to whom and why—and must also draw inferences and conclusions from those facts, such as whether conduct was "reasonable" or whether a defendant's mental processes were "substantially impaired." Different people receive and interpret courtroom evidence through different eyes and ears, and they attribute significance and meaning to testimony according to their unique perceptions, backgrounds, and experiences. Trial by a "jury of one's peers," or a jury selected from a representative cross-section of the community, is thus a fundamental part of the Sixth Amendment's right to trial by jury (*Taylor* v. *Louisiana,* 1976). Nevertheless, this fair cross-section requirement applies only to the large group of people summoned to court for potential jury service (the venire); there is no Sixth Amendment right to have any particular trial jury mirror the demographic makeup of a community (*Holland* v. *Illinois,* 1990). For example, it is not unconstitutional per se to have a black defendant tried before an all-white jury.

However, by invoking the equal protection clause of the Fourteenth Amendment, the Supreme Court has ruled that neither prosecutors in criminal cases (*Batson* v. *Kentucky,* 1986; *Powers* v. *Ohio,* 1991) nor litigants in civil trials (*Edmonson* v. *Leesville Concrete Co.,* 1991) may exercise peremptory challenges to excuse potential jurors from trial duty for racial reasons. This prohibition predictably will be applied to criminal defense lawyers (*People* v. *Kern,* 1990; state constitution), but it remains to be seen whether peremptory challenges based on gender, religious beliefs, and other attributes or attitudes will be deemed constitutionally impermissible. The Court's willingness to impose limits on the exercise of peremptory challenges is of symbolic significance to the commitment for evenhanded justice in American courts, and this commitment may become even more meaningful as trial judges and attorneys collectively reflect greater racial, ethnic, and gender diversity (*Chisom* v. *Roemer,* 1991).

Scientific jury selection (using social science expertise to help choose trial jurors) may become more popular in future trials, even though such techniques are unlikely to influence trial outcomes in most cases. We can expect increased social science participation in other aspects of trials, such as helping lawyers pretest or get feedback on their strategies and tactics through simulating trials or enlisting "shadow juries," assisting in motions for changes of venue, and promoting comprehensible and effective jury instructions. Science can hardly be expected to revolutionize the centuries-old institution of the trial jury, even if scientific research findings are more regularly incorporated into the trial process in the next twenty years. And even if major reforms, legal or scientific, were to sweep over jury trials, it is a safe bet that roughly nineteen out of twenty cases will still be adjudicated by guilty pleas in the criminal courts of 2010.

There are, of course, many other aspects of criminal procedure law that merit attention as we speculate about the law of the future. We must defer consideration of issues such as eyewitness identification, bail and preventive detention, arraignments, double jeopardy, and many others. In general, we can anticipate that the major trends and forces identified earlier—the dominance of fact-finding reliability and finality over due process values, the instability of precedent, restricted access of state prisoners to the federal courts, the Supreme Court's respect of federalism and deference to legislative and executive rule making, the renewed prominence of state courts and increasing diversification in the law—will help determine the shape of specific rules in these and other areas of criminal procedure law.

THE SUBSTANTIVE
CRIMINAL LAW
OF THE FUTURE

We now consider the substantive criminal law, an area every bit as expansive as criminal procedure law and even more diverse, primarily because fewer constitutional principles unify the rules that define crimes and govern criminal defenses. Future crimes and punishments are considered elsewhere in this volume, enabling us to focus on other issues that may be important to the criminal law of 2010.

Justification and Excuse

Criminal defenses (other than "I didn't do it") are of two basic types: justification and excuse. Justification-based defenses, such as necessity and self-defense, focus on the *act*: We condone conduct that normally is prohibited (e.g., shooting someone) when that conduct is a necessary and proportionate response to some triggering condition (e.g., an imminent homicidal assault) that would cause even greater harm if unchecked. Defenses of this nature generally fit into a "lesser evils" framework: The injury resulting from the justified conduct is of a lower order than the harm that would occur if we did not approve of that conduct. For example, it would ordinarily be a crime to set fire to a farmer's field of crops. Such conduct would be justified, however, if necessary to create a fire break to impede a forest fire from engulfing an adjoining village, although setting the village ablaze to spare the farmer's crops would not.

Defenses based on excuse focus on the actor rather than the act: We find that an actor is not blameworthy for conduct (e.g., shooting someone) because some disability (e.g., mental illness, tender years) caused a condition (e.g., impairment of volition or rational thought) that negated the culpability that normally makes criminal punishment deserved. Thus, we excuse certain actors, such as very young children and the insane, from criminal responsibility even for causing serious harm, although we do not condone their conduct (the act).

In the criminal law of the future we may see interesting changes in the application of defenses based on justification and excuse and perhaps accompanying changes in formal legal doctrine. These changes will be stimulated by the "victims' rights" movement, which has captured the country in various forms including victims' bill of rights legislation in numerous states, victim assistance programs, and increased participation of crime victims in criminal prosecution, sentencing, and parole decisions. The interests of crime victims also have been recognized in Supreme Court decisions (*Morris* v. *Slappy,* 1983:14; *Payne* v. *Tennessee,* 1991:2613; Scalia, J., concurring). The widespread public attitude of being fed up with crime should result in justification defenses becoming more widely accepted when the accused has acted in response to threatened criminal conduct. Conversely, the availability of excuses should be constricted in light of the public's unwillingness to countenance unprovoked antisocial behavior.

For example, self-defense claims that incorporate the "battered woman's syndrome" should flourish, and Bernhard Goetz–style subway shootings may be approved if not applauded. Under circumstances such as these, the jury's sympathies can be expected to rest not with the alleged crime victim—the battering spouse or the would-be mugger—but with the defendant who takes corrective measures with his or her own hands, even if that means resorting to deadly force. Far from conforming to the orthodox model of self-defense, which is based on necessity and proportionality, this brand of "justification" risks promoting extralegal vigilantism by allowing punitive force to masquerade as defense force and by letting "he deserved it" take precedence over "she had to do it."

On the other hand, the law in 2010, and jurors who implement it, may not be inclined to look favorably on defenses based on excuse. After John Hinckley, Jr.'s attempted assassination of President Reagan and subsequent acquittal by reason of insanity, we have witnessed restrictions on the insanity defense in many jurisdictions. These cutbacks range from narrower definitions of insanity to placing the burden of persuasion on the accused and to outright abolition of the defense. The "guilty but mentally ill" verdict, which has typically been made available as an alternative to insanity acquittals, is now part of the law in roughly a dozen states.

The social mood seems increasingly less tolerant of excuses for conduct that results in significant harm, and we can expect a jaundiced reception of defenses based on premenstrual syndrome, posttraumatic stress disorders, and the like. This same attitude is likely to condemn to criminal punishment the growing cohort of fetal alcohol syndrome and crack babies who are getting older who may be prone to criminality and who are likely to assert prenatal harm to excuse their alleged crimes. More forgiving views about human nature and the appropriate role of criminal punishment may make jurists less skeptical of excuse-based defenses in the distant future, but such views are not likely to come of age by 2010.

The Domain of the Criminal Law

As the Supreme Court declines to extend substantive federal constitutional protections beyond a limited range of conduct, legislatures will be required to make tough choices about whether the criminal law ought to be employed as an instrument of social policy and under what circumstances. For example, the states are entitled to regulate individuals' "right to die" (*Cruzan* v. *Director, Missouri Dept. of Health,* 1990), many aspects of abortion decisions (*Webster* v. *Reproductive Health Services,* 1989), homosexual conduct (*Bowers* v. *Hardwick,* 1986), and the access to obscene materials (*Paris Adult Theatre I* v. *Slaton,* 1973) and other forms of sexual expression (*Barnes* v. *Glen Theatre, Inc.,* 1991), among many other activities. Most states already have overburdened courts and are plagued by overcrowded jails and prisons and thus are unlikely to engage in aggressive enforcement of laws that address such conduct. With the exception of abortion, where we should see a multiplicity of state regulatory philosophies, and sizable pornography operations, the criminal law's role may be largely symbolic in areas near the borders of constitutional protections where individual victims are not directly harmed.

Where harm is more concrete and tangible, the criminal law will continue to play a significant role. As in every other generation, the criminal law will be used to pass judgment about vexing social problems, some of which may strain traditional legal principles: May (or should) a prospective mother be criminally punished for transmitting drugs to her unborn child? What should the criminal law's response be to intentional or reckless transmission of the AIDS virus? (See *United States* v. *Moore,* 1988.) How can the criminal law cope with the "theft" of computer information? May (or should) expressive conduct such as racially motivated burning of a cross be punishable as a "hate crime?" (*In re R.A.V.,* 1991). Under what circumstances and for what sorts of harm (e.g., toxic gas leaks, massive oil spills, unsafe automobile manufacture) should corporations be punished criminally? The list of issues could go on. By 2010, tentative answers will be available to some of these questions, but a host of new and unanswered questions will certainly be waiting in the wings.

CONCLUSION

"You don't need a weatherman
to know which way the wind blows."

Bob Dylan

Rules of criminal procedure and the substantive criminal law help plumb the balance between social order and individual freedoms. There is a constant tension between society's obligation to protect citizens through effective law enforcement, including the detection and punishment of crimes, and the countervailing need to preserve individual liberties and fairness in the face of coercive state powers. The equilibrium achieved between these competing forces helps give specific form to constitutional rules of criminal procedure and to the law of crime and punishment. The public's short-term fear and frustrations about unlawful violence, drugs, and other crimes will cause a crime-control ideology to dominate the country. Corresponding legislative attitudes and shifts in judicial personnel and philosophy will tilt the law in this same direction.

History suggests that social attitudes are cyclical and that trends toward one extreme of values eventually are corrected and reversed. In the longer term future we should expect a heightened regard for due process norms. This reversal may be somewhat checkered rather than occurring across the country uniformly as individual state courts, legislatures, and administrators respond to the threatened encroachment of personal liberties caused by shrinking federal constitutional guarantees. The year 2010 promises to bring many changes in the law, including in several important areas that we have not considered, such as civil liability suits and civil forfeiture proceedings. But in historical perspectives, 2010 will mark only a single stopping point in an ever-changing ebb and flow of legal rights and protections.

CASES

Arizona v. *Fulminate* (1991) 111 S.Ct. 1246.

Arkansas v. *Sanders* (1979) 442 U.S. 753.

Ballew v. *Georgia* (1978) 435 U.S. 223.

Barnes v. *Glen Theatre, Inc.* (1991) 111 S.Ct. 2456.

Barron v. *Mayor of Baltimore* (1833), 32 U.S. (7 Pet.) 243.

Batson v. *Kentucky* (1986) 476 U.S. 79.

Benton v. *Maryland* (1969) 395 U.S. 784.

Berkemer v. *McCarty* (1984) 468 U.S. 420.

Bivens v. *Six Unknown Named Agents of Federal Bureau of Narcotics* (1971) 403 U.S. 388.

Booth v. *Maryland* (1987) 482 U.S. 496.

Bowers v. *Hardwick* (1986) 478 U.S. 186.

Brewer v. *Williams* (1977) 430 U.S. 387.

Brown v. *Allen* (1953) 344 U.S. 443.

Burch v. *Louisiana* (1979) 441 U.S. 130.

Butler v. *McKellar* (1990) 110 S. Ct. 1212.

California v. *Acevedo* (1991) 111 S. Ct. 1982.

California v. *Ciraolo* (1986) 476 U.S. 207.

California v. *Greenwood* (1988) 486 U.S. 35.

California v. *Hodari D.* (1991) 111 S.Ct. 1547.

Chapman v. *California* (1967) 386 U.S. 18.

Chisom v. *Roemer* (1991) 111 S.Ct. 2354.

Coleman v. *Thompson* (1991) 111 S.Ct. 2546.

Colorado v. *Connelly* (1986) 479 U.S. 157.

Colorado v. *Spring* (1987) 479 U.S. 564.

Coy v. *Iowa* (1988) 487 U.S. 1012.

Cruzan v. *Director, Missouri Dept. of Health* (1990) 110 S.Ct. 2841.

Duckworth v. *Eagan* (1989) 492 U.S. 195.

Duncan v. *Louisiana* (1968) 391 U.S. 145.

Edmonson v. *Leesville Concrete Co.* (1991) 111 S.Ct. 2077.

Fay v. *Noia* (1963) 372 U.S. 391.

Furman v. *Georgia* (1972) 408 U.S. 238.

Gideon v. *Wainwright* (1963) 372 U.S. 335.

Gregory v. *Ashcroft* (1991) 111 S.Ct. 2395.

Harris v. *New York* (1971) 401 U.S. 222.

Holland v. *Illinois* (1990) 493 U.S. 474.

Hoyt v. *Florida* (1961) 368 U.S. 57.

Illinois v. *Perkins* (1990) 110 S.Ct. 2394.

In re R.A.V. (1991) 464 N.W. 2d 507 (Minn) *cert. granted sub nom., R.A.V.* v. *City of St. Paul*, 111 S.Ct. 2795. (1991)

Johnson v. *Louisiana* (1972) 406 U.S. 356.

Jones v. *Murray* (1991) 763 F.Supp. 842 (W.D.Va.).

Katz v. *United States* (1967) 389 U.S. 347.

Kaufman v. *United States* (1969) 394 U.S. 217.

Ker v. *California* (1963) 374 U.S. 23.

Kirby v. *Illinois* (1972) 406 U.S. 682.

Kuhlmann v. *Wilson* (1986) 477 U.S. 436.

McCleskey v. *Zant* (1991) 111 S.Ct. 1454.

Maine v. *Moulton* (1985) 474 U.S. 159.

Malloy v. *Hogan* (1964) 378 U.S. 1.

Mapp v. *Ohio* (1961) 367 U.S. 643.

Maryland v. *Craig* (1990) 110 S.Ct. 3157.

Massiah v. *United States* (1964) 377 U.S. 201.

Michigan v. *Chesternut* (1988) 486 U.S. 367.

Michigan v. *Lucas* (1991) 111 S.Ct. 1743.

Michigan v. *Tucker* (1974) 417 U.S. 433.

Michigan State Police v. *Sitz* (1990) 110 S.Ct. 2481.

Miranda v. *Arizona* (1966) 384 U.S. 436.

Moran v. *Burbine* (1986) 475 U.S. 412.

Morris v. *Slappy* (1983) 461 U.S. 1.

Murray v. *Giarratano* (1989) 492 U.S. 1.

New York v. *Quarles* (1984) 467 U.S. 649.

Oregon v. *Elstad* (1985) 470 U.S. 298.

Oregon v. *Hass* (1975) 420 U.S. 714.

Palko v. *Connecticut* (1937) 302 U.S. 319.

Paris Adult Theatre I v. *Slaton* (1973) 413 U.S. 49.

Patterson v. *Illinois* (1988) 487 U.S. 285.

Payne v. *Tennessee* (1991) 111 S.Ct. 2597.

People v. *Kern* (1990) 75 N.Y. 2d 638, 554 N.E. 2d 1235, 555 N.Y.S. 2d 647.

Pointer v. *Texas* (1965) 380 U.S. 400.

Powell v. *Alabama* (1932) 287 U.S. 45.

Powers v. *Ohio* (1991) 111 S.Ct. 1364.

Robinson v. *California* (1962) 370 U.S. 660.

Schad v. *Arizona* (1991) 111 S.Ct. 2491.

Schmerber v. *California* (1966) 384 U.S. 757.

Skinner v. *Railway Labor Executives' Association* (1989) 489 U.S. 602.

Smith v. *Maryland* (1979) 442 U.S. 735.

South Carolina v. *Gathers* (1989) 490 U.S. 805.

Spaziano v. *Florida* (1984) 468 U.S. 447.

Stanford v. *Kentucky* (1989) 492 U.S. 361.

Stone v. *Powell* (1976) 426 U.S. 465.

Swain v. *Alabama* (1968) 380 U.S. 202.

Taylor v. *Louisiana* (1975) 419 U.S. 522.

Teague v. *Lane* (1989) 489 U.S. 288.

Terry v. *Ohio* (1968) 392 U.S. 1.

United States v. *Calandra* (1974) 414 U.S. 338.

United States v. *DeLeon-Reyna* (1991) 930 F. 2d 396 (5th Cir., en banc).

United States v. *Henry* (1980) 447 U.S. 274.

United States v. *Janis* (1976) 428 U.S. 433.

United States v. *Leon* (1984) 468 U.S. 897.

United States v. *Moore* (1988) 846 F. 2d 1163 (8th Cir.).

United States v. *Place* (1983) 462 U.S. 696.

United States v. *Wade* (1967) 388 U.S. 218.

Wainwright v. *Sykes* (1977) 433 U.S. 72.

Washington v. *Texas* (1967) 388 U.S. 14.

Webster v. *Reproductive Health Services* (1989) 492 U.S. 490.

FOR FURTHER READING

Donald Black. *The Behavior of Law.* New York: Academic Press, 1976.

This classic study of social control examines variation in the extent of the law as social control according to stratification, differentiation, culture, and other variables. The theory developed can allow for predictions of changes in law as other social changes occur.

James McGregor Burns and Stewart Burns. *A People's Charter: The Pursuit of Rights in America.* New York: Knopf, 1991.

This book explores the historical roots of legal rights and their applicability to modern society. The text also discusses the difficulties of developing rights within the context of larger social issues, such as economic justice, equal rights, and human rights. This thought-provoking analysis of rights in contemporary society also discusses the process of contracting, nurturing, and empowering rights.

Alan Dershowitz. *The Best Defense.* New York: Random House, 1982.

This book explores specific and controversial cases handled by one of America's preeminent lawyers. It describes in detail the battles of individuals against large societal institutions such as prosecutors and bureaucracies. It also highlights the questionable practices of governmental officials to gain convictions in criminal courts.

Norval Morris. *Madness and the Criminal Law.* Chicago: University of Chicago Press, 1982.

This book's subject is the insanity defense in the United States. The origins of the defense are described, and the work includes fiction to illustrate conflicting views of individual responsibility. It also offers suggestion for reform.

Samuel Walker. *In Defense of American Liberties: A History of the ACLU.* New York: Oxford University Press, 1990.

This book provides a history of the ACLU, detailing the development of this membership organization, which has taken on the responsibility of protecting constitutional liberties through legal action. The book uses exacting analysis to examine many controversial cases, including those protecting the freedom of speech and assembly for self-proclaimed Nazis and other often-criticized groups.

DISCUSSION QUESTIONS

1. Discuss the importance of the "due process revolution" in the criminal courts. How has this changed the nature of criminal justice case processing?

2. Comment on the "general themes" of the 1990s and how they will influence criminal procedure into the next century.

3. What role will state courts and nonjudicial authorities have in criminal proceedings in the year 2010?

4. How might the nature of criminal defenses change in the next twenty years? What implications will this have for the disposition of criminal cases?

5. Consider the nature of substantive criminal law. What issues may be significant for the constitutional protections of criminal defendants?

5

The Nature of Common Crime in the Year 2010

CHESTER L. BRITT, III

University of Illinois at Urbana

In the movie *Blade Runner*, the main character is an ex–police officer working in the year 1999. The portrait of society in this movie is one of a dark and gloomy world, in which criminals have basically overrun the entire city of Los Angeles. No one can be trusted, and virtually everyone is involved in some form of criminal-like behavior. Hollywood's portrayal of the future of crime notwithstanding, the future of crime in the United States appears to be much less disconcerting. We know, for example, the major correlates of crime rate trends— those factors that seem to correspond best with trends in the various crime rates in the United States since World War II. Based on these correlates, we can have reasonable expectations about crime rates over the next two decades. The goal of this chapter is to describe recent trends in crime rates and crime rate projection and perhaps provide the reader with a realistic picture of the nature of crime in the year 2010.

TRENDS IN CRIME DATA

There are two major sources of crime data on which predictions about the future of crime can be made. The *Uniform Crime Reports* (UCR) is one source; it is published annually by the Federal Bureau of Investigation (FBI) and represents crimes known to the police. The second source is the *National Crime Survey* (NCS), which presents the results from an ongoing victimization survey conducted by the Bureau of the Census in which approximately 50,000 households are polled every six months for a total of seven interviews over a three-year period. Respondents are asked about any victimization experiences in the past six months, and, if they have had any, they answer a series of follow-up questions that describe the circumstances of the victimization.

The rates of crime given by these two sources are quite different— since less than one-half of all crimes are generally reported to the police by the victim, the official rate of crime presented in the UCR seriously underestimates the volume of crime in the United States in a given year. But, at the same time, the two data sources also show a great deal of similarity in whether rates appear to be increasing or decreasing over time. In other words, when the official crime rate shows a drop, there is usually a drop in the victimization rate, once differences in percent reporting to the police have been controlled. In short, regardless of which source of data we choose to use, the trend and direction of annual changes will likely be similar, although not necessarily identical. Recent research has established the similarity of burglary and robbery trends in the UCR and NCS from 1973 to 1988, for example.

Figure 5.1 presents the UCR trends in index crimes (homicide, rape, robbery, aggravated assault, burglary, larceny–theft, and motor vehicle theft) for the period 1960 to 1989. The figure clearly shows that total index, property, and violent crimes all show a similar pattern of a rapid increase in the rate from 1960 through 1980, where the rates peaked, followed by a slight decline through 1984 and an increase from 1984 to 1989.

At first glance, it might appear as if serious crime were on the increase, with the only significant difference being the rate at which the increase was occurring. However, results from the NCS reveal a somewhat different picture. The rates of property and violent victimization for the period 1973 to 1989 are presented in Figure 5.2. For this period, the victimization rates were relatively constant. What, then, accounts for the more pronounced trends in official statistics? Primarily, the changes in the UCR crime rates can be accounted for by changes in the

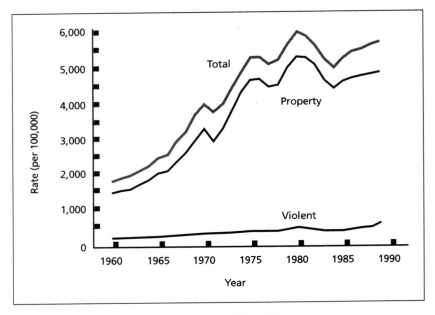

FIGURE 5.1   Trends in Official Crime Rates, 1960–1989

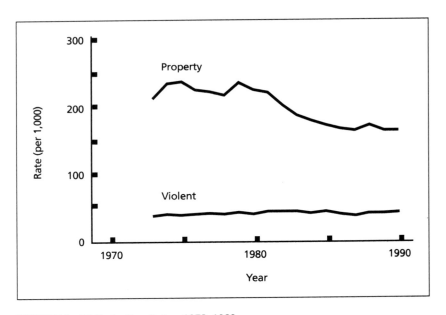

FIGURE 5.2   Victimization Rates, 1973–1989

percentage of victims who were reporting crimes to the police. For example, in 1973, 32.4 percent of all crimes were reported to the police. By 1989, this percentage had increased to 36.8 percent. When crimes are broken down by type, the rate at which violent offenses were reported to the police increased from 45.5 percent in 1973 to 49.6 percent in 1986 but declined to 44.9 percent in 1989. In 1973, 22.1 percent of personal property crimes and 37.8 percent of household property crimes were reported to the police, with both report rates increasing to 28.7 percent and 40.7 percent, respectively, by 1989.

The trend in crime in the United States, based on a combination of UCR and NCS data, suggests that crime rates have been stable. The more pronounced changes in the official rate of crime can be largely attributed to changes in reported victimizations. The victimization rates obtained from the NCS would therefore seem to offer more accurate estimates of the true trend in crime rates in the United States over the last two decades. However, to say that the level of crime in 2010 will be approximately the same as the level of crime in the late 1980s, based only on the trends in crime, will be unsatisfactory. A large body of research has established that a limited set of social factors can explain much of the annual variation in crime and victimization rates. We now turn to a brief summary of this work.

EXPLAINING CRIME RATE TRENDS: A REVIEW OF PREVIOUS RESEARCH

In what has been called the "routine activities" or "opportunity" approach to explaining crime, three general factors are claimed to account for the occurrence or prevention of crime: (1) supply of motivated offenders, (2) supply of suitable targets for victimization (both persons and property), and (3) lack of a capable guardian to prevent the crime from occurring. The significance of these three factors is that they suggest that a crime can only occur when a motivated offender and potential victim coincide in time and space and when there is no perceived credible threat to the offender's successful commission of the crime. Should any of one of the conditions not be met, then a crime is unlikely. For the first two conditions, this assertion is self-apparent: If there is no motivated offender or target for the crime, then a crime cannot occur. For the third condition, the relationship is more probabilistic, where the assumption is that offenders will give at least cursory attention to the circumstances in which a potential target is located, and if a person or physical structure is seen as a threat to completing the crime successfully, then the likelihood of the crime occurring decreases.

The routine activities–opportunity approach has been used to explain trends in post–World War II crime and victimization rates in the United States. Collectively, this work has found four factors to explain much of the variation in the official crime rates as well as the victimization rates in Figures 5.1 and 5.2. The following presents a brief summary of this work.

Age Structure

The age of a person is one of the strongest predictors of the likelihood of criminal behavior. Some researchers have argued that the age distribution of crime is stable across social and cultural conditions. This claim is based in part on evidence showing the age distribution of crime in nineteenth-century England following the same general pattern as crime in the United States in the early 1980s. Other research has documented the stability in the age distribution of index crimes in the United States from the 1950s through the 1980s. Although there has been some disagreement in the criminological literature over the degree of stability in the age distribution of crime, this body of work generally shows that crime has become only somewhat more concentrated among young people in both England and the United States from the 1930s through the 1980s. In other words, virtually all forms of crime have been concentrated among youth, and with few exceptions (e.g., gambling), the proportion of all crime committed by youth has continued to increase without altering the basic shape of the age–crime relationship.

It is not surprising, then, that the age structure of a society has the strongest predictive effect on the current level of crime in a society. Thus, in those societies with large proportions of young people, there tend to be much higher rates of all types of crime. Conversely, in societies with a larger older population (that is, older than 30 years), crime rates tend to be lower. In the United States, for example, trends in the age structure have had major effects on crime rate trends. Although a change in the age structure of a society, such as the proportion of the population aged 15 to 25 or 29 years, is not perfectly correlated with a change in crime rates, the correspondence is close.

One recent study found that changes in the age structure in the United States from 1946 to 1984 accounted for 58 percent of annual changes in the homicide rate and 26 percent of annual changes in the motor vehicle theft rate. The difference in the level of explained variation for these two crimes is likely attributable to the different measurements of age structure used by the researchers. For homicide, they used the proportion of the population aged 15 to 29 years; for motor vehicle theft, age structure was measured as the proportion of the population aged 15 to 25 years.

The general conclusions reached in this work suggest that as the "baby boom" generation (that group born in the years 1946 to 1960) reached adolescence in the 1960s and 1970s, the rate of property crime skyrocketed and then declined when this group reached ages above 20. But at the same time the property crime rate was declining, the violent crime rate continued to increase slightly, since the age distribution of violent crime is slightly older than for property crime, and has only recently declined as this generation has aged out of its twenties and into its thirties and forties.

Unemployment

Many studies have been able to document significant effects of the total unemployment rate on property crime rates and a weaker relationship with violent crime rates. The effect of unemployment is mixed, however, as unemployment has both opportunity and motivation effects. In terms of opportunity, the relationship between the unemployment rate and crime rates for the same year is negative. In other words, as the unemployment rate increases (decreases) in some year, there is a strong tendency for crime rates to decrease (increase). Apparently, as more people become unemployed due to an economic slowdown or recession, many more people remain at home during the day. The effect of more people staying at home during the day when not working is unintentionally to provide an extra degree of protection for their property and person. Specifically, by their remaining in the home during the day, the chances of some form of household theft are then greatly reduced, since slightly more than one-half of these crimes, when the approximate time of offense is known, occur during the day (6 A.M. to 6 P.M.). Similarly, most violent victimizations occur outside the home, and by not working and remaining in the home, unemployed persons reduce their risk of violent victimization by reducing their exposure to potential offenders.

Unemployment also has a delayed, or lagged, effect on crime rates. The magnitude and direction of change in the unemployment rate from one year to the next has a positive effect on crime rates for the second year. In other words, if the economic slowdown lasts for an extended period of time, indicated by stable or increasing unemployment rate, forms of economic assistance, such as unemployment benefits, begin to disappear. The overall effect of long-term unemployment seems to be an increase in the number of persons motivated to commit crimes out of either frustration or a perception that they could subsist on criminal behavior. The increase in the size of the population motivated to commit crime then places many more potential offenders on the streets looking for suitable targets, ultimately resulting in an increased rate of crime.

Unemployment thus has two rather conflicting effects on the crime rate. Contemporaneously, unemployment decreases opportunities for property crime by providing a larger population of capable guardians for surveillance and the protection of person and property. But if the increase in unemployment lasts for an extended period or continues to increase, then people may begin to run out of financial assistance and see criminal behavior as one way to survive.

Incarceration Trends

A theoretical tradition with an interesting history in criminology has argued that incarcerating individuals at higher rates will reduce the crime rate through either deterrent or incapacitative effects. The link to the routine activities–opportunity approach is that higher levels of incarceration should have the effect of reducing the number of motivated offenders in society. Since we cannot know with any degree of certainty why incarceration should lower crime rates, it is worth noting that several studies have found a significant negative relationship. Unfortunately, from a crime-control perspective, the magnitude of this effect ranges from weak to moderate. In a recent study of homicide and motor vehicle theft rates in the United States from 1946 to 1984, the total incarceration rate had negative relationships with both crime rates, even after introducing statistical controls for age structure and unemployment.

Opportunity Factors

In addition to the factors noted above, there is also the effect of opportunity or the presence of guardians, which may prevent crimes from occurring. Obviously, the nature of the opportunity effect will vary with the specific type of crime. For example, motor vehicle registrations per capita have significant positive relationships with the motor vehicle theft rate. In other words, the more cars there are circulating in society, the greater the chances of a theft occurring. In addition, the residential population–density ratio has significant positive relationship with crime rates. The residential population–density ratio is an indicator of household victimization risk due to people either living alone or with unrelated persons or due to changes in labor force participation that removes both husbands and wives from the home during the working hours and that increases the risk of all types of victimization for the household.

In summary, these four correlates of U.S. crime rates provide evidence that supports the idea that crime is a function of the number of motivated offenders, the number of suitable targets for victimization, and the lack of capable guardians to prevent such offenses. The supply of motivated offenders is influenced by the effects of long-term unemployment and prison experiences. The supply of suitable targets is influenced by unemployment, both short- and long-term, which influences peoples' ability to purchase new goods that are attractive to people interested in stealing them. Similarly, for offenses such as auto theft, the unemployment situation in the United States will influence people's inclination to purchase a new vehicle, which exposes them to a different victimization risk. Finally, the absence of capable guardians will be influenced by short-term unemployment, which increases the number of people in their homes, meaning the residential population density has also decreased.

PROJECTING CRIME RATES

Since we cannot know with great precision the state of the national economy, the incarceration rate (especially if it continues to increase at an exponential rate), and attendant opportunity factors in the year 2010 in the United States, the projection of crime rates rests primarily on trends in the expected age structure. Since many of the people who will fall into the age group of 15 to 29 years through the year 2010 have already been born, we can be reasonably confident in population pro-

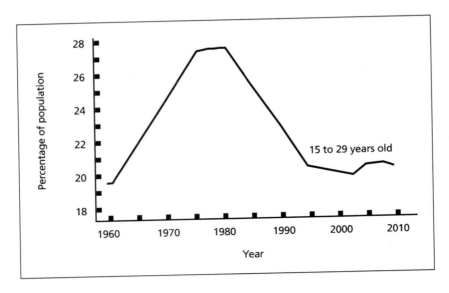

FIGURE 5.3   Trends in U.S. Age Structure, 1960–2010

jections two decades from now. Two factors that would upset these projections, which are discussed in more detail below, are increased levels of immigration and changes in birthrates and death rates that would alter the size of the youth population relative to the rest of the population.

The proportion of the population aged 15 to 29 years for the period 1960 to 2010 is presented in Figure 5.3. The values for 1960 to 1990 are based on census counts (for 1960, 1970, 1980, and 1990) and estimates for the population published by the Census Bureau (1981 and 1987). From 1991 to 2010, the population estimates represent the Census Bureau's middle-range estimates for the population (Bureau of Census, 1990). These estimates assume that the growth in the total population will stabilize early next century. While this assumption is debatable, the population estimates do provide a baseline for projecting trends in crime.

The trend in age structure revealed in Figure 5.3 clearly shows the youth population to have peaked in 1980, followed by a gradual decline in the year 2003, when the youth population is again expected to increase slightly through the year 2010. That age structure had a strong relationship with crime in the United States as seen in Figures 5.4, 5.5,

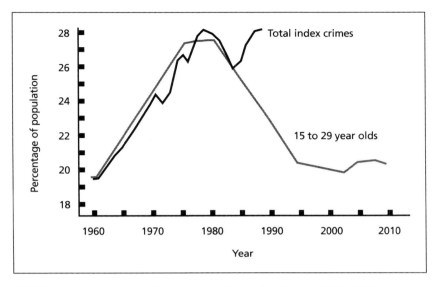

FIGURE 5.4   Trends in Age Structure and Total Index Crimes, 1960–2010

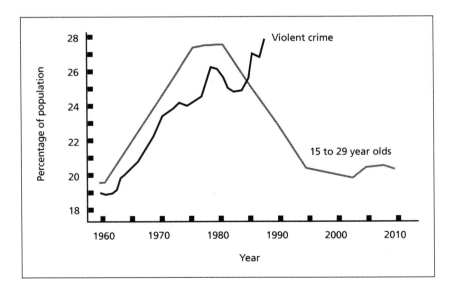

FIGURE 5.5   Trends in Age Structure and Violent Crime, 1960–2010

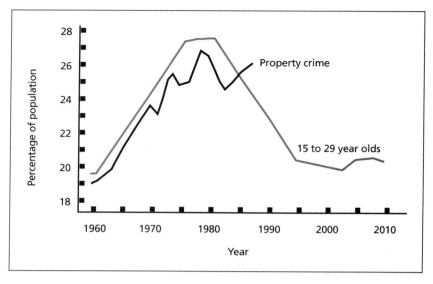

FIGURE 5.6   Trends in Age Structure and Property Crime, 1960–2010

and 5.6, which show trends in age structure and the total index, violent, and property crime rates, respectively, from 1960 to 1989. Since the age relationship with criminal behavior is so stable, there is no reason to suspect that crime rates will not continue to follow the age structure. If this pattern continues to hold, then we should see a slight decrease in these crime rates throughout the 1990s and the first two years of the next century, followed by a slight but not dramatic increase in crime rates through the year 2010.

The trend toward a decreasing and then stable crime rate is seen more clearly with data from the National Crime Survey. Figures 5.7 and 5.8 show the relationship between age structure and total personal violent and property victimization rates, respectively, from 1973 to 1989. Since the NCS data takes into account the level of reporting to the police, these rates presumably present a better depiction of overall trends in "true" crime. If this presumption is granted, then there is no reason to suspect major changes in the violent and property victimization rates over the next two decades.

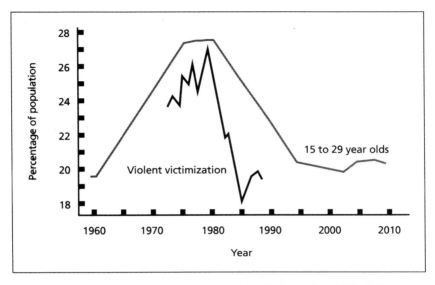

FIGURE 5.7   Trends in Age Structure and Violent Victimization, 1970–2010

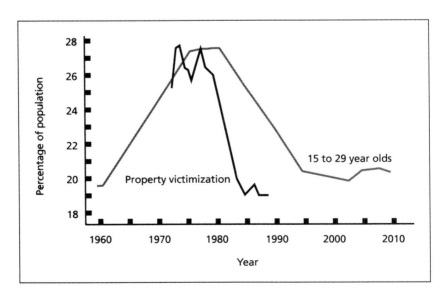

FIGURE 5.8   Trends in Age Structure and Property Victimization, 1970–2010

Caveats to the Projections

Three issues cannot be known at this time which may have the effect of drastically altering the trend in crime or victimization rates discussed above. First, as briefly noted above, changes in the unemployment rate, incarceration rate, and opportunity factors will have significant effects on the rates of crime in any given year. Should the United States experience a severe economic recession, the rates of crime and victimization will likely be much higher than projected. Conversely, if the unemployment rate is declining just before 2010, we might expect crime rates to be lower than projected. Similarly, if incarceration strategies change in ways that deter or incapacitate more persons from committing crimes, then we might observe crime rates much lower than expected or find that the rate is higher than expected if the rate of incarceration drops over the next two decades.

Second, the United States has been experiencing a high rate of immigration from Latin America in recent years. If the rate of immigration remains constant or increases, then estimates of the population aged 15 to 29 years will be off considerably. Birthrates are higher among Hispanic populations—meaning the size of both the total population and the youth population—and will be much higher than those recently projected by the Census Bureau. In addition, changes in individual lifestyles and advances in medicine have increased life expectancies of all persons in the United States. If these advances continue to increase the length of people's lives, then it is also possible that the elderly population will be much larger than expected by the Census Bureau, with the effect again being an incorrect estimate of the proportion of the population aged 15 to 29 years.

Third, claims have recently been made that drug use increases the likelihood that the drug user will commit other crimes. Although the evidence for this relationship is scant, should the relationship be shown to exist and should more people begin to use drugs more often, then we might expect crime rates also to show an increase that reflects increased drug use. At the same time, if drug use continues to decline, as it did during the 1980s, and if there is indeed a relationship between drug use and crime, then crime rates might drop even further than expected.

CONCLUSION

The purpose of this chapter has been to suggest what crime will look like in the United States in the year 2010. At one level, the answer offered in this chapter is not frightening or provocative; crime and victimization rates are expected to be quite similar to crime rates in the United States in the late 1980s. There is no evidence that violent or property crimes will increase dramatically over the next two decades, and all indications would seem to be that the rates will actually undergo an overall decline. Again, the justification for this claim rests on the stability of the age relationship with criminal offense and projections of the size of the youth population (15 to 29 years) through the year 2010. Since the proportion of persons aged 15 to 29 years has been decreasing since 1980 and is expected to continue to decrease until the year 2003, the crime rate is also expected to show an overall decrease for this time period. From 2003 to 2010, as the proportion of the population aged 15 to 29 years begins to increase slightly, there should be a corresponding increase in crime and victimization rates.

While futuristic movies portray a society completely overwhelmed by crime, a more realistic view of the future of crime is that it will likely not be too different from today. Although the crime rate in the United States in the mid-1990s does not generally make the average citizen feel comfortable with the chance of being the next victim, we should be able to take comfort in the expectation that the situation will likely not worsen and may improve slightly.

FOR FURTHER READING

Georgette Bennett. *Crime-Warps: The Future of Crime in America*. New York: Anchor-Doubleday, 1987.

This popular book examines crime over the next fifty years by considering trends in demographics, politics, economics, and other areas. The author looks at changes in street crime and white-collar crime and the movement of crime to sunbelt cities. She also chronicles the rise of new forms of crime and new restrictions on constitutional protections.

Paul Brantingham and Patricia Brantingham. *Patterns in Crime*. New York: Macmillan, 1984.

This book examines patterns of crime around the world with particular emphasis on the United States, England, and Canada. It describes the methods by which crime is measured and focuses on patterns of violent and property crime as they vary across time and geographic space.

Robert M. O'Brien. *Crime and Victimization Data*. Beverly Hills, CA: Sage Publications, 1985.

This text details the best known sources of data on crime in the United States: the *Uniform Crime Reports, National Crime Survey,* and *Self-Report Surveys*. There is also a discussion of the similarities and differences in the crime problem that are revealed by these different measures.

Samuel Walker. *Sense and Nonsense about Crime: A Policy Guide*. Pacific Grove, CA: Brooks/Cole, 1989.

This book focuses on the policy debates over crime and its control. It discusses the ways in which unproven beliefs about crime influence policy choices, and it exposes common myths about crime and criminal justice.

Neil Alan Weiner, Margaret A. Zahn, and Rita J. Sagi. *Violence: Patterns, Causes, and Public Policy*. New York: Harcourt Brace Jovanovich, 1990.

This collection of articles covers a wide range of topics related to violence. Research is presented ranging from historical studies of violent crimes to statistical studies of particular offenses. Specific sections also look at collective violence and the causes, prevention, and treatment of violence.

DISCUSSION QUESTIONS

1. What are the strengths and weaknesses in the two main ways in which crime is measured?

2. How would you describe recent trends in the amount of crime in the United States and in your community? Is your description consistent with popular opinion? Why or why not?

3. What is the "routine activities–opportunity" approach to explaining crime and how does it help to predict crime trends?

4. Discuss the ways in which age, unemployment, incarceration trends, and opportunity factors influence the amount of crime in society. Which factors will be the most important in explaining future trends?

5. How does immigration influence the amount of crime in society? What implications will immigration have for the delivery of criminal justice services in the future?

PART II

★

Criminal Justice System Response in the Year 2010

In this section, our experts tackle the heart of the criminal justice process, from police to corrections, trying to answer the question, What will justice be like in the year 2010? The authors approach their tasks with varying degrees of trepidation. In looking to the future of policing in Chapter 6, John Crank first acknowledges the difficulty of his task. Arguably, it is more difficult to see clearly into the future of policing than into the future of other areas. Although much of criminal justice, including policing, has been remarkably stable, some theorists would argue that we stand at the threshold of a new era—the so-called community-policing era—in which a new and different approach to policing will take hold. As Crank points out, not everyone is so optimistic. The argument lingers as to whether this approach represents a fundamental shift in the role of the police or only a change in rhetoric. Crank's concerns go even farther as he examines the dark side of the order-maintenance mission of community policing. Police officers, with a mandate to maintain order and new reserves of discretionary power, could find themselves responding to community needs in ways that do not reflect the current level of restraint imposed by the law.

Still more frightening, however, is Crank's view of the potential of education. In his flight into the future, educational credentials are used to free police officers from the traditional restrictions that rein in their considerable powers. It is a definition of professionalism that all students of the field should consider.

In Chapter 7, which addresses the future of the courts, Candace McCoy deliberates fundamental questions that the justice system will face. Her concerns are driven by already observable trends. In some ways, she examines not how the courts will change, but how they will struggle to maintain their basic principles in the face of a changing world. In particular, she is concerned with what the face of justice will look like in an increasingly diverse and multicultural country. Clear patterns of changing demographics already have emerged, and those patterns will be further affected by immigration. The courts will increasingly contend with volatile issues of race, ethnicity, and gender.

How well will the courts cope with these changes? This is the important question. McCoy suggests that greater attention to explaining the business and process of the courts, as well as alternatives to judicial processing, can preserve and strengthen the courts. She also considers the possible consequences of the courts' failure to adapt to changing circumstances.

In Chapter 8, Lynne Goodstein and John R. Hepburn use a fictional future judge, Tamika Watson, to reveal their expectations of criminal sentencing in 2010. Judge Watson confronts dilemmas that are common to today's students of criminal justice. What goals should govern sentencing? How can rationality drive criminal sentencing? How can large caseloads and full dockets be accommodated? What will sentencing be like when all of the choices have been made—that is, when the courts are governed entirely by rationality?

Goodstein and Hepburn document the efforts that may be made in the hopes of increasing rationality. In 2010, indeterminate sentencing has been abandoned, as has much of the rehabilitative ideal. Plea bargaining has been eliminated. All of this has been replaced by a computer-driven sentencing system. But in this future scenario, the answers to fundamental issues are not so easy. Judge Watson seems troubled by many of the same issues that today's judges confront. The doubts and conflict that this system of rationality was to have replaced have not disappeared.

David B. Kalinich and Paul Embert examine the enduring role of the jail in a changing world in Chapter 9. They focus on the social service function of jails in communities that are grappling with growing social problems. Jails will increasingly confront problems of communicable disease, poverty, and homelessness. But the most troublesome part of this scenario is not in increasing social needs but in how we might respond to them. Kalinich and Embert see jails as greatly influenced by the increasing disparity in our society. As the problems of a growing urban underclass mount, a split system of jails and justice may emerge. Private, well-run facilities will be found in affluent suburbs, while underfunded, overpopulated, and deteriorating jails will serve the cities. It is a critical view of the impact of privatization on criminal justice. But if it seems extreme, one need only consider the current problems of public education.

In Chapter 10, Lucien X. Lombardo integrates many of the issues discussed in previous chapters. His analysis of imprisonment provides a new theme to consider. Although much can be learned from history and current context—and we should be aware of the ways in which theoretical and philosophical developments will help shape the future—we should not view our own influences as unimportant. Lombardo assures us that although powerful factors are at work, and the circumstances surrounding imprisonment are changing in important ways, we can manage change effectively. If we can think of prisons as more than mechanistic organizations responding to their own environment and if we can appreciate our own power to effect change, then we can create a desirable future. For Lombardo, that future is one of progressive, humane institutions in which learning and reform take place. That future is ours to create.

One sentence that Judge Watson might use is probation or, as Todd R. Clear suggests in Chapter 11, its high-tech counterpart in 2010, a privately owned enterprise known as "community control." Probation also has confronted basic questions about its role. Even now the emphasis on supervision has overtaken the treatment focus and yet, even as a Community Control Specialist II in the future, Ophelia plays an important treatment role. But a returning emphasis on treatment is not the most significant theme in Clear's essay.

Perhaps the most important and most onerous theme is that of accountability. Most of Ophelia's day is driven by such a system. Her work schedule is predetermined. Specific tasks are assigned, and their completion is recorded. But most significantly, there has been a dramatic reduction in discretion, something that has been regarded as an important element in probation work.

The theme of accountability is tied to several important trends that Clear foresees. Privatization of community supervision will usher in more of the tools of traditional business enterprise, including close supervision. More important, however, legal liabilities will be reduced and proven regimens will be more closely followed. But such systems will never completely guard against the problem of a probationer committing a serious offense while in the community.

As different as Ophelia's day may seem to today's probation officer, Clear is certain that some things will not change. Technology will not diminish the need for human relations skills. These can be seen in Ophelia's interaction with her cases and their family members. For Clear, the technology and accountability systems that seem inevitable will never overwhelm the task that will continue to require keen human skills of judgment and discretion.

6

The Community-Policing Movement of the Early Twenty-First Century:

What We Learned

JOHN CRANK

Boise State University

This essay is on the future of policing. Any such effort is self-evidently preposterous, and therein lies the sheer delight of it. The notion that anyone can hope to predict the future of his or her own life for even the proximate moment, let alone the future of a social institution over the next eighteen years, is pretentious. What I have written here is a story, crafted from what I believe to be current events that may affect the future of policing, but a story nevertheless. My goal has not been to divine the future—I will leave that task for police psychics of the twenty-second century. I have instead attempted to provide the reader with an entertaining and semiplausible story of what might be: a trip through the looking glass of time, as it were.

There are particular themes in this essay. The first one is historical. Thorstein Veblen described history as "mass blind causation." This suggests a process of incremental although unpredictable change. In this essay, I have presented education as continuing its current evolution in the policing sector and culminating in a highly esteemed "doctor cop" who does "community wellness."

The second theme is that there are shocks to systems that may change those systems forever. These are one-time events that appear random when they occur and yet have a far-reaching and systemic effect. The riots of the 1960s and the ensuing Crime and Kerner Commissions marked the decline of the police professionalism movement and the beginning of the community-policing movement; they also changed the way in which many people thought about the role of police in society (Mastrofski, 1991). In this essay, two major shocks to the system are introduced as random events that change policing: the Madison Nuke Fizzle and the Ox-Bow Assassinations. The point in introducing these shocks to the system is not simply to provide entertainment, though that is the goal of this essay, but also to suggest the sheer impossibility of divining a future made unpredictable by unanticipated shocks to the system.

The essay provided here is not, however, a purely episodic accounting of a blind future adrift. Human agency affects the course of events, even at the institutional level, though outcomes may not be quite those anticipated or sought by original agents of change. In this essay, the third theme is that particular ideas of community-based policing sought by influential reformers become institutionalized by the year 2010. Yet the impact of these ideas on police organization and behavior occurs in a particular historical matrix, and the results do not come out quite the way intended. Ideas of police–community reciprocity, reorientation of patrol, and area decentralization of command are presented in this regard.

The fourth theme is context. According to this notion, the enterprise of policing occurs in a broader crime-control context, which in turn occurs within a broader political context, and on and on. These are all systems within systems, all turning on their particular historical axis and all affecting one another. The organization or behavior of the police is affected by its broad institutional environment, and analyses of police organization and behavior should take that institutional context into account, whether that context is local and is described by actors in the municipal arena or includes the whole of the institutional environment of policing. Changes in these contexts over the next eighteen years, I believe, will affect police work. This essay thus develops a variety of interesting contexts (edge ghettos, national crime-control mandates) that interact with and affect the police institutional environment.

A final theme is, simply put, that politics really does make for strange bedfellows. Liberal and conservative crime agendas are presented as subtly different, with unanticipated players and stages.

In all, I have presented an image of policing in 2010 that simply could not have been foreseen and that makes perfect sense when viewed in retrospect. If any of this story is borne out with the passage of time, I am sure it will be with different twists and spins from those described here. I hope you enjoy the tale.

"THE COMMUNITY-POLICING MOVEMENT OF THE EARLY TWENTY-FIRST CENTURY: WHAT WE LEARNED" *

The return to law and order on the part of the police in this year 2010 is being hailed as a new era of policing in America. This surprising movement, in sharp contrast in legitimacy and role to the community-policing era of the turn of the twenty-first century, is gaining momentum nationally. Reformers recall nostalgically the policing professionalism movement of a century ago as the golden age when police did something about "bad guys, not social problems." Advocates of police reform today, calling the movement the "police neoprofessionalization movement," are hailing the return to the "pure mandate" of law enforcement.

The neoprofessionalism movement is resisted by traditional, highly educated line officers steeped in community-policing (commonly called "com-pol") training and what they call the intuitive, common-sensical com-pol nature of their work. These officers argue that police officers have to be street-level community managers who understand the fundamental social, racial, and ethnic ecologies of their beats, the network of formal and informal community resources available to them, and how to solve complex social and order-maintenance problems on the streets. However, contemporary reformers are, with increasing political support, articulating a more focused law-enforcement police mission than the service and order-maintenance mandate that is practiced by com-pol organizations today.

Before we as an academy jump too fast on the neoprofessionalism bandwagon, I would like to take this time to reflect on policing's past in the hopes that we might gain insight from the mistakes of earlier eras of

---

*Keynote address at the 2010 annual meeting of the Academy of Criminal Justice Sciences

police reform. What I wish to avoid is the natural tendency toward a reaffirmation of a catechism of police history that presents a sort of internally driven, evolutionary history of policing and instead critically consider the broad context that affected the development of policing into the com-pol style and organization of policing we tend to take for granted today. We need to remember that neoprofessionalism is the latest in a series of reform movements, none of which had much effect on crime or on how street-level officers did their work on a day-to-day basis. Further, the current era of community policing, considered by many to be highly institutionalized today, was itself in its infancy in 1970, only forty years ago. What I wish to do is examine the history of com-pol policing until the present time, from its infancy to 2010, in the hopes that we can gain some sense of where policing has been and the implications of that history for the emerging neoprofessionalism policing movement.

The Era of Community Policing

We are emerging from an era of reform commonly referred to as the "community-policing era." This era emerged from what were perceived to be broad crime-control problems of the 1960s. These problems— big-city riots from 1963 to 1967, public perceptions of sharply increasing crime since the 1930s, and political turmoil brought about by the Vietnam War—were perceived by the public as symptomatic of a fundamental breakdown in social control in general and big-city crime control in particular. The police had failed by many accounts to do much in the way of controlling street crime and disorder associated with these events and, moreover, were implicated as more than a spark factor by the Kerner Commission in the most violent of the 1960s' urban riots.

The Kerner Commission (1967) and the President's Crime Commission (1968) recommend sweeping changes in police-service delivery, changes that oriented police work toward precisely what professionalized departments disdained—reciprocal communication and involvement in the affairs of the community. In these commission reports were sown the seed of the com-pol movement.

Community-based policing emerged as a new theory of police organization and activity, not only for its potential for crime prevention, but also for its seeming potential to alleviate a broad range of social and moral dilemmas overwhelming contemporary urban society. In other words, community policing was an effort by police organizations to regain the legitimacy ceremonially revoked by the Kerner and Crime Commissions. The focus of the community-based policing mandate was in the area of order-maintenance activity, and it provided a new legitimating theory for police organization and activity when traditional justifications in terms of enforcement-oriented professionalism no longer were seen as legitimate by the public, the courts, and the police themselves.

Community-based policing diffused across the municipal landscape with as much energy as the neoprofessional movement today. The state of Washington, for example, explored a strategy to convert more than fifty municipal and county police agencies in the state to a community-based policing model. Similar support for community-based policing was provided by the National Institute of Justice, with its allocation of a special granting category for research and experimentation on community-based policing. Textbooks and readers on policing in the United States today universally contain sections on community-based policing. Experiments containing community-based elements were conducted in many major cities in the United States by 1995, and by 2000 virtually every municipal department in the United States was "com-poled"—that is, converted to structures, activities, and mandates that made the department look like what community policing was expected to look like. In short, community-based policing rapidly became institutionalized at the end of the last century and during the incipient years of this one.

Astute observers raised many questions about the community-policing movement. As early as the late 1980s, many scholars challenged the image of the watchman and his work, community-based policing. Some challenged the linkage between aggressive order-maintenance patrol practices and the quality of urban life. Others questioned the existence of institutions that represented the interests of or acted as informal systems of control for communities. Positive, rather than negative, relationships were noted between aggressive order-maintenance behavior and victimization. Still others charged that the community-policing movement was a circumlocution whose purpose was to obscure the principal role of police as a mechanism for the distribution of non-negotiable coercive force. Thus, a large body of literature emerged to challenge many facets of community policing. Yet the vigor with which the movement gained momentum through the 1980s made all the dark clouds of criticism seem like will-o'-the-wisps, until the real problems with community-based policing began to emerge.

The Ox-Bow Assassinations

Retrospect often provides a sense of historical inevitability to events that, when they occur, seem like savage and unpredictable shocks to the system. So it was with the critical blow to the community-policing movement, which was called, for obscure historical reasons, the "Ox-Bow Assassinations." A series of execution-style murders of known criminals occurred in Jefferson City over a six-year period, from 2002 to 2008. What confounded many observers was that many of the murdered criminals, apparently aware of their own danger, were traveling with bodyguards when they were killed. A leak to the press revealed, amid a great deal of public controversy, that a special squad within the Jefferson City Police Department was acting as an assassination squad to, in its members' words, "make Jefferson as safe to live in as any rural American community." Jefferson was exceptionally violent, and they argued that they were simply reinforcing the informal norms that governed the city anyway.

At their trial, the officers charged with the assassinations contended that aggressive order maintenance was a part of their training protocol. The use of training protocol was carefully presented by defense counsel using videotapes that officers themselves had made of some of the assassinations. The shocker, as you of course recall, was when the jury found them innocent. Announcing her outrage, the President in 2009 called for a full-blown investigation and appointed the President's Commission on the Investigation of Police Misuse of Community-Based Authority. The commission called for a sweeping reconsideration of police training, oversight, mission, and role. The role of the police, the commission contended, must be law enforcement. Training should not emphasize service and order-maintenance frills, especially in this third consecutive decade of budgetary crises. It is the conclusions of this commission that are providing the impetus for the neoprofessionalism movement today.

The Madison Nuke Fizzle

The second shock to the system was, of course, what we call today the "Madison Nuke Fizzle." In 2004, a caller to the Madison Police Department announced that a terrorist group had hidden a nuclear device in downtown Madison that would detonate in twenty-four hours. Ransom was not mentioned, and efforts to negotiate were not reciprocated by the terrorists. A massive search by the Madison Police Department located a ten-kiloton nuclear device at the last minute, just sitting in the open between two parked cars, but concealed by the deep shadows of the elevated railway overhead. The priming device exploded, killing fourteen police officers and three National Guardsmen. The nuclear device itself had, it turned out, been vandalized and just fizzled out, although some leaking radiation caused a great deal of public fear.

In the next month, the police stopped and searched those automobiles on major roads in the Madison vicinity "that had suspicious people inside," as they said. One of the terrorists was caught and subsequently appealed the search of her vehicle. The Circuit Court established what is now called the "community safety standard"—that is, due-process protections could be superseded in the event that the police were taking into custody any person whom they believed presented a perceived present or potential danger to the community order and safety. The circuit court case provided the basis for the Stocklin Supreme Court decision, in which the Court ruled by a narrow margin that com-pol trained officers could use arrest as a "tool to maintain the community safety and order even if there was not at the time evidence that an arrestee had technically broken the law." The current debate, of course, is whether arrestees for extralegal violations have to be Mirandized, since they technically did not violate any law.

Internal Dynamics

In addition to random shocks to the system, there were inherent problems in community-based policing. The movement, a stepchild of the 1960s urban riots, always had identity problems. At the outset, it was incomprehensible to the average police officer. Like the poem "Jabberwocky" in *Alice in Wonderland,* there were lots of words that created a nice poem, but none of the words had any denotative meaning. Beyond putting a mechanical hand on the side of the squad car or bike that automatically waved to people on the street, officers spent most of their time doing what they had since the turn of the previous century—covering their asses and dealing with people's everyday problems.

Four areas of innovation in police organizations served as a rallying cry for the com-pol movement. These were *police–community reciprocity* (the idea that the police must communicate a general feeling that the public has something to contribute to the enterprise of policing), *area decentralization of command* (a phrase loosely referring to geographical decentralization of decision-making authority), *reorientation of patrol* (a movement to foot patrol), and *civilianization,* that is, using civilians to perform tasks traditionally reserved for sworn officers. The first three of these goals were realized, but only with twists unexpected by community-policing advocates at the outset of the com-pol movement.

Reorientation of Patrol

During this era, police officers changed their style of service delivery. They returned to walking the beat. This was accompanied by a great deal of public fanfare and often led to celebrated events. Municipal governments were glad for any method of offsetting the tremendous expense of automobiles, especially after the gas tax was put into place and gasoline prices rose to four dollars a gallon. Moreover, citizens enjoyed the easy banter and the visible presence of police officers, especially the relatively prestigious doctor cops. Return to a walking beat thus was a natural move for big city police.

A latent consequence of the return to walking beats was a change in the relationship between police and gangs. Initially, when police were assigned to neighborhoods frequented by gangs, they feared victimization and tended to band together in gang neighborhoods and to over-react to perceived threats. And gang members were quick to capitalize on this fear by intimidating and threatening police officers. Yet a surprising thing occurred—"police rap." Police and gang members began to exchange verbal spars as contests of wit, and these sparring contests served to establish a sort of grudging mutual respect between police and gangs. Then a group of police officers called "Boz-man 'n' the Hogs" became famous as rap music stars in 1999. They toured from city to city, rapping to the accompaniment of local gangs. This changed the police–gang relationship. Gangs began to work with police to maintain social control in neighborhoods, facilitating the community-policing mission (though, it should be noted, at the expense of other gangs). In this way, one of the components of police innovation sought by reformers, police–community reciprocity, came about, although not in quite the way intended.

Today, a concern expressed by critics of the neoprofessionalism movement is that current levels of community control, aided and assisted by gangs, might disappear with the return of police with a "pure" (law-and-order) mandate. A second area of patrol innovation was the reorientation to cycle patrols. Bicycle patrols were especially popular in business areas, and the colorfully dressed cycle patrol officers were a hit among the business elite. Many big-city departments initiated or dramatically expanded bicycle patrols with cycle races. By 2010, the idea of a motorized vehicle patrol in high-population-density areas was obsolete.

Rapid Response Penalty Fees

The reorientation of patrol toward foot and bicycle patrol was facilitated by the shift away from the heavy use of rapid-response (911) systems in urban departments. By the mid-1990s, departments were so overwhelmed with pressure to respond to calls for emergency assistance that efforts to reorient patrols into other, potentially more effective crime-control practices initiated in the late 1970s and mid-1980s were abandoned. A few big-city departments at this time put in place a user-fee structure: 911 callers were assessed a nominal user fee, with the charge in proportion to the priority assigned to the call. Needless to say, the idea of a user fee for emergency public calls for assistance was not well received by the public. Opponents contended that they were already paying taxes for the use of municipal services, and that the police were giving callers from wealthy neighborhoods, who could afford to pay higher user fees, a higher priority, thereby providing the wealthy with more and better police protection. The idea of a user fee was subsequently abandoned, but it was replaced by a "penalty fee" whereby individuals who made bogus emergency calls were charged the estimated cost of the police response together with an additional fine. With police departments using their powers derived from the drug wars of the 1990s to confiscate the property of those who failed to pay penalties for 911 misuse, calls for emergency response finally began to drop. By the turn of the century, they were half of what they were in 1990.

Decentralization of Command

Efforts to decentralize the police command structure also had unexpected consequences. No one realized the enormous growth in organizational complexity that would accompany geographical decentralization. The idea of decentralizing police organizations did not reduce the size of bureaucracy, they simply added the dimension of geographic complexity. After Kansas City shifted its command to substations, the entire command structure previously in place in the headquarters was replicated at each substation. In effect, there were fourteen independent Kansas City police organizations complete with organizational chart, personnel system, and command hierarchy. Kansas City replaced three chiefs in four years trying to find someone who had the sheer tenacity and tough-headedness to take over the police organization. Who would have thought in 1992 that Darryl Gates, the bloodied chief of the Los Angeles Police Department, would ever again assume the leadership of a major police organization? Yet he directed that organization so well that he became the darling of the com-pol reformers and later presidential advisor for the "Keep It Down" campaign.

Civilianization

Civilianization as an element of com-pol reform did not occur. The attraction of civilianization had always been cost savings: Why hire relatively expensive gun-toting officers when civilians can be hired to perform tasks that do not require guns? Well, civilians unionized and became expensive. But that was not the worst of it. Probably the death knell to civilianization was the famous public employee strike in 2003. After a prolonged contract dispute, the public employees' union ordered all civilians in police organizations on strike in New Jersey. When the governor ordered the National Guard to take over the work done by the civilians, the union called for a general shutdown of state municipal services. For three weeks, the ability of the state to deliver fundamental services was effectively blocked. Ultimately, under a general order from the governor, all of the striking civilians were fired and replaced by National Guardsmen and auxiliary police until regular sworn officers could be found to replace them. Civilianization as a goal of com-pol reform was effectively abandoned after the strike.

Crime Trends

The community-based policing movement failed to take into account historical and institutional features of the broader context in which policing occurred, and that context had profound effects on police organization and activity. One of the great conundrums of criminal justice history is witnessed here. It will be recalled that, from the 1970s through 1990, crime went steadily down across virtually all offense classifications, yet political leaders from the local to the national level sold a bill of goods called the "crime wave" to the American public. Who can ever forget that poor criminal justice teacher being savagely beaten by his students in 1993 for failing to change their test grade when they all got the question "Is crime going up or down?" wrong?

The reverse situation occurred after 1990, when community policing was in a period of intense institutionalization. At the core of the community-policing mandate was order maintenance and service. Com-pol leadership argued that, according to research over the previous twenty years, crime was going down, and police organizations needed to engage in crime-prevention programs that would keep it down, instead of archaic law-enforcement strategies that had served their purpose in lowering crime through the '70s and '80s but were inappropriate for the current period. "Keep It Down" became the slogan of the day. I still remember the jokes made about the President when she wore a "Keep It Down" button. The federal government, seeking any excuse to cut into service programs in big cities, willingly abandoned the severe social problems to the police. Yet, especially in inner cities, crime was beginning to rise and sharply so for violent crime offense. Thus, like the law-and-order era before it, the community-policing era justified its flawed policies on perfectly misunderstood crime trends.

Big-City Economic Retrenchment

Another contextual element that profoundly affected police activity was the continuing stagnation of big cities. In 1975, who would have foreseen how bad inner cities would become? Few heeded the warning presented by conditions in East St. Louis in the 1980s, where garbage had been piling up on city streets for years for lack of services and where some streets were literally closed to transportation because of huge piles of garbage. The situation was so bad that the city was placed into receivership to pay the fine for litigation resulting from the beating of a jailed inmate by another inmate. Yet there it was. By the year 2000, at least thirty cities and three states were in severe retrenchment. Curiously, this had an anomalous effect on the collection of crime data. UCR data collected in these cities revealed relatively low levels of crime, contributing to the turn-of-the-century myth that crime was going down. Police services were so sharply curtailed in these cities that an image of dramatic reductions in crime was fostered. We now know that crime was, in fact, increasing rapidly in those areas after the 1990s. Of course, victimization data revealed the sharp rise in crime in these areas even though official statistics did not, but no one outside academia ever took victimization data seriously anyway.

Edge Slums

The continuing stagnation of the economy contributed to the "edge-slum" phenomenon. A number of writers in the late 1980s were writing about "edge cities," or the shopping and community-service delivery centers that emerged in areas peripheral to city centers. They prospered in areas where bedroom communities grew in the 1950s and 1960s, and they provided all the functional needs for those areas, including centers for city-service delivery. The entrenched recession of the 1990s turned many of these areas into "edge slums," full of largely abandoned buildings, which were occupied primarily by cigarette junkies, and dispensaries for municipal services. Police organizations, decentralizing geographically so that they could "look like" com-pol organizations, found in these edge slums natural communities for community-policing work. They were in areas of concentrated populations, and thus were amenable to foot and bicycle patrol. Property values tended to be low, and departments could frequently acquire free rent for substation space in exchange for keeping a watchful eye on the property. Moreover, crime concentrated in these areas, so police officers won public support when they established beats in these areas. Thus, the edge-slum phenomenon provided a natural sort of geographic dispersal that facilitated the community-police movement.

Percorders

The camcorder revolution of the early 1990s was quickly followed by the "percorder" (personal recorder) revolution. Following a now-obscure event regarding police brutality in Los Angeles in 1991, by 1995 every major department in the United States had added roof-mounted camcorders to their vehicles. However, toward the turn of the century, departments were converting en masse into walking and cycling beats, and the roof-mounted camcorder became obsolete. Its function, recording officer–citizen interactions, was performed by the percorder. The percorder was a video recording device, placed in police officers' tie clips, that provided a visual recording of all interactions involving citizens. Percorder files were kept and periodically monitored by the police dispatcher (with union authorization). When a small multiple-band radio device with its bands modulated by voice command was added to the percorder, the automobile-based two-way radio was virtually eliminated as a communications technology for the police.

Crime-Control Politics

It is said that politics makes for strange bedfellows. The turn of the century was marked by a shift in the liberal crime-control perspective that would have been incomprehensible a decade previously. Liberals argued that the conservative crime-control argument, that criminality was located in the criminal, was actually a condemnation of the conservative crime-control agenda. Liberals, in a crime-control about-face, contended that the problem with contemporary policy aimed at rehabilitation did not work in large part because many criminals could not be rehabilitated—there were indeed many very bad people out there. This was a profound indictment of conservatives, they contended. Because the conservatives refused to recognize that a hostile social environment breeds criminality, they had allowed a class of criminals to come into being in the inner cities who were extraordinarily dangerous and who could not rehabilitated. The only solution was incapacitation. The indictment of the conservatives was that their policies had been a powerful stimulus to crime, and the only viable policy, incapacitation, was an enormous expense to the system. Thus, the turn of the century saw liberal crime-control advocates espousing incapacitation, and, in doing so, being embraced by that icon of crime control, James Q. Wilson.

Education

Probably the most significant changes in policing during the com-pol era were in the area of police education. The doctor cops, the shift of postgraduate criminal justice education to colleges of education, extension of Peace Officer State Training (POST) into four-year college programs, and the Stocklin decision previously discussed represent profound changes in education during the current era of policing.

Doctor Cops

The first change of interest was the appearance of street-level police with doctorate degrees. This was a continuation of a historical trend of education among police officers. Surprising, however, was the dramatic improvement in the status of college-educated police associated with the doctor cop. The idea of a doctor cop, because of its metaphorical resonance with the idea of community wellness, provided those with doctoral degrees high status among both community leaders and com-pol reformers.

Historically, college cops were accorded peripheral status, were cited for their cynicism, and were scorned by other police officers. However, this changed dramatically by the turn of the twenty-first century. As in the 1930s, a sustained period of economic hard times had made an increasing number of well-educated persons seek employment with police organizations. The near disappearance of the middle-class job market during the 1980s and 1990s had resulted in a pool of highly educated individuals available for police work. This era, however, differed from the 1930s in that the literate word, in the form of tests, extensive paperwork, POST, computer terminal use, and the sheer quantity of electronic or hard copy information routing invoked by police bureaucracies, was now integral to the performance and recording of police work. Interestingly, "CYA" in this era became the art of paperwork. Noncollege employees simply could not compete. The new elite of the police core became the highly educated. Especially in the era of community policing, when no one had a clear idea of what they were doing, highly educated police—especially doctor cops—were seen as those who could "give good community" (i.e., provide community wellness).

Postgraduate Police Education in Schools of Education

The doctor cop was only one of the ways in which the linkage between the police and educational sectors affected police change during the heyday of the com-pol era, 1990 to 2010. Related institutional development occurred in higher education in many centers of graduate and undergraduate education. The proliferation of M.A.-degree criminal justice programs in the 1970s and 1980s was paralleled by growth in the number of doctoral programs in the next two decades. What could not be foreseen in 1980 but appears inexorable from the vantage of historical retrospect was the shift of graduate-degree criminal justice programs out of liberal arts schools and into colleges of education. By 1988, there were twelve institutions that provided Ph.D.s in criminal justice and two that provided Ed.D.s. By 2010, there were only five Ph.D. programs in criminal justice, but there were eighteen Ed.D. programs in criminal justice.

What marked the shift toward advanced education in colleges of education? The answer was surprisingly simple. Liberal arts has always been an uncomfortable home for application-oriented criminal justice programs. Criminal justice programs were uneasy bedfellows with the liberal arts and humanities components of liberal arts schools, who typically thought of criminal justice programs as the intrusion of politically oriented crime-control activity into the core academic enterprise of freedom to engage in the pursuit of knowledge, even if that pursuit placed one in questionable relationship with the law. Simply, most liberal artisans thought of criminal justice faculty as academic Neanderthals intellectually ill-equipped to understand the foundations and goals of higher education. On the other hand, those criminal justice programs that espoused the pure pursuit of knowledge and sought academic prestige through traditional channels of research and publication were viewed by the criminal justice community as sterile: They contributed nothing to the preparation of individuals for their future work in the field of criminal justice.

The model for service was found in schools of education. A model was already in place in these schools that linked research and publication in higher-education training preparation for practitioner fields and did so in a way that was well received by the professional nonacademic audience in the criminal justice field and was esteemed by colleagues in the university environment. Simply, the purpose of higher education was to train teachers and prepare programs for credentialing, and emphasis in those programs was on heavy service commitment, but it was not as important as in liberal arts colleges that simply had no other way to gauge the relative merit of their faculty. Criminal justice faculty, in these schools, could commit to community, regional, or national service and receive academic recognition by other faculty in the school in which they participated. Thus, it was not surprising that many programs in the early twenty-first century initiated graduate development in criminal justice in colleges of education.

POST Training and
Community Policing

Another development in higher education was the continued expansion of Peace Officer State Training (POST) preservice and in-service programs. The enterprise of POST training received a powerful stimulus at the 1997 annual meeting of the Academy of Criminal Justice Sciences, which formally incorporated into a mission statement support for preservice and in-service peace officer training and established a Board of Educators to coordinate national information regarding developments in POST training. By the turn of the century, with this and the parallel development of the doctor cop, many POST training academies were actively recruiting Ed.D.s (in preference to Ph.D.s, who were seen as temperamental) to provide leadership in com-pol training.

By 2010, the advances in education resulted in the most highly educated police force in the world and highly articulated relationships among universities, police training academies, and community-based criminal justice organizations that employed police officers.

In the professionalism era in the early and mid-twentieth century, the police perceived their mandate in terms of law enforcement. In this regard, the police were creatures of the law, and the idea that arrest could occur when the law had not been broken was unthinkable. However, the shift to community policing redefined the legitimacy of the police in terms of community needs rather than in terms of legal code. As police, in the name of order maintenance, operated more and more outside the parameters of the legal code, they were increasingly likely to engage in behavior that was not strictly legal.

The dilemma was this: How could the police do aggressive order maintenance, community-based policing, especially make arrests to re-solve order-maintenance problems, if every time they did so they became the object of expensive litigation? The answer was in legitimiz-ing extralegal enforcement to the courts. This was done ceremonially, through educational credentialing. The police expanded pre- and in-service training in the area of criminal, civil, and constitutional law; in theory and principles of community-based policing; in criminological perspective, cultural awareness, and local, regional, and national history; and in many other related classes. These were called "com-pol" pro-grams, and by being incorporated into a formal training protocol, these programs ceremonially demonstrated to the courts and judges that police officers had the necessary credentials for extralegal aggressive order-maintenance policing. The Supreme Court, in the Stocklin deci-sion, cited the extensive com-pol training of police as the basis for its decision.

As formal com-pol curricula expanded, preservice training increas-ingly resembled undergraduate education offered at four-year institu-tions of higher learning. From 2005 to the present time, an increasing number of police departments have recognized a four-year degree in a criminal justice program as equivalent to com-pol training. Thus, in many states, POST training and a four-year education became the minimum requirements for entry into police work.

The A-Cig Wars

The drug war finally ended shortly after the turn of the century, not because there were any winners or losers, but because the American public was weary of hearing about it. It all ended with a press conference and announcement of victory. Besides, the police were being reluctantly drawn into the new anticrime effort: the cigarette wars. In 1998, formally acknowledging the severe health risk and staggering death toll associated with the smoking of cigarettes, the Congress of the United States passed a law banning "the importation, manufacture, sale, and use of any tobacco product or tobacco substitute containing tobacco tars or nicotine."

Fortunately, already in place were models for the anticigarette wars—the strategies and tactics used in the drug wars. Unfortunately, they were not very good models and were no more successful in keeping cigarettes away from the American public than they were regarding marijuana, heroin, and cocaine. Although the cigarette czar plied the media with impassioned speeches on the evils of smoking and "a-cig" (anticigarette) units regularly released to the media footage of high-profile multiple-carton busts, cigarette use continued unabated. Some blame the resurgence of organized crime in the United States during this era to the anticigarette laws and the resulting highly prosperous black market. However, the cigarette wars had their excesses. Even the strongest supporters of the anticigarette laws thought the government was going too far when it ordered mandatory drug testing for the presence of nicotine in the blood of all lung cancer patients. Today, many of the neoprofessionalist reformers in this year 2010 are calling for an abandonment or decriminalization of cigarette laws to, as they say, "refocus our efforts on real law-and-order issues."

Lessons of the Com-Pol Era

What is the lesson of this brief overview of the history of policing from 1990 to the present? Police movements come and go, but the real shapers of police organizational behavior are largely beyond the control of the police. Even when fundamental change sought by reformers occurs, it is deflected by historical shocks to the system and modulated by the influence of other institutions at both the local and national level. There is no way that advocates of community-based policing could have foreseen the end result of their reform efforts, even where, in principle, elements of those reform efforts were successful.

There is one final theme in this essay. It is said that the best predictor of the future is the past. So it is here. For all the reform, for all the change in police structure, for all the education, for all the change in criminal code and in technology, line officers are doing basically what they did forty and even one hundred years ago. They act like street-level bureaucrats, they cover their asses from the command hierarchy, they try to protect other officers from public and departmental oversight, and they just generally try to do what they think is right in hostile and potentially dangerous situations. They are well educated today, so they tend to do those things better than they did one hundred years ago. But they still make arrests where nothing else works or where it helps their career, they provide service if it does not take a lot of on-line time, and they generally maintain order as best they can. The institution of policing swirls around them in constant change and variation, yet what they do on a day-to-day basis on the street is largely unaffected.

FOR FURTHER READING

Herman Goldstein. *Problem-Oriented Policing.* New York: McGraw-Hill, 1990.

This book is by one of the leading scholars in the new design of police organizations. It covers criticisms of traditional styles of policing and the rationale for new approaches in which police officers reduce crime by solving problems rather than relying only on arrests.

Jack Greene and Steven Mastrofski. *Community Policing: Rhetoric or Reality.* New York: Praeger, 1988.

This series of essays on community policing addresses many practical, philosophical, and conceptual issues associated with the implementation of the community-policing ideal. The problems of redesigning police organizations using community-policing principles are emphasized.

Jerome Skolnick and David Bayley. *The New Blue Line: Police Innovation in Six American Cities.* New York: The Free Press, 1986.

The authors provide case studies of innovative police practices ranging from changes in police practices in sections of cities to larger-scale reforms.

They also cover organizational and management issues as well as the changing role of the police officer.

Samuel Walker. *Police in America.* 2nd ed. New York: McGraw-Hill, 1991.

This collection of essays examines the role of police in a democratic society. Of particular emphasis among the essays are the central problems police face within a diverse society. Many of the articles address the issue of defining the police role in American society and offer suggestions on how policing can meet the needs of complex communities.

Robert Trojanowicz and Bonnie Bucqueroux. *Community Policing: A Contemporary Perspective.* Cincinnati, OH: Anderson, 1989.

Based on research done in Michigan, this book explores the many practical issues facing police administrators who attempt to implement community-policing ideas within their departments. Included in the examination are concerns of police officers, administrators, and citizens in the implementation of community policing.

DISCUSSION QUESTIONS

1. What things have helped the community-policing movement achieve popularity in recent years?

2. Often people think of predicting the future as drawing a straight line from where we are today. What kinds of critical incidents do you think could occur that might dramatically affect the way policing is done? Can police planning take into account such possibilities?

3. Does the community in which you live show signs of urban stagnation? If so, how is policing being affected by these changes?

4. If community policing involves greater use of discretion to solve community problems, will difficulties arise over the abuse of that discretion? How can police maintain order while ensuring that discretion is not used inappropriately?

5. What role do you think education should play in preparing students for entering the world of policing? What are the strengths and limitations of the approach you describe? What things should you emphasize to prepare for a career in criminal justice?

7

☆

The Future of Criminal Court:

Due Process, Crime Control, Optimism, and Pessimism

CANDACE McCOY

Rutgers University

The year 2010 is not far off; it is less than two decades away. Barring cataclysmic events, social trends that are gathering momentum right now will exert their full influence on the operations of our governmental institutions.

A lot can happen in two decades. In the past twenty years alone, a multitude of technological innovations have influenced our daily lives. Do you remember how to live without microwave ovens, pocket calculators, disposable diapers, VCRs, aerobic classes, cable TV, panty hose, personal computers, word processors, or Mexican and Chinese food easily available for takeout in any remote hamlet in the nation? If you are under 20-years-old, you probably do not remember a time when these things were absent from your normal environment. If you are older than 20, you probably marvel that you were able to function at all before they appeared on the consumer scene.

Old-timers know, though, that the fundamental structure of American daily life, and the consumerism that supports it, is basically unchanged. Even though you can microwave the Szechuan beef or chicken burritos in two minutes and eat while watching a VCR movie, the basic activity of coming home for dinner and enjoying some mindless diversion remains the same as when the only entertainment was radio. A parallel observation holds true for the basic structure of American governmental institutions. Over the past two decades, crime rates fluctuated, weaponry became more lethal and gun-related violence surged, awareness of the differential treatment of ethnic minorities and women in the justice system heightened, and attitudes toward drug use among the middle class changed. But the basic structure of the justice system remained mostly fixed as criminal courts continued to absorb and process a pressing flow of people accused of committing crimes.

The basic structure continues to be, and will continue to be, that a person accused of a crime will be arrested, booked, taken before a court, bailed out or jailed pretrial, pronounced not guilty or guilty by a judge, and, if guilty, sentenced to punishment. More fundamentally, the basic precepts underlying this procedure will undoubtedly continue to be those that have been characterized by Anglo-American tradition since the days of the Magna Carta: due process of law, the requirement that guilt be proven beyond a reasonable doubt by credible evidence, and the argument that punishment may not be cruel or unusual. The nineteenth-century American legal invention that the law must be applied equally to all will continue to exert great power. But, as any casual observer of criminal courts knows, these grand ideals are difficult to carry out in practice, and they may become increasingly attenuated in decades to come.

Also as any casual observer knows, U.S. Supreme Court decisions significantly affect the degree to which these ideals are painstakingly upheld. The Court has been recast from its due-process-oriented mold of the 1960s and 1970s into a powerful supporter of hard-line crime-control ideology.[1] Understanding exactly how this change will affect the daily work of trial courts in this nation is not simple. Although the Court sets standards for trial court operations through interpretations of the constitutional guarantees of the Fourth, Fifth, Sixth, Eighth, and Fourteenth Amendments, putting those standards into practice is not a one-dimensional enterprise. The Court's case law interacts with demographic and ideological trends. Its holdings are applied in a shifting social environment, and it is only when these legal and cultural vari-

---

1. See Chapter 4, "The Law of the Future," by James Acker, for a description of trends in Supreme Court case law.

ables come together that change occurs in the daily work world of criminal courts.

What are these cultural and social variables likely to be? How will they connect with the law so as to produce particular procedures and programs in the lower criminal courts? What will those procedures and programs look like by the year 2010?

Variables describing the social and cultural background to which the courts apply the law can be divided into three categories.[2] Perceived over time, they constitute trends: criminological, demographic, and ideological. The criminological trend most likely to affect courts is the rate of crime committed in various categories. The demographic trend most likely to affect courts is the continuing increase in that proportion of the nation's people whose ethnicity is nonwhite or foreign-born. And ideological trends are what they always have been: a tug-of-war between retributivist, crime-control ideology and a sociologically based credo that would control crime primarily through social engineering. (The latter approach holds that, realistically, courts and prisons can do little to control crime; their tasks are to provide due process and penal fairness.) While we can observe the criminological and demographic trends in empirical data and thus can tentatively predict their courses and effects into the year 2010, ideology is exceedingly difficult to observe or measure until its actual effects are apparent. So this essay will not contain a prediction of how political opinion will regard the court system—indeed, the entire criminal justice system—in ideological terms in the year 2010. Instead, the reader is invited to formulate "optimistic" and "pessimistic" scenarios about how courts will address the problems they face, and then to imagine how ideologically based choices would affect them.

CRIMINOLOGICAL TRENDS

There are many explanations of why people commit crime—indeed, it is the ultimate issue that practicing criminologists must continually address. From the viewpoint of the criminal justice system itself, however, the most important question is not why anybody commits crime (except for the issue of how often criminal defenses based on justifica-

---

2. These are simply handy ideas that spring to mind and are not by any means a definitive list. The reader is invited to imagine many other social factors, predict how they will change in the next two decades, and match them up with our knowledge about lower criminal courts to achieve a picture of future court functioning.

tion, excuse, or lack of *mens rea* are raised),[3] but rather *how many* people are accused. The mission of criminal trial courts is straightforward: determine the guilt or innocence and possible punishment of every person brought to court. If the number of criminally accused people increases or decreases significantly, the courts must respond administratively with revised budgets, program requests, and staffing levels.

The criminological theory of primary importance to criminal courts, then, has to do with how many people will be expected to commit crimes and therefore require court processing. Assuming that poverty causes crime, courts could expect more work if the poverty rate increases. By contrast, rates of crimes with biological bases (if any) would remain constant because presumably the distribution of biological criminogenic traits would remain constant throughout the population.

The criminological explanation with by far the most intuitive cogency for court administrators is the theory that crime is correlated with the age of the offender. Youths tend to commit violent crimes, desist as they age, and are considerably less likely to resume violent behavior the older they grow. "One thing all participants in the criminal career debate agree on is the age–crime relationship: aggregate arrest rates increase steadily with age until they reach a peak, after which they steadily decline."[4] Given this relationship, we would expect the rate of violent crime to increase if the proportion of teenagers in the population increases. Violent crime rates in the past few years have fluctuated within the normal expected range,[5] as has the median age of the population. But by the year 2010, the children of the 1950s baby boomers will be teenagers and young adults. This "baby echo" of children born in the mid-1970s, the 1980s, and the early 1990s is approaching its high-crime-prone years right now, in 1995, and it will not fully mature into its "crime desistance" years until about 2015.

---

3. See James Acker's discussion of justification, excuse, and self-defense in the future (Chapter 4).
4. Arnold Barnet, Alfred Blumstein, Jacqueline Cohen, and David P. Farrington, "Not All Criminal Career Models Are Equally Valid," *Criminology,* Vol. 30, No. 1 (February 1992), p. 136. Also see other articles in that issue exploring recent research on the correlation between crime and age of offenders.
5. Despite sensational headlines about a perceived rise in violent crime, recent UCR data show only the usual expected fluctuations in "index" crimes. Crime is certainly increasing, but so is the population. And while homicide rates have indeed gone up, the latest public perception of skyrocketing mayhem on the streets is probably attributable more to isolated bizarre cases such as that of Jeffrey Dahmer, the Milwaukee serial murderer and cannibal, than to actual increased risk. In addition, a glut of new cases brought to court for prosecution is attributable not necessarily to increased criminal activity, but to campaigns to increase arrest rates in selected crime categories. That has been so with drug arrests and prosecutions over the past few years.

Furthermore, there seems to be no reason to believe that the rate at which guns are used in committing these crimes will decline. Indeed, assuming a constant rate of technological improvement in firearms as well as other consumer goods, we would expect violent acts committed with guns to get deadlier and deadlier.

Thus, assuming the "baby echoers" commit crimes as their parents did, and assuming the violent crimes will be efficiently accomplished with firearms, the criminal courts in the year 2000 will probably experience a surge in business—at least in the prosecution of violent crime.[6] At about the turn of the millennium, the criminal courts will be called upon to respond either creatively or with heavy-handed assembly-line justice to this expected increase. That response will have been institutionalized by the year 2010, and its imprint will still be strong.

The exact character of that initial response, of course, is still unknown. Predicting what it will be is almost an act of faith. The most pessimistic scenario would be to predict that judges will refuse to handle the increasing caseload, dismissing great numbers of cases of defendants the police bring to court, even when successful prosecution seems likely on the evidence. The result would be to return great numbers of offenders immediately to the streets, which would not only be an unjust result in each case but also would probably encourage vigilante justice. Few judges would take so unprofessional an approach.

A more likely but also pessimistic scenario, would be to predict that courts, overwhelmed with the sheer numbers of accused people presented for prosecution, will respond by speeding up the assembly-line justice that is the prevailing model today. The most likely method of speeding up the assembly line is to speed up the guilty plea process.

By contrast, a more optimistic scenario would be to predict that courts will respond creatively by developing alternatives to criminal trials, which would be possible in nonserious cases, and using the resources thus freed to provide a careful, participative guilty plea process in serious felonies.

---

6. This is not to discount the effect of crime rates on nonviolent crime, but we know little about criminal careers in white-collar crime, so predictions about court case loads in prosecuting economic-based crimes are nearly impossible to make. The same can be said for crime that is basically the result of legislative changes. If possession of marijuana or cocaine were made legal, for instance, the aggregate crime rate would dive because drug arrests would no longer be included. The courts, naturally, would experience a significant drop in caseload. It is impossible to predict what state legislatures will do, and in any event the prediction would have to be made for fifty states—a daunting task, considering how difficult it is to predict legislating actions for the next fiscal year, much less for the year 2010.

No matter which scenario you favor, the major response of the courts to an increase in violent crimes will be to elicit guilty pleas efficiently. Whether these guilty pleas will be not only efficient but also fair is the question raised by demographic trends and ideological trends.

DEMOGRAPHIC TRENDS

There is one overwhelming demographic trend that will significantly affect courts and, indeed, all of our social institutions in the decades to come: The fact that the United States is becoming increasingly multiethnic and multicultural:

> Immigrants were responsible for a third of the population growth (in the United States) in the 1980s. More arrived than in any decade since the second of this century. . . . Still, foreign-born residents constitute only about 7 percent of the population today and . . . the black share has grown rather slowly—9.9 percent in 1920, 10 percent in 1950, 11.1 percent in 1970. 12.1 percent in 1990.[7]

This sweeping overview, while accurate for the nation's population as a whole, does not account for geographic variation (many cities and even entire states, such as California and Florida, have high concentrations of foreign-born ethnics, while the population of other locales is overwhelmingly native-born of European descent), nor does it take account of the ethnics whose families have lived in the United States for generations and been assimilated into the dominant culture while still carefully retaining their own unique cultural folkways. Tensions among them, native-born blacks, and the newer immigrant groups will be apparent in the political arena of the year 2010. And the courts are an important part of this political system.

Of course, a multiethnic population is nothing new in criminal court. Indeed, a common criticism of the entire criminal justice system is that ethnic minorities, particularly blacks, are overrepresented "clientele"—a reflection of the racism inherent in American society in general and the justice apparatus in particular. No honest observer can deny that people of color are prosecuted and imprisoned in numbers far

---

7. Arthur M. Schlesinger, Jr., *The Disuniting of America: Reflections on a Multicultural Society* (New York: Norton, 1992), 120–121.

greater than they would be if people of all ethnic backgrounds were prosecuted in numbers exactly proportionate to the ethnic composition of the overall population. But courts are essentially reactive—that is, they must accept the criminal suspects brought to them by the police and prosecutors. What the court then does in deciding the fate of a criminal suspect may or may not be affected by that person's ethnic background—indeed, it probably often is—but the "raw material" that the court is asked to "process" in the first instance can scarcely be regarded as a product of the court's own racism.

The next rejoinder would be to say that the reason a disproportionate number of minorities are prosecuted is that police and prosecutors are mostly racist in choosing which people to send to court. The theory states that whites who commit crimes are not prosecuted, while minorities are. Surely, some police and prosecutors practice such shameful ethnic discrimination, and surely there is a tendency to err on the side of too many arrests in situations where an ethnic minority is accused of wrongdoing but the evidence is ambiguous. But generally, most police and prosecutors are responding to an observable, objective phenomenon,: racial and ethnic minorities do indeed commit more "street" crimes than their numbers in the general population would predict. The reasons for this may be debatable, but the generally accepted explanation has been that "conditions still existing in urban ghettos will serve as a driving force funneling more and more of the minority poor into . . . the system." As long as great numbers of people in our cities continue to be ill-educated, underemployed, underparented, and kept at the margins of participation in the wider society, the justice system from the police through the prisons will be presented with a disproportionate number of minority "clients." Few demographic trends—at least, none that I know about at the time this essay is being written—point in any other direction.

Furthermore, the demographic trend toward a multiethnic society covers much more than the chronic marginalization of our inner cities. It springs also from immigration of peoples from every spot on the globe into the United States. While the influx of immigrants' talents and energies has in the past produced our tremendously powerful economy, absorbing these varied social groups into traditional American cultural and political values has always been a difficult sociological undertaking. "What happens when people of different ethnic origins, speaking different languages and professing different religions, settle in the same geographical locality and live under the same political sovereignty?"

Unless a common purpose binds them together, tribal hostilities will drive them apart."[8]

The challenge for American society as a whole is to find common ground, to forge the "one out of many" to which the motto *E pluribus unum* urges us. Somehow, in the twenty-first century, as in the previous two centuries, Americans must develop a shared understanding of democratic institutions and self-government but not sacrifice the cultural endowments of the many people absorbed into the common *polis*.

The most powerful leaders in this development must be the democratic institutions themselves. Their credibility and utility, demonstrated in their daily operations, will eventually touch the lives of all these ethnic groups. As schools strive to educate a multiethnic population, as legislatures set standards for providing basic services to all, courts will struggle to provide justice in individual cases. The challenge for criminal courts is to be prepared for the minority composition of the criminally accused and of victims of crime to expand into a wider variety of ethnic and racial minorities, and to respond creatively, compassionately, and constructively to the inevitable increase in racial friction.

Increasingly, the parties in criminal cases will be people whose cultural backgrounds are not congruent with the Anglo-American adversary system, or at least who are likely to resent the opposing party not only because of the events that landed everybody in court, but also because the other party is of a different heritage. Dissimilar ethnics arrive into criminal court playing a variety of roles. They are victims, witnesses, defendants. They are judges, lawyers, jurors. They are police and probation officers.

The ethnicity or cultural background of any particular participant is unlikely to affect the overall character of the court or the justice of its decisions. We assume that the court professionals, no matter what their ethnicity, will support the traditional structure and vision of American criminal law and procedure. Similarly, the ethnicity of nonprofessionals in court is traditionally relevant only insofar as it must be considered in providing a fair trial. A jury, for example, can hardly be said to represent a community in which the defendant lives if none of its members are of similar ethnic heritage (assuming the defendant himself or herself is of a racial or ethnic background typical in the area). Judges, lawyers, and police officers of the same race as is typical of the court's community are often recruited because, it is assumed correctly or incorrectly, victims and witnesses are more open and communicative with people of

---

8. Schlesinger, p. 10.

their own backgrounds. This goal fits perfectly with an adversary notion of criminal law: The right to bring into court evidence demonstrating the truth of what actually happened in an alleged criminal act is the most fundamental underpinning of due process. Any device that may increase the quantity and quality of fact-finding is supported, and a trust-inspiring ethnicity of court professionals is regarded as such a device.

For courts in 2010, the greatest challenge in accommodating an increasingly diverse population will not be to attract dedicated professionals of minority heritage into careers in the criminal courts. That challenge is already being met in 1995, and it will continue to be met. The much more difficult task is to provide "justice for all," for defendants and victims of all ethnic backgrounds, under prevailing court procedures. Perhaps even more difficult is not only to make just decisions, but also to communicate and demonstrate to all the people caught up in the court drama that the case outcome is indeed fair and just. When litigants and court professionals share the same ethnic heritage, participants may not exactly understand why a court has done what it has, but at least they are unlikely to blame it on racism. In the courts of 2010, that blind, unfortunately reflexive response will be more likely because ethnic divisions will be more likely. Courts must take creative and unprecedented steps to prevent it.

But trial courts are ill-equipped to explain why they make the decisions they do. A judge and perhaps a jury listen to evidence brought into court to prove or disprove the defendant's guilt beyond a reasonable doubt. Each fact is analyzed and weighed on the scales of justice, and attorneys forcefully argue about the reliability and implications of this evidence. Whether each fact is credible or not, however, is not recorded, and the court's reasoning is not described. All the defendant, the victim, and the public know at the end of the trial is whether the accused is guilty or not guilty.

Deficient though the trial courts may be in explaining their decision-making processes to litigants, if a case is tried, the evidence and witnesses have at least been presented in public for all to see and judge for themselves. But few cases go to trial. Most end in guilty pleas in which the defendant admits guilt after the attorneys have discussed the evidence and determined its credibility and import between themselves.

Approximately 90 percent of all criminal court cases in the United States end in guilty pleas, and under such conditions there is scant opportunity for anybody to know exactly which facts resulted in the conviction. The charges are read, the defendant pleads guilty under advice of counsel, and the judge accepts the plea on the facts submitted by the attorneys. Later, a sentence based on those facts and others gathered by the probation officer is affixed to the conviction.

Under these conditions, most laypeople suspect that something may be wrong. The defendant may claim to have been railroaded, the victim believes the defendant hoodwinked the court or that the sleazy lawyers made unethical backroom deals, and interested community and family members are mystified as to what the criminal activity really was. Although the guilty plea is probably an accurate reflection of the actual criminal wrongdoing that could have been proven at trial, nobody but the lawyers and judge know that. It is hardly surprising that this system is distrusted, and that, lacking information and hard proof, victims and defendants alike strain for explanations of the outcome that have little to do with the actual evidence. In a diverse society, racial or ethnic discrimination, and not the real facts of alleged criminal activity, is often claimed to be the determining factor in trial court convictions and sentences.

Of course, victims or defendants or anybody can claim anything. Even if evidence of terrible criminal wrongdoing is brought into an open trial, presented carefully and convincingly, and relied upon in convicting an offender, that person can claim to have been the victim of the court's racial prejudices and not the recipient of just punishment. Conversely, if an accused person is acquitted because evidence is flimsy, the crime victim who is of a different racial background can claim racial favoritism.

These allegations are most certainly groundless, but it is the court's task to explain that to the litigants and—ever more critically—to the community. Ordinarily, the evidentiary airing in the trial itself is all that the court offers, under the assumption that objective observers will understand the import of the evidence once it has been aired. Nevertheless, even when a case goes to public trial, themes of racial, ethnic, and gender frictions will resonate in interpretations that different people make of the evidence. It has been said of one recent highly publicized trial:

> Even though a jury will reach a verdict, only the most needle-nosed of lawyers will interpret it as truth. A trial is not so much a rendering of scientific truth as it is an accommodation of social policies, a balance of interests, and, of course, a game akin to cat-and-mouse. Nobody could mistake the [William Kennedy]

Smith trial for a dispassionate inquiry into what really happened at the Kennedy compound last Easter weekend.[9]

As with many cover stories in popular magazines, this passage is probably overstated. But the point is important: Even if the trial brings out all the evidence, which is then carefully and scientifically evaluated, the social tensions that so completely permeate the factual situation will appeal to emotion, not logic. They invite us to infuse the events described with meanings that we ourselves bring to them rather than to strive for some ephemeral objectivity. The Smith case, for example, involved an alleged rape. The evidence that proved or disproved forcible sexual intercourse was not only brought into the courtroom, but also broadcast on Court TV and summarized every night on every news show in the country. At base, how the public (if not the jurors) regarded the truth of the allegations was influenced as much by attitudes toward sexual politics and social class stratification as by the evidence produced. That is to say, observers interpreted the facts using their own beliefs and knowledge, including their attitudes toward gender and status.

A trial, then, is sometimes more like a morality play or social parable than a test of the truth—whatever that may be. When volatile emotions about race, ethnicity, or gender are stirred because a person accused or the crime itself raises the issue, the trial court is asked to do something for which it is not well equipped: explain the problem fully and demonstrate the justice of a particular outcome.

Criminal trials are increasingly becoming morality plays in which great issues of equal justice among races and genders are staged for the media and an aroused public. The awesome power of the criminal law, when brought in full force against an accused person, labels that person as bad not only for his or her acts but also because of *who he or she is*. It is no wonder that advocates of social division latch onto criminal trials as convenient rallying tools and as outlets for their own brand of racism. The Tawana Brawley case, in which a young black woman in New York claimed to have been raped and racially vilified by white men whom she said were from the Ku Klux Klan, is an example. The case is surprising not because a confused young woman concocted a story to try to cover up her own slight transgressions (she had been out past curfew and was probably sexually active despite her family's wishes), but because purveyors of racial animosity grabbed it and used it as a

---

9. "The Trial You Won't See," *Newsweek,* Dec. 16, 1991, p. 18.

platform to preach hatred. The actual evidence, and eventual acquittal of the defendants, mattered little next to the posturing of Ms. Brawley's advocates.

Even in many situations in which the racial component of the case is quite real and incendiary—such as recent cases in which a Korean grocer shot a young black man who he suspected was going to rob him, or the Rodney King case in Los Angeles where four white police officers were accused of criminal assault on an unarmed but uncooperative black motorist—the criminal trial serves as a place where the actual facts of the alleged acts are analyzed, not a place where the social conditions in which these actions were taken may be confronted. Courts are reactive: They accept what police and prosecutors bring to them, and they can do little to change or even explain the social problems that gave rise to the criminal cases in the first place.

Yet the courts become the focal point for these social problems because they are public and dramatic. If the demographic trends toward a multicultural society continue, by the year 2010 ethnic tensions may reach their breaking points, and criminal courtrooms will be one of the places where the ruptures become evident. But it does not have to be that way. Courts can take steps to explain their decisions more carefully, to demonstrate that the evidence on which a defendant is convicted or acquitted has little to do with ethnicity or gender and a lot to do with the facts as presented. For the preachers of social division, that will not be enough. But nothing will ever be enough for them, and in the end all the judges can do is to trust the voice of reason and be sure it is heard.

These dynamics are most evident in the example of the criminal trial, as discussed above. The need for explaining the justice of case outcomes, however, is even more pressing when cases are plea-bargained. With guilty pleas, evidence is not even aired publicly. While this may bypass the problems associated with grandstanding and the use of criminal trials as social parables, it more clearly raises the issue of how victims, defendants, and the public in general can come to understand the justice of case outcomes. The courts must find a way not only to weigh evidence in the adversarial courtroom, but also to give explanation and meaning to verdicts.

This will require reforming the guilty plea process, but not much. Nobody seriously advocates eliminating plea bargaining—not because to do so would swamp the courts with trials, although that is true, but because in most cases the negotiated guilty plea does indeed match the actual, provable criminal wrongdoing. The reform must be that judges and prosecutors will explain to litigants, in open court and on paper, exactly what facts were found to be convincing and what conviction and sentence was thereby produced. Every case must have some kind of open court hearing, so that all people connected to the alleged crime, including the victim and the defendant and their families, can come into the public arena and actually see justice being done. Ordinarily, a preliminary hearing will suffice. A guilty plea will usually follow, but this will be a guilty plea based on facts actually produced in the court. The judge, on accepting the guilty plea, must then state exactly which facts were found to be convincing beyond a reasonable doubt. Facts will then be recorded as proving or disproving every distinct element of the crime. The victim, the defendant, and the public will each be given copies of these documents.

In practice, many if not most courts already have procedures that approximate these steps. The point is that their explanatory function, as distinct from their prosecutorial function, must be emphasized more. This is all premised on the belief that democratic institutions serve all the people, that governmental actions cannot be made arbitrarily, and that the power of information will help people of varied social and ethnic backgrounds understand the reasoning behind institutional acts. Cynics will say that it will not matter, that racial animosities are too incendiary to be dampened by a sprinkling of words. But we will not know unless we try it, and if ethnic divisions persist in the courtroom, at least court professionals and the American public will know that this is because the divisions are too deep outside the halls of justice to be improved by events inside. The court events themselves, at least, will not be to blame.

IDEOLOGICAL VARIABLES

The problem is that more careful explanation takes time and effort. It slows down the conviction process. To crime-control advocates, the entire guilty plea process is premised on the concept of swift, unobstructed conviction short of trial, and adding these requirements to the court's procedures for accepting guilty pleas will be regarded as silly at best and criminal coddling at worst. By contrast, the due process advocates' response to the recommendation that courts explain their plea-bargained decisions more carefully is, "Good! Plea-bargained cases generally move too fast to probe very deeply into the evidence, although the opportunity to challenge the charges against you is the most fundamental underpinning of the right to due process. Slowing guilty pleas down somewhat would allow more careful assessment of the facts of each case, and this is all to the good."

This minidebate characterizes the final "trend"—ideology. Herbert Packer's classic dichotomy, dividing criminal justice values into due process and crime-control orientations, is obviously involved in any debate to reform plea bargaining. Whether courts in 2010, in an effort to prevent racial and ethnic animosities from blossoming unwarranted in the criminal courtroom, begin to emphasize an explanatory function of criminal procedure is dependent mostly on whether court professionals are willing to expand due process. That ideologically based outcome cannot be predicted one way or another. It is up to the reader, and eventually all citizens, including court professionals, to decide whether such a change would be good or not.

PREDICTED PROCEDURES
AND PROGRAMS

We come now to the part of our inquiry that is both the most difficult and the most fun. Given the trends outlined above, and given what we know about the current operations of the criminal courts, what scenarios would we predict for the year 2010? Current knowledge of criminal court processes tells us that felony and misdemeanor cases are (understandably) handled very differently. Current knowledge also tells us that the criminal justice system itself, from police through court and probation services and all the way into the correctional system, is overloaded and likely to remain so. Given these realities, the task for 2010 will be the same as it is in 1995: process a crushing load of people accused of crimes, and do so as fairly as possible. The difference in 2010 will be that the process will be even more strained by demographic factors of age and ethnicity than it is now.

Felony justice and misdemeanor justice are different today, and the question for the future is not whether they will continue to be different (they will), but how much more different they will or will not become. In felony adjudication, naturally, more is at stake. A lengthy prison term is much more important to a criminal defendant than is a monetary fine, which is the likely outcome of misdemeanor conviction. Defendants resist pleading guilty the higher the possible punishment is: In other words, you might plead guilty quickly if you are facing a $200 fine or even a month in jail for shoplifting, but you would be more likely to fight vigorously a conviction that brings ten years in prison for assault with a deadly weapon.

As Malcolm Feeley has said, in misdemeanor courts today "the process is the punishment." Once a defendant has been arrested for a low-level misdemeanor, perhaps held in jail before being released on bail or recognizance, arranged to get through court (which may include taking off work), and gone through preliminary court hearings, defending the case is more of a hassle than pleading guilty and paying the fine would be. These incentives are unlikely to change in the future, so misdemeanor courts will likely not change much.

The more difficult cases involve the higher-level, serious misdemeanors and nonserious felonies—the cases that are called "wobblers" in California. These are cases of drunk driving, minor assaults, possession of drugs for sale, and so on. These cases are serious enough that defendants do not want to plead guilty quickly just to get it over with. Yet they are not serious enough that full trials are ordinarily contemplated, unless there is some obvious mistake or ambiguity in the evidence and the prosecutor will not make concessions for it. These are also the kinds of cases that, given the trends presented above, are likely to become very important in the future. Already drug cases especially are flooding our courts and straining the system's capacity to process them (see Chapter 12 in this book). Add to this the fact that the baby echo defendants will most likely commit these crimes at a greater rate beginning in 1995, and that these crimes like all others will raise issues of ethnic friction, and the picture for the future appears either discouraging (assuming the courts do not respond creatively) or very interesting (assuming they do).

An optimistic scenario would involve justice professionals assessing their needs and the quality of justice the courts provide and figuring out how to reform. "Justice professionals" include legislators and judges, primarily. Legislators would decide that some of the less serious felonies are too harshly prosecuted—mostly, this would mean that drug problems would be handled outside the criminal justice system and that the criminal sanction would be reserved for only the serious offenders who are dealers and importers. Judges, who are currently swamped in drug cases, would surely appreciate such a legislative response.

The judges themselves could ease the baby echo caseload and heightened ethnic tensions by applying a "dispute-resolution" approach to serious misdemeanors and perhaps many low-level felonies. This program, which has been pioneered in the civil courts, is generally regarded as an alternative to litigation to which the negotiating parties (in this case, the criminal defendant and the prosecutor) both agree to be bound. Although there are real problems in applying the dispute-resolution model to criminal adjudication (primarily that the rights of criminal defendants are, and should be, considerably more extensive than those of civil defendants), nevertheless we would expect that defendants who are now willing to plead guilty after extensive plea bargaining would be equally willing to plead guilty after dispute-resolution sessions. The caseload impact would be about the same, but the quality of justice might improve. Defendants who want to plead guilty in the old-fashioned way could do so, but defendants or victims who want fuller participation in the case and deeper understanding of its facts—presumably a good thing for confronting ethnic tensions—could urge the prosecutor to engage in the criminal equivalent of binding arbitration. A dispute-resolution session would replace the plea bargaining discussion ordinarily held between the prosecutor and defense attorney. Court time would be about the same, but public understanding of the case and its reasoning would be greatly enhanced.

A pessimistic predicted scenario for the bulk of felonies (i.e., those at the lower end of the felony seriousness scale and upper end of the misdemeanor scale) would be that crushing caseloads and unpleasant ethnic tensions would prompt the police and courts to prosecute fewer of these crimes. Police would look the other way more often, and courts would find spurious reasons to dismiss or reduce the charges. The result in court would be a more manageable caseload and steadfast adherence to established norms of court functioning. But on the street, the result would be a breakdown in civility and, perhaps, such a negative social reaction that incidents of vigilante "justice" would increase. The traditional reason for engaging in violence that vigilantes from the Ku Klux Klan to Dirty Harry give as a justification for their illegal acts is that existing institutions of law enforcement do not provide justice, and that therefore they must take the law into their own hands. Few of us would approve of this pessimistic scenario.

Scenarios about prosecution of serious felonies—rapes, murders, aggravated assaults, residential burglaries—are also either optimistic or pessimistic. They are generally outlined above, in the discussions about reforming the guilty plea process. Optimistically, the courts in the year 2010 will continue to include almost all cases through guilty pleas, thereby accommodating the baby echo increase in violent crime to be expected around 1995. But to address ethnic tensions, the courts could reform the process somewhat so as to offer litigants more explanation of the reasons for the guilty plea and resulting sentence in each case. (Incidentally, the one fact that will probably become more and more important in serious felonies is whether the defendant is armed. In the past, the fact of "carrying" during the commission of a felony was something that could be the subject of a plea negotiation. But if gun-related crime continues to soar, judges in the year 2010 will be like the public in general and swiftly and fully condemn anybody who commits a crime involving firearms.)

A pessimistic scenario for serious felony adjudication would be to predict that, under the burden of ever more crushing caseloads, the courts will place even more emphasis on achieving swift guilty pleas. The reduced due process that would result would be regarded as permissible because U.S. Supreme Court cases on the Fourth, Fifth, and Sixth Amendments by that time will have moved to a hegemonic reliance on crime-control ideology. The reader may not regard this scenario as pessimistic, but it would be regarded as such if "optimism" is defined as the capacity to confront the dual trends of increasing crime rate and heightened ethnic frictions and to make a difference in improving the quality of justice. "Improving" existing guilty plea processes by speeding them up and driving them even farther out of the public view cannot be said to even acknowledge the trends, much less address them.

Of course, predictions are inexact. The most that can be done is to offer two scenarios, one hopeful and one pessimistic. The reader is invited to choose which outcome he or she thinks is more likely and to do whatever possible to move the courts in that direction. Are you a pessimist or an optimist?

FOR FURTHER READING

James Eisenstein, Roy Flemming, and Peter Nardulli. *The Contours of Justice: Communities and Their Courts.* Glenview, IL: Scott, Foresman, 1988.

This book provides a comparative analysis of nine felony courts in three states. It develops the idea of court operations reflecting local communities in their history and political culture. The processing of cases, their resolution, and sentencing patterns are influenced by such local factors as political development and traditions.

Michael Gottfredson and Don M. Gottfredson. *Decision Making in Criminal Justice: Toward the Rational Exercise of Discretion.* Cambridge, MA: Ballinger, 1980.

This book focuses on how decisions are made throughout the criminal justice system. Its chapters on the courts provide strong reviews of research on decision making and the results of decisions.

Joan E. Jacoby. *The American Prosecutor: A Search for Identity.* Lexington, MA: D.C. Heath, 1980.

This classic study of prosecutorial decision making examines the pressures on prosecutors in processing and disposing of cases. It also offers a typology of decision makers based on the information they need and their goals in making decisions.

Lisa J. McIntyre. *The Public Defender: The Practice of Law in the Shadows of Repute.* Chicago: University of Chicago Press, 1987.

This look at the other side of the adversarial process focuses on the pressures on public defenders. In particular, it deals with how defense attorneys must deal with their role in providing legal services for clients they often know are guilty as charged.

Robert Satter. *Doing Justice: A Trial Judge at Work.* New York: Simon & Schuster, 1990.

This work examines the third member of the courtroom work group: the pressures on them and their concerns with justice. The book provides a good analysis of the differences between the ideals and realities of a career on the bench.

DISCUSSION QUESTIONS

1. What criminological trends have you seen that are already influencing the criminal courts?

2. Describe the changes in the demographic characteristics of our society that are expected to occur by 2010.

3. How will increases in racial and ethnic diversity affect the court system? How can the court demonstrate that it is fair and just in such a diverse society? Will increasing diversity among court personnel have an impact?

4. What does it mean to argue that a trial is sometimes more like a morality play than a test of the truth? Do you agree or disagree?

5. Do you think that justice will suffer under the weight of increasing caseloads and racial tension or that there will be improvements in understanding the courts and in the quality of justice? Are you an optimist or a pessimist?

8

☆

The Trials of
Tamika Watson:

*The Future of
Criminal Sentencing*

LYNNE GOODSTEIN
Pennsylvania State University

JOHN R. HEPBURN
Arizona State University

amika Watson prepared herself for her first day on the bench as the newest judge of the Metro County Criminal Court. She couldn't wait to get into the courtroom to hear her first case. After twenty years of working in the criminal law field—first as an assistant district attorney, then as district attorney, and finally working on the other side of the room as a private practitioner who quickly became known as one of the best criminal defenders in the business— she felt she was well prepared to take on the responsibilities that came with being called "Your Honor."

She put on her black robe, the traditional uniform of jurists since the European Middle Ages. She noticed that it was too long and figured that it, like the continuing shortage of women's lavatories in the criminal court building, still reflected the former dominance of men in the business of criminal law. This was changing rapidly among her contemporaries, with half of all criminal court judgeships now held by women, a full fifth by women of color like herself. But it seemed like some of the simplest things took the longest to change.

She took out her voice-activated diary, which recorded all entries both in her own personal computer and in her secretary Peter's computer, and made notes about shortening her robes and looking into the addition of more washrooms for women personnel. Then she checked the hardware she would need to be wearing for all court proceedings. She put her personal bail-setting calculator in her pocket, first checking to see whether it was functioning properly after yesterday's practice session. She knew that her seat in the courtroom was equipped with a built-in calculator, left over from the years when judges were responsible for applying the sentencing guidelines, but she knew she would feel more comfortable with her personal model.

With passage of the Sentencing Experts Act, sentencing authority had been shifted from judges to three-person sentencing committees, so the built-in calculators in the courtrooms were retrofitted to aid judges in the only discretionary decision that was still under their domain—whether to set bail and, if so, for how much? In some ways she was disappointed that she would not be setting sentences, since that was what she had been brought up to believe was the judge's role. But she recognized that her training and experience in the law made her an expert in dealing with procedural issues in the courtroom, not in offender behavior. That expertise was represented among the members of the sentencing committees.

Criminal sentencing in 2010 was certainly different from the system in place when she first studied the topic as an undergraduate criminal justice student in the late 1970s. She recalled that a rather simple formula then governed criminal sentencing: The severity of the offense determined the time served—whether in jail, in prison, on probation, on parole, or some combination of these. Now, with the Sentencing Experts Act, the system that had been slowly evolving over those thirty years was fully operational.

The act created the Offender Retribution and Rehabilitation Program (ORRP), which called for a comprehensive and integrated range of sanctions. The entire system could be viewed as one large, elaborate staircase, with each step reflecting a different degree of supervision, contact, restriction, and privilege. At the lowest level of sanction were monetary fines and assessments. This stage was followed in order by the three stages of probation, jail confinement, and prison confinement. Each stage was broken down into different substages or levels. Probation, for instance, consisted of four levels: summary probation, standard probation, community probation, and intensive probation. Each level of probation had a different degree of supervision and constraint over the offender. Similarly, there were two levels of jail: regular jail time and night or weekend jail, a work-furlough option that allowed people to work in the community and return to jail for nights or weekends. Prison sentences also were used in a variety of ways—from short, intensive confinements followed by immediate probation to intermediate confinements followed by parole.

The sentencing committee was responsible for applying the results of sophisticated computer programs to determine two aspects of the sanction for each offender sentenced. One was the exact length of time the offender would be under the ORRP's control; the other was the initial placement of the offender (stage and level) on this staircase of sanctions. Once placement was assigned, movement up or down the staircase was determined by the offender's performance within the ORRP. Following a specified minimum time at this initial placement, each offender had the opportunity to "walk the staircase" toward less constrained and more privileged stages within the ORRP. That is, offenders could not earn early release from ORRP, but they could earn the right to progress to the least restrictive condition (Stage 1, Level 1), where they remained until they had completed their sentences.

The foundation of the system was something called the Offender Retribution and Rehabilitation Program Profile Index (ORRPPI), which actually determined the appropriate sentence for each offender. Apparently, social scientists had been working on these profiles for quite some time, but until the passage of the Sentencing Experts Act, few people had realized how much of the job of sentencing offenders had actually been passed on to computers. The point of the profile was to match the offender to the retribution–rehabilitation level that would be both commensurate with the seriousness of the criminal offense and supportive of rehabilitation. The ORRPPI did not treat all offenders the same. Instead, it prescribed the same treatment for all offenders who shared the same profile. By placing similar offenders in the same stage and level of the ORRP, it assigned to each the same initial degree of retribution and rehabilitation.

Tamika was impressed with the complexity and rationality of the system, but she had to admit that she was a bit overwhelmed by its technology. Supposedly, the ORRPPI was a completely objective instrument that gave weights to factors such as the offender's criminal, social and employment history, psychological traits, and readiness for ORRP. Presumably, it was superior to more subjective assessments by judges, probation officers, or other professionals because it did not allow personal biases to creep into the sentencing decision. It seemed almost ironic that the sentencing committee was as powerful as it was, considering that its members also did not actually set the sentences. With collective backgrounds in computer science, social science, and applied legal studies, those sentencing committee folks still had to be pretty knowledgeable about offender behavior, classification systems, and the multitude of steps in the staircase. Their job was to constantly monitor the profiles of the offenders they had sentenced, ensuring that offenders were evenly distributed along the rungs of the staircase. If some levels or phases of the ORRP system began to be over- or underused, they were supposed to make suggestions for changes in the computer programs to the appropriate legislative committees.

Sentencing by computers certainly did cut down on opportunities for individuals to be subjective and did produce consistent and uniform profiles regardless of who administered the instruments. The result of this scientific approach to sentencing was that offenders scoring the same on the ORRPPI received the same sentence, as measured in terms of both total length of sentence and stage and level of initial sanction.

Tamika had to admit that she was a bit wary, though, because she knew that all decisions reflected the subjective position of some person or group, including the algorithms of the ORRPPI. She worried about so much power being put into the hands of social and computer scientists. They might be knowledgeable in their fields, but did they really understand the concerns of victims—or of offenders, for that matter? And were there some differences, perhaps subtle but nonetheless important, among offenders, that should be recognized? She wondered whether what was being gained in uniformity was worth what was being lost by not letting individual voices—of victims, offenders, and even sentencing committee members—speak for themselves.

Continuing to prepare for her first day as judge, Tamika put on the nearly invisible earphone for the simultaneous translator. One of the newest devices used by criminal court judges, the translator enabled her to understand defendants and witnesses in twelve languages. This was especially necessary now after passage of the Native Language Bill, which guaranteed all American citizens the right to conduct legal proceedings in their native language. When she was born, the common conception of the United States was as a melting pot in which people sought to assimilate into the bland, white middle-class culture of the suburbs and shopping malls. But with the waves of new immigrants from South America, Asia, and Eastern Europe in the 1990s, coupled with the emphasis on multiculturalism, people seemed to recognize the importance of their roots and the value of cultural differences in strengthening a society. This was not to say that the new appreciation for diversity was without its pitfalls, as evidenced by the rejuvenation of the Ku Klux Klan and the American Nazi Party in the 1990s as well. But overall, the increased acceptance of groups who never would have been there fifty years ago into the "towers of power" was seen by many as enabling the United States to retain its position of political and economic world leadership.

Checking the digital readout on her personal diary, Judge Watson noted that she still had fifteen minutes to wait before it would be time to enter the courtroom. Her mind drifted back to law school days in the late 1980s when she first became fascinated with the criminal law and the prospects of working in the law-enforcement field. She had grown up in the 1960s in what was then called the "Projects" of a Midwestern city, and she had been raised by her grandmother and aunt to work hard, study hard, and give all she could to her community. She excelled in school and enjoyed it too, and so she was encouraged by her family and friends to avoid the street scene by staying inside and studying. Even so, she was very much aware of the crime around her. Her own home had been burglarized several times, and most devastating of all, her best friend had been killed at age 10 on her way home from school by a drug dealer's stray bullet. She knew that many of the people responsible for this mayhem had been arrested more than once, and she couldn't figure out why the police and judges let them stay out of jail. At an early age, she became determined to do something to fight the criminals who seemed to be destroying her community.

As a criminal justice major at the community college in the mid-1970s, she learned about why known offenders were often returned to her community rather than being sent to institutions for long stays. The rehabilitation model was popular in those days of the 1960s and early 1970s. The prevailing notion, which actually had been in effect for about one hundred years, was that crime was much like a disease. Offenders needed treatment not punishment, and properly treating a criminal for the condition that gave rise to his or her criminality would prevent its recurrence. Advocates of this approach reasoned that different offenders needed different amounts of time to be successfully treated, even if they had committed the same crime; therefore, it was not sensible to assign sentences simply on the basis of the seriousness of the offense. The rehabilitation model also assumed that some offenders would respond to treatment more quickly than others, so the decision about a person's release from treatment could be made only after the person had demonstrated its effects. Incorporating these principles into a sentencing model, judges sentenced offenders to indefinite lengths of prison time, or indeterminate sentences, and when the offenders showed prison staff and parole boards that they had been appropriately rehabilitated, they were released. This was the essence of "individualized justice," that each offender had to be responded to as an individual and that judges were the people who had primary authority for deciding whether a person would be sent to prison at all (the disposition decision) and broadly for how long (the duration decision).

On the face of it, from an intellectual standpoint, this had struck Tamika as a reasonable approach. She knew that people committed crimes for different reasons, and if professionals could develop programs to address those reasons, then offenders might really stop committing crime. But knowing what she did about the communities that appeared to be sending disproportionate numbers of young people, mostly men, into the criminal justice system, she was also cynical about the ability of corrections professionals to help. She knew how skilled many of these offenders were at manipulating other people; she figured they would simply use this skill to "get over" on the corrections professionals and parole boards, convincing them that they had been rehabilitated so that they would be released from prison more quickly.

Evidently, she was not the only one skeptical about the rehabilitation model. She learned that since the early 1970s it had been under attack from academicians and politicians alike, both liberals and conservatives. For liberals, the problem was that the discretion inherent in the indeterminate-sentencing model often resulted in inequities that discriminated against ethnic minorities and the powerless. Conservatives, in contrast, viewed the same discretionary latitude as permitting too much leniency toward offenders. Both groups shared a dislike for the fact that the indeterminate sentences did not provide for certainty of release, that is, an exact and inviolate date set at the time of sentencing for the offender's release. Furthermore, several studies of the effectiveness of correctional programs had called into question the ability of the correctional system to rehabilitate offenders, and rehabilitation was the principal basis for indeterminate sentences.

As she suspected, corrections professionals were not as expert as they had claimed in identifying when an offender was ready to be released from treatment. Parole boards made many mistakes in releasing dangerous offenders while keeping less risky inmates in prison. In focusing on what offenders did during treatment, parole boards actually made poorer decisions about who would succeed after release than if they had simply used information available at the time of sentencing (e.g., prior criminal records and the seriousness of the offense). Her readings of interviews with prisoners confirmed her suspicions that inmates tried to manipulate the system. Rehabilitation programs in prison often were viewed by offenders as "time games" to be played in hopes of reducing their time in prison rather than because they were genuinely interested in helping themselves.

Her studies also revealed that judges were no better than parole boards in making decisions about offenders' sentences. If scientists said it was impossible to specify the length of treatment time each offender needed, at least offenders should be treated consistently. There was no excuse for different judges giving whoppingly different sentences to the same types of offenders in the name of individualized treatment, but that was essentially what was happening. This point was especially upsetting to Tamika when she remembered that her brother had been sentenced to one year in the county jail for possession of marijuana, while her classmate at the college had been given probation for the same thing. And when she read that judges treated some defendants more severely than others because they were black or could not make bail, she was convinced that reformers were right in trying to move away from the rehabilitation model.

As a person who had experienced her own share of victimization, she also felt strongly that the criminal justice system had not been doing an adequate job of protecting the public. She thought of the long hours of waiting to testify after the police had arrested the person who mugged her, the many delays and missed days of school and work. And then the defendant had plea-bargained to a charge of simple assault so that there was no need for her to testify anyway! It angered her that offenders who had committed serious crimes in her neighborhood were sent to prison, only to return in what seemed like a matter of months. She sympathized with the conservatives who argued that the criminal justice system, especially with its emphasis on treatment and not punishment, was too easy on criminals. When she thought of how many hours she had worked behind a counter at McDonald's to earn her college tuition, she became even more angry knowing that prisoners could get not only their GEDs but also even their college degrees without paying a cent.

That was why Tamika had been so encouraged when she learned from her criminal justice professors in the late 1970s that the field was undergoing a revolution in sentencing from the rehabilitation model to a system people were calling "determinate sentencing." This model of sentencing was supposed to correct many of the failings of the old indeterminate-sentencing model by concentrating on two goals. First, the determinate model emphasized fairness in sentencing so that sentences would be proportionate to the seriousness of the offense, and offenders convicted of similar crimes would be treated the same. That should take care of the problem that had happened to her brother. Second, the length of the sentence was to be determined by the judge at the time of sentencing, not by some corrections or parole official. She thought this system sounded a lot more sensible, making sentences more uniform and more fair, and not promising more than it could deliver.

As it turned out, soon after she first heard about determinate sentencing from her professor, she had a chance to experience it firsthand, or actually secondhand. Her brother Robert, who had been released from jail about two years earlier, was rearrested for another drug-related offense. It happened that Minnesota, where Tamika lived, was one of the first states to adopt a determinate-sentencing approach, using what were now called "sentencing guidelines" to determine whether and for how long a convicted offender would spend time in prison. Tamika figured her brother would be sent back to jail, considering that this was his second conviction, but she was surprised when her brother's lawyer told the family that the sentence would be only fourteen months in a county facility, considering that both the current and previous offenses were relatively minor. She had no idea that judges would be so restricted in their sentencing to the "guidelines grid," which spelled out the sentence for each type of offense, considering the defendant's prior criminal history. She also was pleased to hear that his time could be reduced by more than one-third if he earned "good time" and was able to work certain jobs in the institution. From what Robert said, he also was relieved to know his definite release date and was motivated to earn the additional days off.

But Tamika found later than Minnesota's system was not typical of all determinate-sentencing models. In fact, there didn't seem to be any model that could be called typical. Some states, such as Maine and Indiana, seemed to adopt sentencing reforms that actually made it more possible for defendants to be treated unfairly, because judges were given wide latitude in assigning a sentence for a particular offense, while the corrective factor of the parole board was removed from the picture. In other states, such as Pennsylvania, judges were more restricted in the sentences they chose, but the parole board still had the option of overriding a judge's sentence by keeping an offender in prison beyond the minimum specified by the judge.

Then she found that what occurred in a number of states, along with the adoption of so-called reform, was an increase in the length of time a person would serve for a given crime. When the legislators began to revamp the rehabilitation model, ostensibly out of a concern for increasing the equity and certainty of sentences, they also agreed to increase the severity of sentences at the same time. She remembered all too well the Reagan and Bush years of the 1980s and 1990s, when the criminal justice pendulum swung sharply toward the side of political conservatives. She had supported the lengthening of sentences, considering her own experiences with repeat criminals in her neighborhood. She also thought that some of the other statutes that appeared at about the same time were good ideas. It seemed reasonable, for example, to have mandatory sentences with no possibility of parole for certain crimes. After all, criminals who committed felonies while in possession of a firearm should certainly be locked up, as should those "habitual offenders" who had been convicted of repeated serious felonies.

As a citizen, she had been concerned about the growth of crime and, like the governmental leaders of the time, thought that anything was worth trying to eradicate it. Thinking that rehabilitation didn't work, the only solution was to "get tough" on criminals and go after them with a vengeance. The hope was that by scaring criminals with long prison sentences and keeping them off the streets when they were caught, the criminal justice system would eventually regain the upper hand. Ironically, in the 1990s, corrections professionals aided by scientists rediscovered the value of rehabilitation and became more effective in applying the techniques to specially targeted offenders—but that's another story.

The only thing that was apparently overlooked back in those days was the pressure this approach would put on the court system, which was faced with increased numbers of cases. There was no alternative for most criminal cases other than the "assembly-line justice" created by the extensive use of plea bargaining. So many felony cases were resolved by a plea of guilty that only about 10 percent of all felony convictions resulted from a jury or bench trial. Actually, given the rules of the game in those days, it was often in the interests of both defendants and prosecutors to arrive at guilty pleas rather than risk the expense or uncertainty of a trial.

For defendants, pleading guilty could mean a reduction in the charges—their number, their severity, or the sanctions following conviction. Since most defendants wanted the least serious sanction they could receive, they were more often concerned about the degree of sanction than with the legal formality of conviction. Thus, defendants were willing to settle with a plea bargain, even if it did not exactly reflect "the truth" of what they had done.

Prosecutors also had interests other than simply uncovering "the truth." Plea bargains were quicker and less costly than trials, but that was not the major reason for their widespread use. The main benefit of plea bargaining was in reducing uncertainty. With a plea, the outcome is certain; the unpredictability of witnesses, juries, and trial judges is avoided. Moreover, since defendants who plead guilty waive all claims for appeal on the basis of due-process protections pertaining to the investigation, arrest, or prosecution, the plea brings finality to the case. Prosecutors were evaluated by the public on the basis of their conviction rate, not by the penalties imposed, so it was not surprising that they sought the certainty and finality of guilty pleas. Besides, they could always argue that they agreed to reductions in criminal charge or punishment only when warranted by mitigating circumstances.

Tamika was troubled by the extensive use of plea bargaining for several reasons. On the one hand, thinking back to her studies of the way the judicial system was supposed to function, she couldn't help thinking that serious offenders willing to "cop a plea" should not be let off so lightly just because they were helping to keep the wheels of justice turning. On the other hand, she wondered about the poor and powerless defendants who might not have been convicted at all if their cases had been resolved on their merits at trial. And what about the fact that those who bargained did not receive the due-process protection that governed the criminal investigation, arrest, and representation by counsel? This whole process seemed a slippery way of undercutting the ideals of the criminal justice system.

Court backlogs. Plea bargaining. Prison crowding. Memories of days when she was just getting her start in the criminal justice system. In many ways, things were still the same; in others, they were so different that it was almost hard to believe that only twenty years had gone by from the 1990s' days of crises to the streamlined, rational sentencing process of the twenty-first century. Judge Tamika Watson knew it was time for her to proceed to her courtroom. Taking one last look around her chambers, she stood, took a long breath, and walked the corridor to Hearing Room 74.

"Order in the court," the bailiff shouted, echoing thousands of bailiffs over the centuries. Judge Watson punched a few keys on the personal computer built into the console before her to get a readout of the docket cases for the day. The first case was a preliminary hearing for 23-year-old Donald Romelli, a college student accused of raping a woman he had met one evening at a party after she had passed out. When she punched up the screen outlining the police investigation, Judge Watson noted that the details were consistent with most of these "date rape" cases and should lead to a decision to bind this one over for trial. She knew she shouldn't try to prejudge the case, but as a prosecutor of almost a hundred such cases over her fifteen years, she had a pretty good sense of how they went.

She did remember the days in the 1970s and 1980s when these cases infrequently came to the attention of the authorities, were rarely prosecuted, and, when they were, almost never resulted in guilty verdicts. Back then, people seemed to think that the only ones who could be criminals were poor minority men committing "street crimes" such burglary or robbery or operators involved in drug trafficking. It was amazing to think about the changes that had occurred in people's thinking about criminals. About the turn of the century, people began to be convinced that crime did not occur only among strangers but involved situations in which one person exerted coercive power over another, even in the most intimate of relationships. She credited feminists with changing people's minds about sexual victimization so that now women's experiences of sexual victimization were taken seriously by the law, criminal justice professionals, and even juries. There had also been remarkable changes in the prosecution of other formerly invisible crimes such as domestic violence and child abuse.

As she read the investigator's report, she listened to the prosecutor question the 19-year-old alleged victim about what had happened the night of the alleged rape. The young woman recounted a typical scenario—going to a party with friends, meeting a guy, drinking too much, going to his room for a drink and to listen to music, getting tired and falling asleep on his bed, then waking up to the realization that someone was on top of her and having sex. The evidence presented at the hearing provided clear justification of the need for a trial, despite presentations by the defense attorney. After the fifteen-minute hearing, Judge Watson proceeded to the next case on the docket.

When Judge Watson called up the next case for the morning on her console monitor, she couldn't believe what she saw. Reginald Silver was being tried for grand computer theft, and she would be the trial judge since Judge Susan McClintock had taken maternity leave from the bench. The last she had heard, Silver had left the country and established a profitable corporation producing and marketing narcotics in Sweden. That must have been about ten years ago. Silver had been a notorious drug dealer through the early 1990s, with estates in Palm Springs, Miami, and New York; and several yachts, a Lear jet, and contacts with more connected people than the president. Unfortunately for him, he got caught in what at the time was called the nationwide "war on drugs," a national panic to achieve the unrealistic goal of a "drug-free America."

It seemed strange to think about the national preoccupation with "zero tolerance" for drug use from the mid-1980s to the mid-1990s, especially considering that the prevalence and use of illicit drugs had been decreasing during those years. Attitudes were so different in 2010, with drug use legalized and production regulated two years ago.

She remembered reading about what happened to Silver. It wasn't that the government was ever able to convict him of any criminal offense. He was simply harassed to the point of deciding that the only thing he could do was leave the country. During those times, the government may not have been good at getting convictions of major drug dealers, but it was expert at applying administrative rules and civil laws with such force that it made the dealers' lives miserable. Following an arrest for some drug-related offense (unlikely, as Judge Watson recalled, ever to lead to a conviction), Silver's house and boats were impounded under the Asset Forfeiture Act on the pretext that these properties were instrumental to carrying out his illegal business. Municipal building codes and health codes were used to close down his restaurants, even though they were allegedly legitimate businesses.

What struck Judge Watson as interesting was that although the trafficking in drugs, which had inspired the various "creative" law-enforcement strategies, was no longer illegal, the strategies had survived and were currently being used on what appeared to be an ever-widening range of minor crimes. She knew that people suspected of prostitution or distribution of pornography and such street crimes as theft, burglary, and minor assaults were routinely handled "out of court." Judge Watson knew that this strategy was hailed as a means for controlling the number of cases that had to be dealt with in court, and as a brand-new judge, she should probably be grateful. Still, she wondered about the "justice" in using municipal building codes, health codes, and fire codes to harass those thought to be engaging in crimes. What had happened to the old saying, "Innocent until proven guilty"? When state and federal entitlements such as Social Security and medical care, as well as driver's licenses and other permits and licenses needed to work, were denied because of the government's suspicion that a person had committed a crime, something was just not right.

Punching a few keys, Judge Watson quickly familiarized herself with the government's current case against Reginald Silver. Evidently, when Silver returned to the United States, he found that the tobacco and pharmaceutical industries already had such a stranglehold on the infant narcotics industry that the profit margin simply was not attractive enough for a man used to an unfair advantage. So he became interested in the possibilities of computer crime. Despite the fact that the government had begun to define new forms of crime involving computers as early as the late 1970s, technology had advanced at such a rapid rate that even now creative criminals continued to find new ways of benefiting from the unscrupulous uses of computers. And the "take" could be extraordinary. Whereas robbers and thieves netted only a few hundred dollars on average for their crimes, and a million-dollar robbery was record-setting, routine computer-related crimes cost hundreds of thousands of dollars, and the potential harm of just one criminal act could easily reach into the hundreds of millions. Silver, true to form, had allegedly hit the jackpot by transferring funds over the past three years from several major pension plans into hidden bank accounts in unnamed countries.

From a perspective of deterrence, what penalty would be so great that its threat would outweigh the benefits to be had by this crime? From a rehabilitation perspective, what treatment could possibly be used to "restore and rehabilitate" Silver? And, finally, from a retribution perspective, how great a penalty would offset Silver's harm to those thousands, perhaps hundreds of thousands, of pensioners? Of course, these questions all assumed that Silver would be found guilty. Given his track record, Judge Watson somehow had her doubts. But today's proceeding was only to set the trial date, so as she banged the gavel and called the next case, she mused to herself that she would just have to wait and see.

From their looks, Judge Watson's next two defendants certainly should have been in school rather than in criminal court. Natasha

Collins and Jeffrey Jenkins couldn't have been older than 17. As she scanned the readout on her console, she saw that she was right—Jeffrey would be 17 next month; Natasha had just turned 16. The nonverbals they displayed while waiting for the proceedings to begin were certainly not those of obedient school children; however, one look was all she needed to tell her that these youngsters would not be easy to handle.

A quick review of their files told Judge Watson that Natasha and Jeffrey, codefendants charged with four counts of burglary apiece, were not newcomers to the justice system. Each had been adjudicated delinquent at least three times before, otherwise she would not be seeing them today in adult court. Thanks to the Serious Juvenile Offender Act, which was passed in the mid-1990s, all juveniles were automatically remanded to adult court after three serious adjudications.

Reading on, she learned that Jeffrey and Natasha were accused of making repeated visits to the home of their elderly neighbor, Ms. Claire DeBrow, while she attended her weekly bingo game. Each time, according to the report, they left with another item of value to Ms. DeBrow, first her prized multimedia unit, then the camcorder, the audio system, and finally her heirloom gold bracelet. Given that she was living on the meager allowance the U.S. government afforded Social Security recipients and that she was unable to afford the hefty insurance rates that would have protected her possessions, the loss of these items must have been pretty traumatic to the older woman. Judge Watson looked up as the prosecuting attorney introduced the codefendants and, sure enough, in the first row sat an elderly woman, looking proud but obviously distraught, who must have been Ms. DeBrow.

Judge Watson learned that this was not the first time these youths had been confronted about this string of burglaries. In fact, according to Judge Watson's console readout, the case had initially been referred to criminal court more than six months ago. Why were they back in criminal court again? Of course, she thought to herself, this case fit the profile for mediation perfectly—perpetrators and victim who had an ongoing relationship as neighbors, nonserious (at least from the vantage point of the court) property offenses, and alleged perpetrators without serious adult criminal records.

This case, like an increasing number over the past ten years or so, reflected efforts to offer an alternative method to the adversarial system for resolving problems and concerns among people. Rather than focusing on the punishment of the "criminal" who has "offended" society due to some moral weakness or social deficiency, mediation sought to restore the status quo between codisputants through discussion and, hopefully, reconciliation. Its increased popularity reflected the acknowledgment by many in the criminal justice system that criminal courts and legal sanctions simply could not be used to resolve all crimes. Obviously, this approach had the advantage of diverting many cases from the busy criminal court dockets. But besides the benefit of court efficiency, mediation was viewed as a desirable means of dealing with conflicts among people who must maintain ongoing social or working relationships, as is true for family members, co-workers, neighbors, and friends.

The goals of the parties to mediation were twofold. For the offenders, the goal was to understand the consequences of their crimes on the lives of real people and to take actions to rectify what they had done to their victims. For victims, the goal was to get to a place in their relationship with the offenders where they felt satisfied that justice has been done. Since most cases in which mediation was used were property crimes, mediation often led to agreements by which an offender would attempt to restore a victim's lost or damaged property. While it might not be possible for the offender to replace the exact item stolen, the offender and the victim might agree that the offender would repay the victim either in money or by performing some compensatory service, such as working extra hours for an employer or painting the victim's house.

Looking at the two defendants and Ms. DeBrow, Judge Watson did not have to wonder why the mediation did not work out. Jeffrey and Natasha kept turning around in their seats and shooting stares at Ms. DeBrow that, if they had been bullets, would certainly have killed. Interspersed with the aggressive nonverbals, the defendants taunted the woman with comments that would have raised the blood pressure of any adult. Meanwhile, Ms. DeBrow kept her eyes fixed on Judge Watson; her expression conveyed clearly her anger and exasperation at these insolent juveniles.

Today there would not be a trial, merely a fact-finding hearing designed to determine whether a trial would be scheduled. The prosecutor called Ms. DeBrow to the front of the courtroom. After being sworn in, she recounted her experiences in mediation with the two defendants. She said she had agreed to the mediation in the first place because she and Natasha's mother, Blair, had known each other for years and Blair had begged her to try to handle the case out of criminal court. Ms. DeBrow said that Blair had mentioned that she knew her daughter would be put in jail if convicted through the courts, and that she couldn't bear the thought of her only daughter in a jail cell.

Ms. DeBrow reported that Natasha's mother confided to her that she knew her daughter had been involved in the burglaries. She told about the day she herself had returned home from work to find Blair waiting for her at the front door with a brown paper bag in her hand. Crying, Blair removed the bracelet from the bag—the bracelet that had once belonged to Ms. DeBrow's great aunt. Blair said she had found it while cleaning Natasha's room and realized right away where her daughter had gotten it. She said that she had called the authorities to tell them her suspicions about who had committed the burglaries, and later in the day her daughter and her daughter's friend Jeffrey had been arrested. After telling Ms. DeBrow about what had happened to Natasha, she hoped Ms. DeBrow would try mediation rather than insisting on the criminal court for her daughter since, after all, she was getting at least some of her property back. Ms. DeBrow had agreed, and a court hearing had been scheduled for Ms. DeBrow and the defendants the following week.

That was six months ago. Since then, Ms. DeBrow, Jeffrey, and Natasha had met every other week with Ms. Cummings, who had been assigned by Mediation Services, Inc., to work with them. At first, it seemed to Ms. DeBrow that they were making some progress. After a few more sessions of "give and take," however, Ms. DeBrow decided that mediation was not going to work for her. So she called Ms. Cummings, told her to cancel the next session, and asked for another hearing with the judge.

Judge Watson knew that the rules of the mediation process allowed the victim to break off the mediation any time and to refer the case back to the criminal court. Now Tamika was faced with a challenge: Could she get the youths to plead guilty to their crimes—and therefore receive the reduced sentences the ORRPPI allows for defendants who did not tax government resources with costly trials—or would she have to proceed with plans for a criminal trial? There was no question they were guilty; the return of the bracelet by Natasha's mother validated that fact. And the kids had returned at least some of what they took from the burglaries to the victim. Judge Watson looked down at the boy and girl, rebellious and at the same time rather vulnerable, and banked on the chance that they would not insist on a trial. She set a time later in the day for a meeting with the youths, their attorney, and the prosecutor and instructed all parties to use the intervening time to make a decision about a guilty plea.

Striking her gavel and calling for a fifteen-minute recess, she glanced at the console readout and couldn't believe it only registered 9:54 A.M. Already, it had been a very long day.

POSTSCRIPT

Tamika Watson's reflections about her work dramatize important changes in sentencing that have been occurring since 1980. These changes, and the critical issues involved in making these changes, are highlighted in this brief review.

First, throughout most of the twentieth century, sentencing decisions were based on a rehabilitation model that called for individualized justice. Convicted offenders received sentences of indeterminate length, with the possibility of early release on parole. In her reflections, Tamika considers again the arguments for and against this model of sentencing and why both conservatives and liberals finally agreed to seek alternatives. What were they?

Second, in the 1980s, determinate sentencing was adopted by several states and the federal government. Why? Tamika remembers that there was great variation among the different formats and guidelines adopted and that many states added mandatory sentences for certain crimes and increased the length of incarceration for most crimes. Did determinate sentencing resolve the problems of indeterminacy? Did it create any new problems?

Third, for Tamika, plea bargaining no longer exists. This widespread practice offered something to both the defendant and the prosecutor. What? How did it work under indeterminate sentencing? Was it eliminated by determinate sentencing?

Fourth, Tamika works with a new sentencing model—the ORRP. But is it really any better than the others? Should offenders be sentenced to a comprehensive range of punishments? Can we base sentences on both retribution and rehabilitation? Even though judges are not (and never have been) trained to determine appropriate sentences, should some other agency, group, or individual make that determination? If yes, then who? What factors should be important in determining the profile used in sentencing? Can this be done solely on the basis of objective factors?

Tamika notes that alternatives to prosecution have emerged. When civil and administrative laws are used instead of criminal laws to regulate and deter criminal activity, what legal and sociological questions arise? And when mediation is used rather than adjudication, do the parties involved really get their "day in court"? What other alternatives to prosecution might arise before Tamika retires from the bench?

FOR FURTHER READING

Lynne Goodstein and John Hepburn. *Determinate Sentencing and Imprisonment: A Failure of Reform*. Cincinnati, OH: Anderson, 1985.

This book analyzes the movement toward sentencing offenders for fixed time periods rather than for indeterminate sentences. It looks at the justifications for the changes and focuses on sentencing reform in Illinois, Connecticut, and Minnesota.

John Irwin and James Austin. *It's About Time: America's Imprisonment Binge*. Belmont, CA: Wadsworth, 1994.

The United States leads the world in its use of prison sentences. This book examines the use of incarceration during the 1980s and 1990s. The authors review the causes, costs, and consequences of our growing use of imprisonment.

Jack M. Kress. *Prescription for Justice: The Theory and Practice of Sentencing Guidelines*. Cambridge, MA: Ballinger, 1980.

This book describes an important alternative to the sentencing guidelines approach adopted by the federal government. Judicial discretion is structured by patterns of past decision making in the court. Judges are expected to explain variations from common practice by mitigating or aggravating circumstances.

Norval Morris and Michael H. Tonry. *Between Prison and Probation: Intermediate Punishments in a Rational Sentencing System*. New York: Oxford University Press, 1990.

This book describes a rational sentencing process that provides options between incarceration and release in the community under traditional probation. The authors argue that the current range of sentences is too limited, and they review a range of intermediate punishments.

United States Sentencing Commission. *Guidelines Manual: Incorporating Guideline Amendments*. Washington, DC: U.S. Government Printing Office, 1989.

This is the main document outlining federal sentencing practices. Its sentencing guidelines have been widely criticized by many federal judges as overly restrictive of their discretion.

DISCUSSION QUESTIONS

1. How does Judge Watson think computerized sentencing has affected discretion? Has the computer algorithm eliminated the potential for bias in judgment or simply moved it to a different level?

2. How did the goals of sentencing evolve during Judge Watson's career from becoming a student in criminal justice to becoming a judge?

3. How have the reforms to increase fairness and consistency in sentencing affected the severity of sentences for criminal offenses?

4. What tensions exist between the need for processing cases and the need for individualized justice? How will these tensions be addressed in the future?

5. What role does mediation play in contemporary criminal justice? How may that role change in the future?

9

☆

Grim Tales of the Future:

American Jails in the Year 2010

DAVID KALINICH
Northern Michigan University

PAUL EMBERT

A window to the future of jails—and perhaps the past—was provided for us during one author's recent visit to the Fulton County, Georgia, jail system. We caught a glimpse of the future of jails as a result of a tour through the jail given to attendees of the American Jail Association Conference in Atlanta during the spring of 1991. The tour took us through the one-year-old "indirect supervision" jail built by the county. This brand-new jail was, of course, overcrowded shortly after it was opened.

Our tour guide, a correctional officer assigned to our group, was asked about the current condition and use of the old jail. Specifically, we were concerned that the old jail would be reopened to alleviate the overcrowding in the new jail. Our tour guide assured us that the old jail would not be used to house the potential overflow from the new jail. In fact, the old jail had been modified and opened as a "shelter" for the homeless and other vagrants. The tour guide also advised us that most of the "homeless" or "vagrants" who were living in the old jail were also regular inmates or revolving-door clientele for the system. An efficient system had been created: The members of the underclass who were the community's revolving-door offenders relied on the resources of the jails—whether by plan or inadvertently—did not have to pass through the rituals of arrest and court proceedings to gain entry to the jail. They just had to show up.

This scenario makes a significant point relevant to our discussion about the future of jails. Jails have always served the community as more than detention or correctional centers to detain criminal offenders for the protection of society or to serve the court and local criminal justice system (CJS). The multiple roles of the jail go well beyond contributions to the "war on crime." Most of the inmate residents of local jails have almost always been members of the underclass who were considered to be society's rabble. The jailed rabble have included the unemployed and underemployed, substance abusers, the undereducated, and the mentally ill. During winters, jails have served as refuges for the homeless or other marginal individuals. For an unfortunate few, jails have been the social service agency of last resort. They will continue to have multiple roles in the future. The pivotal question for the future is the magnitude of the social service role played by the jail.

That magnitude will be a function of the social problems of the future, which will be, in part, a function of today's public policy. The public policy decision, for example, made more than a decade ago to empty the state mental hospitals under the rubric of community mental health has increased the number of mentally ill individuals who are being housed in jails. Also, it can be argued that the economic policies of the 1980s have shifted wealth upward, decreased the size of the middle and working economic classes, and increased the numbers of homeless, which, in effect, increased the numbers of homeless who find their way into local jails.

In addition to the magnitude of the social service role imposed on jails, the conditions of jails—mission, management philosophy, resources—must be considered. These issues will be bounded by the prevailing social philosophy toward offenders, our benefits toward the management of our public enterprises, and our economic ability to provide resources.

INTRODUCTION

The coercive force of the criminal justice system and its jails and prisons is routinely used to solve or address our social problems. The use of jails to participate in or provide solutions to prevailing social problems might be deliberate policy, but it often is an unintended consequence of higher-order policy. Their multiple roles reflect clearly the social problems being addressed by society through the CJS. Jails house the homeless, mentally ill, vagrants, and runaway children as well as individuals whom we would consider criminal. Jails also have held typhoid carriers, political protesters, rock concert participants, drunks and other substance abusers, and a host of others whose criminal status we would debate. We could spell out more categories of individuals who are now or who have been housed in local jails over the years. The point is, however, that the category of individuals held in jail is indicative or symptomatic of our greater social problems.

To predict the future of jails, therefore, requires at least a heuristic prediction of what social problems may exist during the next two decades and the extent to which the criminal justice system and its jails may be called upon to help provide a solution. Our predictions are no more than projections of our assessment of contemporary conditions linked with an understanding of how the projected conditions will affect the nation's jails.

Many historical studies have focused on the rise of the penitentiary in the West. They are not just competing versions of what may or may not have happened 200 years ago. They contain hidden and sometimes not-so-hidden political agendas for the present. That analysis of historical research applies to futurist predictions as well. Any predictions of the future are based on current social conditions and problems and trends projected ahead to some point in time. The social conditions and problems and society's ability to produce change are all up to the perceptions and biases of the particular futurist. In other words, out of necessity, the futurist must provide a critique of contemporary conditions to discuss the future.

To the point: Our prediction of the future of American jails is based on a critique of current conditions projected linearly to the year 2010. That is, we are providing the reader with a future scenario that assumes that a set of social, political, and economic trends will continue unimpeded that will have profound effects upon the structure and function of the jails. It is not likely, however, that current trends within our society will continue linearly. The American public and political system tend to be pragmatic, and after getting slapped in the face with problems, they will produce some policy choices. Specific future alternatives may come to fruition. As an exercise, readers can make adjustments to the trends discussed. They are encouraged to redraw the conclusions put forward here based on their own critique of existing conditions as well as their assessments of our society's capability to identify and solve our most pressing social problems.

We will begin by describing the jails of the future in some detail. We will first describe the inmate population, the problems unique to that population, and then the multiple missions, structures, and operations of future jails. After getting right to the point and describing the future of jails, we will reveal the logic of our predictions: our critique of the present; a discussion of a number of well-entrenched salient economic, political, and social trends; and a heuristic prediction of those trends to 2010.

JAILS IN 2010

The inmate population of the nation's jails will increase by a greater rate than the general population and at a rate exceeding the reported crime rate. The inmates will continue disproportionately to represent the economic underclass, which will have expanded exponentially. The nation's jails, therefore, will be forced to expand to accommodate a significantly higher inmate population rate than today. The inmate population will also be a problem to manage, as inmates will bring a myriad of medical, mental health, and behavioral problems into the jail system with them. It will be strikingly clear that the vast majority of the jail inmate population will have come from the economic and socially disenfranchised underclass. In fact, most of the underclass entering the jail system of 2010 will be classified as homeless. A large portion of the jail population will also be suffering from mental illness, be in poor health in general, and a frightening number will be suffering from deadly communicable diseases such as Acquired Immune Deficiency Syndrome (AIDS), tuberculosis, and so on. Almost all of this group of inmates will remain in pretrial custody unable or unwilling to post bond.

This group of inmates will be a nightmare to manage. In addition to bringing communicable diseases into the jails with them, they will have little to lose and will see the jail as their system. The inmates will, therefore, feel entitled to take control of the jails and maintain them through the corrupt use of power, kangaroo courts, gang warfare, and so forth. A very large number of inmates will be members of street gangs, determined not to become homeless themselves and viewing crime and violence as a means of economic stability. Their view of power, violence, and control will be readily transferable into the jail facility.

As a result of the increased number of inmates and chronic budget problems that will be faced by governments, there will be a shortage of facilities. Therefore, the jails managed by the public sector will be overcrowded, overtaxed, and rundown. This will be true for almost all jurisdictions left to public-sector control. A number of private-sector jails in rather excellent condition will exist in most suburban areas, a twist that we will discuss later. But for the public sector, aging jail facilities will be the core of the system. Urban communities will supplement their systems by renting warehouses and other facilities that can be easily converted into custody facilities. For sentenced inmates, facilities such as old abandoned buildings outside of city areas will routinely be used. In jurisdictions with large inmate populations such as Los Angeles or New York, camplike facilities will be used for chronic vagrants and the homeless who have managed to parlay their criminal behavior into longer sentences.

The bulk of the jails across the country will continue to be managed primarily by county governments. In that regard, the vast majority of jail inmates will reside in public-sector jails. However, the jail system will have evolved into a multiple array of subsystems. Private-sector jails will exist within wealthier suburban jurisdictions. In effect, offenders from "wealthier" areas will have the benefit of better treatment in the private-sector jails. In addition, inmates housed in more affluent private suburban jails will be able to pay for—or have their families pay for—extraordinary goods and services. Inmates in public-sector urban jails will receive minimal services, reflecting relative poverty and the dwindling revenue base of their communities.

The urban public-sector jail systems will be composed of several or a series of physical plants. The main jail containing the administrative unit will be a facility probably built no later than the 1980s. Additional facilities will comprise old dwellings near the main complex such as hotels, old mansions, warehouses, and so on. A camplike arrangement located in the county's rural area will be used for sentenced medium- and minimum-security inmates. The classification system will have a large maximum-security allocation, especially for inmates with contagious diseases or who are severely mentally ill. There will be, of course, the traditional maximum-, medium-, and minimum-security systems for the bulk of pretrial and sentenced inmates.

There will be one more unique classification level: voluntary commitment inmates (VCI). It will occur to policy makers of the future that many inmates enter jail as refuge. When communities face this honestly, the homeless and other "street people" will be allowed to commit themselves to a period of incarceration without the benefit of criminal processing. This, of course, will relieve the overtaxed future CJS of a substantial burden. The voluntary commitment inmates will be housed—when resources permit—separately from pretrial and convicted inmates. Ideally, most VCIs will be transported to camp areas in the rural areas where they can work on farms or be assigned to county road crews. Not all VCIs will be fit for minimum-security level at the camp level. Some will need maximum-security residence because of their health or behavioral problems. Voluntary commitment inmates will be able to choose the length of time for which they will be incarcerated, within statutory limits. However, the law of the future will allow the CJS to require VCIs to remain incarcerated for their chosen length of time.

The jail staff within the public sector will function as turnkeys. Their designated role will be to keep inmates under lockup and protect perimeter security. There will be little status attached to the position of correctional officer. In fact, correctional officers will be perceived by the general public as obtuse and brutal. The pay rates will be extremely low compared to other occupations, even depressed occupations. The poor pay and low status will keep many qualified individuals away from the profession even though jobs, in general, will be scarce. In addition, there will be no funds to provide adequate training for those individuals, who will be attracted to the public-sector jails. The traditional "linear intermittent" supervision—the jail design we now consider traditional—will be used to facilitate the "turnkey" approach to inmate supervision. However, many of the public-sector facilities will be minimum-security or camp arrangements, and inmates in most facilities will have some degree of freedom. In effect, a great deal of interpersonal skill will be needed by the jail staff to promote order and social control. Even the VCI facilities will require supervision to ensure order.

The personnel working in the private-sector jails will receive much higher pay than their public-sector counterparts, have a higher level of education, and receive extensive training. The private-sector staff will manifest the remaining vestiges of the current move toward professionalism in the art of jail management. They will see their role as promoting a humanitarian jail and see the jail's role as helping inmates in some way for the longer term. Most of the private-sector jails will follow what is now referred to as the "new-generation jail" concept, requiring direct supervision of inmates and sound interpersonal skills. Finally, most private-sector staffmembers will have roots in the suburbs, while public-sector correctional officers will come from the inner city.

The private-sector jails will have an array of treatment services. Inmates in the private-sector system will be able to receive additional services—psychiatric counseling, drug treatment, and so forth—as well as additional goods and services beyond those provided routinely to inmates. Services will be limited, and inmates by and large will not be able to afford additional treatment even if it is made available. Also, most public-sector jails will be inadequately staffed with poorly trained and underpaid personnel. This group will face inmates who will be difficult to manage, which in turn will raise stress levels of public-sector staff. The public-sector jails will run on an exchange or corruption model: Inmates who successfully run contraband and can influence officers and inmates will take on leadership roles. Officers will enter into tacit collusion with inmate leaders who keep order in the jail system. This will lead to corruption and bribery on the part of many underpaid public-sector correctional officers. In such a system, weak inmates will be brutalized and exploited, and it will go undetected.

The public and private sectors will also be different from a management perspective. Private-sector jails will have fairly clear missions that will encompass providing rehabilitation, providing sound medical treatment for inmates, and running clean and orderly jails. The private-sector jails will also have clear policies and procedures, invest in planning and research, and, as indicated earlier, have trained and qualified staff. Public-sector jails will emphasize perimeter security, attempt to function as a system closed to scrutiny or reform attempts, give minimal attention to the well-being of inmates, and, in general, be poorly managed.

Our projections about the contrast between private- and public-sector jails is not based on current conventional wisdom that the private sector can do it better. Rather, our projections show a two-tier jail system with the public sector serving the economic underclass, the vast majority of the inmates, with the private-sector jails serving the inmates from the more affluent suburbs or jurisdictions that will be able to afford better services for their inmates. Politically, the urban inmates will be considered criminal, while the inmates from the more affluent communities will be considered victims of drug abuse or other unfortunate circumstances. The future political system's response to the growing diseased and unruly underclass will actively facilitate this perception to allow one jail system for the haves and another for the have-nots.

THE ANTOINETTE COUNTY
JAIL SYSTEM IN 2010

We can perhaps be more instructive by portraying a hypothetical jail system in 2010. Our jail system belongs to Antoinette County, which has a population of 5 million people. The county possesses two struggling industrial cities. Much of the past manufacturing has closed, moved, or gone bankrupt. A number of service industries have sprung up throughout the county, but the unemployment rate is always in double figures. The condition of the cities has caused most of the skilled and professional individuals and families to move to the suburbs. To the extent that new industry has been created, it has located in the suburbs.

The main jail was built in 1985 for a capacity of 1,800 inmates. It was originally built as a new-generation jail. In 2010, the Antoinette County jail system maintains more than 7,000 inmates, with 3,000 of them in the original jail. The main jail holds pretrial inmates pending hearing in the courts in the main urban center. In addition, the main jail houses sentenced inmates who require maximum security control or who suffer from highly contagious diseases and must be held in quarantine. The staffing in the medical wards of the jail comprises student interns from the local medical school who are interested in communicable diseases.

The jail system has been expanded by using a refurbished state office building about three blocks from the main jail and a defunct Holiday Inn in the same vicinity. The office building annex holds 500 inmates, and the Holiday Inn sleeps another 500. The Holiday Inn is used for most of the short-term VCIs. In addition, the county owns several old houses throughout the two main cities in the county to hold minimum-security sentenced inmates who are physically or emotionally disabled. Two of the house units are also used for work-release and furlough inmates. The housing system holds an additional 200 inmates.

For the remainder of the sentenced inmates and VCIs, the county uses three large camp facilities in rural areas of the county. Each camp is an abandoned warehouse converted to dormitory facilities but with a number of maximum security cells to further secure unhealthy or troublesome inmates. The warehouses are also classified, with two being medium security and the third minimum security, where VCIs can get long-term confinement upon request. Fortunately for the county, two of the warehouses were originally built along a commuter train route. Inmates can be transported directly en masse to the two locations in a jail car attached to the commuter train.

The remainder of the Antoinette County jail system consists of several facilities built throughout the suburbs. The suburb jails were built as a result of a move to decentralize the court system. Decentralization took place to create a more efficient court system and, some would suspect, to further separate the inner-city inhabitants from all others. First, county courts were established in the suburbs. Then, to complete the decentralization of the courts, suburban jails were built, and police lockups were expanded and modified to serve also as jails. This was a logistical requirement to avoid transporting inmates from the old urban jails to the new court complexes in the suburbs.

The move toward privatization caught on philosophically with suburban inhabitants and their political leaders. When the jails were constructed, the belief existed that privatized jails would be intrinsically better. In addition, suburban governments supplemented county funds for the new jails, and these state-of-the-art new-generation facilities were constructed. In this system, highly qualified staffmembers are routinely hired and trained, and treatment programs are contracted out to private medical, educational, and vocational-training firms. The suburban jails also have medical wings for inmates with contagious diseases and for the mentally ill. However, in the suburbs, mental and physical illnesses are not nearly as great a problem as they are among the inner-city inmates.

In our hypothetical situation, the suburban jails are part of the county jail system. Theoretically, inmates can be transferred from the suburban jails to the main jail or to and from any of the structures used to create the total jail system. In fact, the suburban jail staff can straighten out any recalcitrant inmates with the threat of transfer to the inner-city jail. However, except in unusual cases, policy precludes such transfers of pretrial inmates for logistical purposes. For sentenced inmates, the "policy preference" is to place them in jails near their residence whenever possible. This, of course, is to facilitate the reintegration model of corrections and to allow ease of visits and other community contacts. This policy preference was also linked to community corrections alternative programs. Incarcerating sentenced inmates in or near their communities would help the many community corrections agencies develop alternative programs for as many inmates as possible to help inmates reintegrate into society. This policy preference also keeps the urban and suburban criminal justice system from overlapping.

More cynical observers considered the policy and policy preference a clever, convenient way to ensure that inner-city rabble—inmates and their friends and families who would visit the inmates—would be kept out of the suburban system. The cynic would say that suburban residents wanted to be kept free of the possible criminal behaviors of inner-city residents who would travel to the suburbs to visit inmates. In addition, the suburban residents are protected from communicable diseases that could be spread into the suburbs through the contacts that would be made between inner-city and suburban inmates if they were housed in the same facilities. Finally, the split system is one more contribution to the cleavage between inner-city and suburban tax bases, populations, and cultures. Whatever the "real" reason, the Antoinette County jail system is divided into two neat subsystems: (1) the large, overcrowded, underfunded system run by the county government that serves primarily inner-city residents; and (2) the well-funded, state-of-the-art, new-generation, private-sector jails that cater to suburban residents.

The Antoinette County court systems, misdemeanor and felony probation systems, and the community corrections bureaucracy are similarly bifurcated. The suburban systems are better funded, run more effectively, and rely upon contracting to private firms to establish an array of community alternatives. The urban system is constantly in a state of madness and confusion as it tries to process and sentence criminal offenders as rapidly as possible. Community corrections is relied upon heavily in the suburban communities. Judges and other decision makers in this setting will have confidence in the community corrections system: After all, suburban offenders have a reasonable opportunity to succeed. Therefore, community alternatives such as house arrest and electronic monitoring are used frequently as alternatives to incarceration in the suburban jail system. The urban community corrections system, which is underfunded and understaffed and lacking in opportunity for offenders, is perceived as ineffective by decision makers and used sparingly by comparison. Urban criminal justice policy makers and decision makers feel much more at ease with overcrowded and inhumane jails than with the use of a poorly structured community corrections system. And keep in mind that the urban jail system caters primarily to the homeless and those otherwise in vagrant status. It is difficult to apply community corrections to those who are homeless. More important, the homeless are often in jail because it is a better place for them to reside both from their own and urban policy makers' points of view.

We have provided a general prediction of jails in 2010 and provided the reader with a hypothetical jail system for Antoinette County. The future sounds bleak and frightening. There are many questions left to be addressed. What happened to inmate rights, to the move to create humane jails run by a highly professional cadre of jail administrators and correctional officers? Why do we predict a bifurcated jail system? On what basis did we predict the expansion and condition of the economic underclass? In the next section, we provide the logic for our predictions.

CURRENT CONDITIONS
AND FUTURE TRENDS

Our premise is that jails, like most institutions, are created by and reflect social and environmental conditions. The most significant environmental factors that will impact significantly upon the CJS and its jails, in our estimation, include the following:

1. the structure and health of the economy;
2. the effectiveness of the educational system;
3. the effectiveness of the system of medical service delivery and its efficiency in providing mass services;
4. civil and criminal law in their application;
5. governments' philosophies toward dealing with social problems; and
6. most important, our cultural values as manifested in the assumptions underlying the way we identify and attempt to solve our social and economic problems.

Our grim prediction about the condition of our nation's jails in 2010 is based upon the assumptions that trends in each area that are present today will continue unabated into the future and will create the environmental conditions and constraints that will create the dismal picture of the 2010 jails that we have portrayed.

Our analysis begins with a discussion of our current economic situation and a projection of the economic situation of the future if current conditions continue. We have seen a dramatic shift of national wealth upward, with those in the top 2 percent of the income level now possessing more than 20 percent of the nation's wealth. Classically, the rich have gotten richer and the poor poorer. The middle and working classes shrank dramatically during the 1980s, and, to no surprise, the size of the economic underclass—the poor street people—grew dramatically. Investment in our nation's infrastructure was about 3 percent of our gross national product before 1970. Since 1970, it has been reduced to about 1 percent. With the debt faced by the federal government and many state governments, it is not likely that the trend will be reduced. Our economic system has been stagnating over the last two decades, and that stagnation will be difficult to reverse.

As a result, employment in the primary labor market—stable jobs with adequate pay and substantial fringe benefits—will decrease, leaving more and more American citizens reliant on secondary labor-market opportunities: unstable, low-paying employment, government subsidies or illegal and quasi-legal income-generating activities. In effect, the nation's underclass will expand. The underclass will also grow as a result of mass immigration, legal and illegal, of individuals from poverty-stricken countries in South America and from Mexico. If both trends continue, our nation's economic underclass will have grown dramatically. We have learned from the literature that both prison and jail populations are highly correlated to the size of the unemployed population. The economic trends described will, therefore, cause the nation's jail population to grow dramatically.

Not only will there be fewer opportunities in the primary labor market, but also the jobs that exist will call for individuals with technical skills and knowledge. In other words, the assembly-line worker will disappear, and those who have the knowledge and skills to work with computers and robotics will gain the opportunities in the primary labor markets. Therefore, the need for highly skilled labor will increase. Our educational system at every level will have to prepare students to be competitive and able to enter the primary labor market with a number of skills beyond sound command of the English language. In fact, 20-year-old immigrants who speak atrocious English but who are skilled in mathematics, statistics, and computer science will have the edge on most Americans in the job market. If we are to believe critics, the American educational system is faltering, yet we have made little substantive effort to rectify our educational system.

It is interesting that, in the face of profound funding shortfalls, many politicians are calling for privatization of the school system, a debate that focuses upon effectiveness issues but begs the fundamental question of resources for the system and the process for resource allocation. If our economy continues to decline, as we have projected, funding for education and training for the American worker will be inadequate. This will be true regardless of the method of educational delivery, whether public or private school systems. However, it is likely that the privatized system, the school system, like the jail system we have described, will become bifurcated, with the lower working class and underclass receiving grossly inadequate training and education. In effect, the educational system of the future may add to the number of citizens who will become members of the economic underclass.

The economic underclass of the future will face severe economic problems and probably will be subjected to an inadequate school system. A more frightening problem that will be faced by the nation in general in the future, especially the underclass, will be the lack of comprehensive medical care. Politicians are now discussing a national health insurance policy. If such a policy is implemented, the poor of the future may receive a fair portion of available medical service. However, medical costs are increasing exponentially. If the cost of medical services is not controlled, then a "fair" share of existing services will be inadequate for anyone. The eroding economy, coupled with the increasing numbers of unproductive and unemployed individuals, will reduce the resources available for medical care.

The advent of the "street person" brings a new dimension to the problem. The number of street people in 2010 will represent a proportionately higher percentage of the underclass. The street people are likely to receive little or no medical services except for emergency room treatment. Therefore, disease and sickness in general and communicable diseases in particular will be prevalent among the underclass. The regrettable conclusion is that the jails will be filled with disease-ridden inmates. And, regrettably, the medical delivery system of the public-sector jails will be woefully inadequate. If we are faced with uncontrollable diseases such as AIDS or some new strain of treatment-resistant tuberculosis, the potential for epidemics within the nation's public-sector jails will exist. The problem may be faced even with good medical care. Currently, for example, communicable and noncommunicable diseases are on the increase in major urban jail systems that expend a great deal of resources on medical care for inmates.

The extent to which jail inmates do receive adequate medical treatment is a function of the profuse expansion of inmate rights granted through civil law, especially from the federal court system. The current trend in the application of civil law, if continued, may well adversely affect the use and conditions of our jails. Recent trends in civil law have made it much more difficult for public institutions to be sued under Federal Statute USC 1983 (see Chapter 4). There also has been a conservative trend within the U.S. Supreme Court, and even the more liberal Court of the 1970s warned federal district courts to limit their involvement in prison and jail litigation and to stop acting as administrators. In addition, a number of federal district court judges have been appointed over the last decade because of their conservative, strict-constructionist judicial philosophy. In effect, these judges were appointed to help keep courts out of the administrative business of government, contrary to the behavior of the Warren Court. We can expect, therefore, a continued erosion of prisoners' rights and a return, at least in part, to the "hands-off" judicial doctrine of the past.

In terms of the application of criminal law, we are currently seeing a trend toward using the law and the coercive power of the CJS to solve social problems. Many would argue that legislation prohibiting certain forms of corporal punishment for children (e.g., spanking) is a good example of using the law to solve social problems. We might see similar criminal legislation created to prevent sexual harassment in the workplace. In many states, the sale and use of anabolic steroids has been made a felony. Also, the prohibition against drug use is a clear example of relying upon the CJS to cope with social problems: If we punish people severely enough, they will cease punishing themselves. The result of the use of the CJS will probably be an increase in the number of individuals considered criminal and an increase in the number of individuals residing in our prisons and jails, many of whom will be drug addicts. We could go on with other examples of the use of criminal law to deal with social problems. The point is, however, that this trend will add to the increase in our nation's jail population in the future.

Many politically astute people are warning that the law is used excessively because our government is managed by professional full-time legislators. If this warning is credible, the trend toward criminalization of our social problems may well continue. Will we see poor laws again? If we arrest the homeless en masse under the pretext of vagrancy and nuisance laws or with new legislation written to "protect" the homeless, we will again see poor laws, and the nation's jails will bear the burden of caring for the poor.

There is an ironic twist to our legislators' tendency to, in effect, utilize the CJS to deal with social problems. While continuing to legislate against personal behaviors and activities, the federal and state governments are touting the merits of privatization and decentralization—or "grass-roots federalism" as it was labeled during the Reagan Administration. Privatization, while having some clear advantages, is, in our opinion, a way for policy makers to avoid resource issues when discussing the effectiveness of our public institutions. For example, privateers argue that the schools do not need more funding to become more effective—they need to be competitive, that is, privatized. If the move toward privatization continues, the logical economic conclusion is that individuals and communities with greater wealth will be able to provide services. Private entrepreneurs will not offer services that do not provide adequate revenues, regardless of the source. Hence, communities with greater per capita wealth will receive better governmental services from the private sector than will poorer communities.

The notion of decentralization is a simple proposition. The state and federal governments continue to tax at the same rate but have delegated their responsibilities for certain public functions to local governments. Emptying mental hospitals is an excellent example of de facto decentralization. Local community mental health and welfare agencies absorb the workload. For clients who do not succeed in their communities, the CJS and local jail are called upon to intervene. Simply put, mental health clients end up in local jails. No matter how poor the jail treatment of mentally ill inmates, we will never return to a policy of benevolent incarceration of the mentally ill in state hospitals. Jails of the future will continue to grapple with mentally ill inmates.

Our last concern relates to the heterogeneous mix of people and groups that produce the mix of values and beliefs we refer to as our culture. Our culture is often accused of being reactive and short-sighted, especially when compared with the German and Japanese cultures. To the extent this is true, this may account for the flight we have seen from the inner cities to the suburbs by industry, white-collar professionals, and blue-collar workers during the last two decades. The flight to suburbia, sometimes referred to as "white flight," has eroded the economic and tax base of many major cities. Cities are struggling to balance their budgets while providing basic services to their constituents.

Along with economic erosion and unemployment, crime, violence, homicides, drug use, and criminal gangs, other problems have grown rapidly within large inner cities. The problems have perpetuated the flight to the suburbs that, in turn, has exacerbated the economic woes of the inner cities. The latter will be composed primarily of the poor, and suburban residents will at least work in the primary labor market. Our prediction is that the cities and suburbs will continue to become culturally and economically divided. Hence, it will be logical to split the jail systems as we have described.

The problems and trends described will be created within our culture, yet the hope for solutions also lies within our culture. Whether the trends outlined above will continue depends on our cultural values and beliefs, especially as they apply to the perspectives we hold toward identifying and solving our social problems. Some solutions may come about as a natural consequence of the free-market economy. For example, with the erosion of inner cities, property values have plummeted; this, in turn, has led to inner cities becoming attractive property for potential industry, and it created a new group of urban dwellers called young urban professionals ("yuppies"). Other problems are more fundamental, and we will need to find long-term planned solutions, such as making medical treatment affordable and universal.

In other words, the structure of the economy, the distribution of wealth, the effectiveness of our educational system, the fairness and efficacy of our medical system, and, ultimately, the way we use the law and our government is based on the mix of values and beliefs that constitute our culture. Some changes in the trends we describe will take place on their own. Concerted effort may be required to alter other trends that will be harmful to the citizens of 2010. To the extent we choose to blame the poor, the homeless, the mentally ill, the unemployed, and the disenfranchised for their plight, then the trends we have outlined may just continue. If they do, then our bleak predictions could come true.

CONCLUSIONS

The premise of this piece is that jails and the CJS will deal with the social and economic problems faced by our society. We boldly projected a worst-case scenario for jails in 2010, which we believe is very possible. The grim tale of the future is possible if some of the trends we have described continue unabated. Specifically, we projected a faltering economic system that would foster a growing underclass and growing numbers of homeless. We also argued that the jail system would be inundated with the underclass and homeless and that the typical inmate would likely be in poor physical or emotional health. The system, we thought, would consist of an urban and suburban jail system that would be physically and administratively divided. The urban jail system would cater to the poor and the homeless, and it would be chronically overcrowded and run-down. We also predicted, for the urban jail system, unrest, corruption, and disease levels chronically on the verge of becoming epidemics. The government will be forced to use warehouses and other available older buildings to supplement the main jail facilities. We also predicted that the jails would be unmanageable, except by inmates, and always on the verge of chaos.

On the bright side, our projection into 2010 shows a rather well-managed jail system in our nation's suburbs. The suburbs will be in sound economic condition and will be able to afford their own criminal justice and jail systems. The split system will manifest the cultural gulf between the future inner city and its suburbs. We also predicted that the privatization trend would flourish in suburbia, where residents would be willing and able to pay for a better jail system.

None of our bleak predictions may come true. We challenge the reader to judge whether our premise and critique of the present is correct. Our predictions are also subject to challenge. For example, the reader should also see John Naisbitt and Patricia Aburdene's 1990 book, *Megatrends 2000: Ten New Predictions for the 1990s,* for a very optimistic view of the future. If they are correct in their projections and the quality of services to jail inmates continues to improve, then our own predictions may be completely off the mark.

AUTHOR'S NOTE

This manuscript is dedicated to my coauthor, Paul Embert, who died November 16, 1991. Paul was the consummate professional. He always gave a great deal more than he received. He will be missed.

FOR FURTHER READING

Ronald Goldfarb. *Jails: The Ultimate Ghetto.* Garden City, NY: Anchor–Doubleday, 1975.

This classic examination of the jail explores their poor treatment and those who reside within them. This is one of the first explorations of the jail, describing its arrival on the American landscape, its many functions including poorhouse and mental health facility, and its continual neglect by politicians, criminal justice officials, and the public.

John Irwin. *The Jail: Managing the Underclass in American Society.* Berkeley: University of California Press, 1985.

Based on personal observations and the records of one California jail, Irwin provides a critical account of the role of the jail in contemporary society. His study explores the process of jailing: disintegration, degradation, and preparation. The outcome of these processes is the reduction of the prisoner into the "rabble class," which has little hope for the future. Irwin concludes with a critical exploration of the role jail plays in the wider scheme of society.

Joel Thompson and Larry G. Mays. *American Jails: Public Policy Issues.* Chicago: Nelson-Hall, 1991.

This volume is a collection of articles on the jail in contemporary society. Topics presented include surveys of jail facilities, use patterns found among jails, and special problem offenders found in jails. The book represents current thinking on a number of issues facing jail managers, politicians, and the public.

Franklin Zimring and Gordon Hawkins. *The Scale of Imprisonment.* Chicago: University of Chicago Press, 1991.

This book addresses the growth of incarceration in the United States during the 1980s. It includes an analysis of the roles of crime, arrests, drugs, and other issues influencing the use of incarceration. None of these issues offers much of an explanation for the phenomenal growth in the prisoner population. Future prescriptions on the role of incarceration in society are provided.

DISCUSSION QUESTIONS

1. What has been the historic role of the jail in the criminal justice system and society at large? How will these roles affect the jail's future?

2. How will social conditions affect the types of jails in metropolitan areas? How likely is a bifurcated jail system in your own community?

3. Discuss the potential problems in both publicly run jails and privately financed facilities.

4. How does the Antoinette County jail system represent what you think your local jail will look like in the future? What local and national factors will influence the type of jail found in your community?

5. Discuss the relationship between economic conditions and jails in the future. What does this suggest about the ways in which current jail conditions have been influenced by the economy?

10

The "Pen" and the Pendulum:

Finding Our Way to the Future of Incarceration

L U C I E N X . L O M B A R D O
Old Dominion University

The character and quality of life in correctional institutions (the "pen") has often found itself inextricably tied to the continuing shifts in political and public sentiment between retributive and humanitarian philosophies (the pendulum). My goals in this chapter are two: (1) to describe and analyze some of the forces and processes that have kept this pendulum in motion and which have created the correctional present, and (2) to offer suggestions for stopping the pendulum and developing dynamic penal practices that can bring penal life more under our control as we move toward the year 2010.

In trying to achieve these goals, I will identify some historical trends in the forces and processes that have shaped the evolution of institutional life and conditions. I will assess the current context, which will provide the baseline from which we will move toward the future. Finally, I will present two views of the future of incarcerative institutions and discuss ways of thinking about organizational change that might help us actively create the incarcerative life of the next century. In doing so, I assume that the correctional future is one that we as a society and polity have the ability to shape by the choices we make between now and the year 2010.[1]

As I look to the future from 1995, I look to other attempts to describe the penal future. I do this in the hope that by not ignoring the past, we can choose not to repeat it. In 1931, the American Academy of Political and Social Science published a volume entitled *Prisons of Tomorrow*. The foreword, written by editors Edwin H. Sutherland and Thorsten Sellin, is as timely now as it was sixty years ago:

> The riots and disturbances which have in recent years oc-
> curred in our prisons have served to focus public attention on
> our methods of dealing with criminals. Many persons have
> come to wonder if we have not, after all, been pursuing false
> idols. We have begun to lose faith in the mighty citadels of im-
> penetrable walls which once made our prisons showcases of
> civic architecture. We are realizing that they have failed us in
> their true task of protecting us against crime.
>
> True enough, the prison has come to be the last resort of penal
> treatment, when all other measures have proved wanting. This
> has made the prison's work a fearfully difficult one. Yet we are
> compelled to conclude that, since the vast majority of prisoners
> will be returned to normal social life at the expiration of their
> sentences, our prisons *must* be rationally adapted, in organiza-
> tions and functions, to the complicated task that faces them. If
> this means the renunciation of vindictive theories and policies,
> let us renounce them. If it means more science in penal treat-
> ment, let us have more science. The fact is that our prisons must
> become effective and dynamic agencies of the social protection
> which, if humanely possible, will return prisoners to society bet-
> ter men then when they entered the institutions.

In my view, these words are as true now as they were then, and I write this essay in the hope that editors of a volume on "prisons of

---

1. In 1969, the American Academy of Political and Social Science published a volume of the *Annals* entitled *The Future of Corrections*. The emphasis in this look into the correctional future was on the expansion and increased support for community-based alternatives to incarceration. In 1985, another edition of the *Annals* discussed *Our Overcrowded Prisons*. Here the impact of crowding and strategies to relieve this condition was emphasized. In reviewing these volumes, one comes away with the perception that correctional change is indeed slow and often moves in directions that are difficult to predict. For other visions of the correctional future, see Leslie T. Wilkins's, "Directions for Corrections," American Philosophical Society, Autumn Meeting, November 8 and 9, 1973; "In Place of Prisons: Some Things Already Done," *The World Tomorrow*, May, 1925, pp. 141–144.

tomorrow" written in 2010 need not introduce their work with the same observations. Indeed, it is hoped that in 1996 (the twenty-fifth anniversary of Attica) we are not again reminded of the folly of our American penal practices by the sight of state authorities extinguishing the lives of confined persons asserting what is left of their humanity.[2]

Between 1995 and 2010 there are fifteen years of history to be recorded. During this time there will be enormous social, political, and economic changes that will affect our society's place in the world and our individual places in society. At the same time, there will be calls for a return to the "good old days" and attempts to hide the future with symbols of a "glorious past." Today, as we see more and larger prisons being built, as we see more and more people being sent to prisons, we indeed should wonder: "What will be happening to those who live and work in these institutions? What is it that we are creating? What will be the human legacy of the correctional practices of the late 1970s and 1980s?"[3] As we think about moving from 1995 to 2010, we must understand that the penal policies and practice of 1995 will be the "good old days" of penal practice twenty years from now. I hope that by then we will not want to return to what we have now!

HISTORICAL PROCESSES AND TRENDS

As we think about the future of life in correctional institutions, I believe there are a number of historical processes (I make no claim to originality here) that will shape the penal future. These are processes that should become part of the understanding and worldview of those who shape correctional policy and practice.

First, I believe it is important to understand that the substantive character of correctional change has been additive. That is, whenever changes occur, they are added on to existing systems. Nothing ever truly disappears. For example, when formal corporal punishment is banned and due-process protections extend to various aspects of prison

---

2. During Attica I was employed by the State of New York's Department of Corrections as a full-time teacher at the Auburn Correctional Facility. This was my reaction as I heard about the retaking of the prison in which forty-three people were killed by state authorities (New York State Special Commission on Attica, 1972).

3. I might say that I am asking these questions out of intellectual curiosity. In today's humanely bankrupt climate, to say that I care what happens to those in prisons is to run the risk of being called "wimpish" or "soft-hearted" or "liberal." However, I must say that I do not approach this question in a detached manner. I do worry when I observe the wanton and needless infliction of pain and suffering. I worry not only about the impact on the humanity of those upon whom the pain is inflicted, but also about the humanity of those who inflict it.

discipline, corporal punishment becomes informal, more indirect, and less visible (often shifting to inmates as control operatives). The introduction of treatment programs in the 1940s, 1950s, and 1960s did not eliminate the coercive aspects of most penal institutions. In the 1980s and 1990s, the return to retribution did not totally eliminate the treatment programs that previously existed.

Prediction 1

Thus, in moving from 1995 to 2010, I believe it is safe to assume that whatever direction we choose will not replace existing practices, but will be grafted onto them in some fashion. The institutional structures that we construct today (and those that we have constructed in the past) will be with us for some time to come.

Second, the traditional dynamic of the correctional change process has been reactive and mechanistic. This means that change occurs only when problems become visible to such an extent that someone must react. It also means that courts, administrators, and politicians have attempted to respond to these visible problems by issuing orders that would change the conditions that are believed to have led to the problem. Relying on the myth that power relations in correctional institutions are hierarchical (courts to politicians to executives to administrators to supervisors to correctional officers to inmates), courts issue orders to correct defects, new policies and procedures are defined, and administrators are changed. To change the machine of corrections, we need only change the parts. Such reactive and often symbolic problem solving assumes that correctional philosophy can be translated into policy decrees and then into a bureaucratic procedure and administrative action. It also assumes that the activities in which the machine of corrections is engaged are indeed the correct activities for the machine to be performing. As we move toward the future, we should be aware that this need not necessarily be the case.

Prediction 2

As we move into the twenty-first century, I believe that more proactive approaches to prison organization and management that involve goal development, information processing and monitoring, and inmate and staff participation in decision making will need to be developed. I will not predict highly visible change-breeding events such as riots, since I hope that processes can be put in place to avoid them.

Third, correctional institutions have always maintained the coexistence of our most humanitarian intentions and our most savage behaviors. That is, practices that purposely inflict pain and suffering on inmates (whether organizationally or individually initiated) coexist with the efforts of some personnel to assist and help change inmates by instilling positive virtues (whether organizationally or individually determined). Our contradictory desires to help the downfallen and punish the wicked will continue to search for an appropriate balance as we move through the next twenty years. These contradictory desires and actions reflect the religious zeal that many in corrections used to (and in all likelihood, many still do) bring to their work. They also reflect the schizoid nature of the penal view of the relationship of the wrongdoer to the community. On the one hand, wrongdoers are seen as fallen members of the community who need assistance to be returned to the community better than they were before. Wrongdoers are also painted as the enemy of the community, outcasts of society, who should be treated harshly to pay for their sins. From this perspective, we feel that the various forms of humiliation, pain, and suffering that accompany confinement are deserved by those who have violated community standards.

This pair of contradictory impulses reflects a dialectic central to the historical evolution of our penal institutions. On the one hand, retribution breeds abuses, which come to the public attention and lead to calls for some corrective. On the other hand, too much humanity toward the evildoer and our response is tempered by reference to the "principle of least eligibility."

Prediction 3

During the next twenty years, we will see the consolidation of the retributive, "just desserts" perspective in the sentencing process and the growing recognition and development of programming and services to support inmate attempts at living lives free of further contacts with the law. These services will not be seen as a purpose of sentencing (that purpose will remain retribution). However, service provision will be seen as a necessary part of effective and efficient correctional management divorced from the sentencing function.

Fourth, penal policy and incarcerative life develop from an interaction with political, social, and economic conditions in the community that surrounds the walls and fences. Changes that will work their way into correctional institutions often have their genesis outside of prisons.

Past research has described the process by which penal concerns moved from the periphery to the center of public concern in the late 1960s and early 1970s. This movement was coupled with response to other newly "discovered" social problems such as the war on poverty and the due-process and civil rights revolutions. This interaction process reflects an open-systems view of correctional life. From this perspective, one comes to understand that the character and dynamics of prison life at any one point in time are shaped by the social, economic, and political contexts that surround them. Thus, in trying to shape the incarcerative institutions of the future, policy makers and administrators must be attuned to the world around them. They must be able to draw on those forces that support the directions in which they wish to move. In addition, they must facilitate the development of those forces that will help them go where they want to go.

Prediction 4

During the next twenty years, domestic problems will emerge as the top national political priority. Education, poverty, housing, health care, and unemployment problems (among others) will again focus attention on practical service provision and issues of fairness and equity in resource distribution. This will provide renewed impetus for giving attention to service provision in incarcerative institutions. By 2010, the fairness, equity, effectiveness and efficiency, and justice of the "crime control" policies of the 1980s and 1990s will be questioned. Links between crime, the questionable effectiveness of repressive techniques of crime control, and other social problems will once again be forged.

Fifth, history teaches us that the character of prison life and the behavior of prisoners and staff are at once responses to the conditions of confinement and reflections of the nonprison experiences of those confined and working in the prisons. In other words, both the importation and deprivation processes account for prison culture and behavior. There is certainly no reason to believe this will change. Prisoners of the 1930s brought their experiences of the economic depression and some experiences gained from coping with Prohibition. In the 1960s and 1970s, challenges to racism and to abusive and unchecked authority in communities brought a new dynamic to prison life. These forces empowered previously powerless prisoners. They engendered feelings of powerlessness in staffmembers who felt their control dissipating. In the 1980s and 1990s, the growth of the violent drug culture, gang behaviors and identities, and the development of AIDS have all had an impact on the size of the prison population and on the nature of social relations and behavior within institutions.

During the next twenty years, the growing recognition of "multiculturalism and diversity" will result from the demographic restructuring of American society with the elimination of any majority group. This change will continue to be intellectually supported by the work of scholars in such areas as women's studies, African–American studies, and ethnic studies programs that give new interpretations and discover values that have been long associated with nonmainstream traditions.

Prediction 5

The changing demographics of crime and criminal justice processing will extend these changes into the correctional system. Inmates, staff, and administrators will bring new experiences of cultural self-definition into prisons. This will provide new self-definitions and needs to interact with conditions of confinement. As these perspectives find their way into public consciousness through the mass media, they will begin to raise questions about our long-standing approaches to power, social control (a consistent theme in these perspectives), and, by extension, the correctional system.

Finally, and most important, it should be noted that life as it is experienced and acted out in prison has both a private and a public character. It is here in the nexus of the symbolic and real world of the prisoners and staff that all of the historical forces and processes mentioned above create the "reality of the incarcerative experience." This is true for both prisoners and their keepers. The private life is determined by the interaction of individual needs and institutional resources. Research has identified many salient prisoner needs that interact with the prison environment: activity, freedom, social stimulation, support, emotional feedback, structure, and safety. For correctional officers, research has identified activity, autonomy, and a need to contribute to the workplace as motivational concerns. Breakdown, stress, and burnout are often seen as indications of a failure to achieve meaningful individual and environmental matches. On the public level, life is acted out and experienced in social groups, playing to the stereotypes of the contemporary prison environment. Officers play the "hack," "screw," and "bull" to the "right guy," "con-boss," "gang-leader," "tough," and "wolf." Here adherence to the "prisoner code" and to the norm of the "guard subculture" shape inmate and staff behavior. Though individuals in their private worlds routinely violate the codes and norms of their group, these public expressions of appropriate behavior shape individual choices in the collective, conflict-laden context in which prison life is often acted out. Such conflict plays itself out in various forms of victimization: inmates of inmates, staff of inmates, and inmates of staff.

Two threads that run through the nexus of these public and private worlds are *authority* (the distribution of real and theoretical power between inmates and staff) and *social distance* (the existence of personal and helping relationships between inmates and staff). These two dimensions provide the "ground" against which both inmates and staff carry out and interpret their own and each other's behavior.

Research has shown us that the authority of the staff to control inmate behavior is a myth, and that the theoretical authority of staff is easily corrupted by the environment and social dynamics inherent in prison life. What has changed is not the nature of the authority relationships, but the context within which they are acted out. New contingencies shape these relationships in the 1990s. Arbitrary authority no longer has the support of a hands-off legal philosophy. Authority of the officer, administration, and the state needs to be legitimized, at least to the level of having formal written policies and procedures to govern the behavior of officers. These policies and procedures also provide inmates with support for appeals when they believe authority is being exercised wrongly. Though inmates' access to the courts may be decreasing (and may continue to be reduced by an increasingly conservative federal judiciary), the policy and procedures approach will be supported and enhanced by the work of professional correctional agencies. Interacting with this legal legitimacy is the personal legitimacy that individual officers gain by implementing the firm, fair, and consistent responses they are taught in training academies. Personal legitimacy is also enhanced when officers find ways to contribute to their workplace that involve service provisions to inmates. Here, attending to inmate stress in ways that alleviate stress-producing conditions and refraining from adding to these conditions allows officers to elicit rather than "maintain" order. This reflects individual officer behaviors that permit and encourage reduced social distance between inmate and staff.

Prediction 6

As we move through the next twenty years, officer legalistic authority and legitimacy will be clarified by the further development of professional correctional standards and the development of written policy and procedures to govern internal prison operations. In addition, officer problem-solving skills will be developed and applied to "victimization reduction," which will become a key indicator of effective correctional management.

CONTEXTS FOR PENAL POLICY AND PRACTICE IN 1995: A BASELINE FOR THE TWENTY-FIRST CENTURY

As we think about the future, we must not only consider the processes and forces that have shaped prison life, but also make some assessment of the current state of correctional life. Recognizing the importance of generational change in corrections, we quickly recognize that the prison environment of the 1990s is the baseline against which those living and working in prisons of the future will measure their condition in 2010.

Policy Context

Today's correctional policy climate is one in which opposition to the dominant retributive philosophy is severely muted; strong spokespersons for corrections are absent; progressive state leadership in corrections has fallen victim to budget deficits and overcrowding; and federal and private funding of experimental correctional research not aimed at enhancing repression is severely limited.

Though I agree with these observations, I believe that ascendancy of the retributive philosophy and the process by which it came to ascendancy (having sentencing policy attacked by both liberals and conservatives) have provided an opportunity for the humanitarian impulses described above to surface. This allows service provision to be developed less as an oppositional force than as a supplementary philosophy that supports activities that sentencing is not meant to reflect or to accomplish.

Here I am not arguing that "treatment" will make a comeback as a purpose of criminal justice intervention. Rather, we will begin to

appreciate the wisdom of voluntary programming alternatives to supplement the punishment associated with the confinement alternative.

The attacks on the indeterminate sentence and the "medical model"
with its uncontrolled discretion and expertise-based authority helped
clear away the underbrush. It is now possible to see that "punishment"
is indeed the purpose of the criminal-sentencing process. But it is
equally possible to see that providing support services for those convicted of crimes and sentenced to periods of incarceration—not as a
reason for their sentence, but as a necessary and, it is hoped, effective
social policy, independent of the sentencing process—may reflect the
less ideological and more practical correctional realism that has characterized the ideals of correctional professionals for decades.

Technological Context

With the rapid growth in the number of prisoners and the numbers of
prisons, concerns with prison architecture and security technology have
resurfaced, as they did during the Auburn–Pennsylvania system debates.
But there is a difference. Whereas the earlier debates had a reform
component associated with the architectural design, today's discussions
revolve almost exclusively around security, control, cost, and mechanisms for dealing with crowding. Here, electronic monitoring, closed-
circuit surveillance, video recording, and computerized data collection
are enhancing the possibilities for increased safety and accountability
for both inmates and staff. In addition, computerized data management
is facilitating the possibility of monitoring various characteristics of the
quality of life. Such capabilities may create the need to identify and
define more specifically the goals of correctional management that can
then be monitored with specific indicators.

Staff Context

Today's correctional staffs are more ethnically and sexually diverse than
at any time in the past. Though it is clear that organizational, cultural,
and legal barriers have surfaced during the process of integration, such
integration will be the norm twenty years from now. It is hoped that the
structural and interpersonal biases and constraints that have characterized this process of staff integration will be reduced by the year 2010
as diversity (gender and ethnic) in the workplace becomes the norm.

In some correctional institutions, staff roles are becoming more
specialized. With the transfer of many of the human services functions
to inmates and professional staff, correctional officer roles appear to be

becoming more security-oriented. Increasing institutional violence has also reinforced this tendency. However, it has only been ten to fifteen years since the human-services contributions and potential of correctional officers were first recognized. If, as I predict, service provision will be a focus of institutional activity as we approach 2010, then correctional officers will be key personnel (they are certainly plentiful) in providing services in cost-effective ways.

Prison Conditions Context

In 1982, John Conrad addressed the question, "What do the undeserving deserve?" In doing so, he observed that many of the pains of imprisonment that characterized prisons of the 1950s had been somewhat alleviated by the 1980s. Inmates received more access to goods and services, more autonomy with the "due-process revolution"; more freedom with the increase of medium- and minimum-security institutions close to inmates' home communities; and more heterosexual contact with the employment of women in positions with direct contact with the population. Where correctional institutions had failed, Conrad noted, was in providing for the safety of the inmates.

There is no doubt that during the 1980s the rapidly expanded prison populations had a retrogressive impact on the gains noted by Conrad. However, the exact nature of this impact has yet to be assessed. In addition, the conditions of confinement have been affected by the changing nature of the problems brought into institutions by the inmate population: drug and alcohol addiction, experience with the subculture of violence, and gang-related activity coupled with administrators' lack of attention to "treatment" programming have made previous gains less meaningful. It is possible that the nature of prison conditions and the problems stemming from crowding and the drug culture might be alleviated by changes in national strategies for dealing with the "drug problem." Decriminalization, the development of drug-treatment programs, or the addressing of social and personal conditions that lead to drug usage might substantially reduce prison populations in the future. In addition, the expansion of nonincarcerative alternative punishment might have a substantial impact on prison populations and, by extension, on the conditions of confinement during the next twenty years.

Legal Context

The law of corrections provides another source of potential conflict and change. With the 1950s as a baseline, there was indeed a due-process revolution in prison life during the 1960s and 1970s.

However, as we move through the 1990s, this revolution will have to some extent been consolidated in policies and procedures that form the baseline as we move to the twenty-first century. During the past ten years, we have seen a shift "back to the future" as courts have taken positions that rely on the expertise of correctional administrators to determine what is and is not appropriate correctional practice. This shift from a recognition of the abuse potential inherent in authority to a preference for expertise contains within it the seeds of change. When administrators are able to rely on the authority vested in their positions to justify penal practices, the legitimacy of that authority comes into question. This may become particularly problematic because the baseline of the arbitrary authority and hands-off approach of the 1950s was replaced by the activist policy-and-procedure bureaucratic approach of the 1970s and 1980s.

Though administrators may win the battle in court and have their expertise reaffirmed, they may lose the war as the censorious behavior of inmates challenges them to justify in person what they are not forced to justify in law. Such a process often leads to greater prisoner "class solidarity" and to increased inmate–staff conflict. It is possible that today's and tomorrow's correctional administrators are and will be more capable of overcoming the bureaucratic tendency to engage in "ritualistic behavior" and abuses of power than were those of the past. However, if history is any teacher, this is highly unlikely.

Cultural Context

As we move from the 1990s and into the 2000s, it is possible that we are beginning one of those periods in which quantum changes in the character of American society and culture are beginning to take place. Writers have referred to the 1960s as an "age of discontinuity." Drucker has identified four areas of discontinuity with the past: (1) new technologies, (2) the development of a world economy as opposed to an "international economy," (3) increasing social and political pluralism, and (4) the development of "knowledge" as a major form of capital.

Today, major discontinuities are again being discussed. Cultural commentators are beginning to question the adequacy of past formulas to solve the problems of the present and the future.

If this observation is correct and the repressively bankrupt correctional philosophies of the 1980s are losing their relevance and appeal just as the "liberal" prescriptions lost their support during the 1970s and 1980s, then it may be time that we think about developing new ways to understand and structure the change process that will lead us to the correctional life of the year 2010.

THE SHAPE OF
PENAL ALTERNATIVES

There appears to be consensus among academic analysts, commentators, and correctional professionals about some of the basic characteristics that should be part of the correctional future. Some advocate a system in which fairness is institutionalized, communications are as open as possible for everyone, and the outside world is welcome to help maintain as natural a social order as possible in the penal environment. These commentators identify four essential goals of prison management: safety, lawfulness, industriousness, and hope. Others argue that to make prison programs relevant and useful, corrections must operate prisons in which stress remains within tolerable limits and is handled maturely, as well as offer a number of programs that enhance the prisoner's capacity to cope maturely with life stresses both in prison and later in the free world. Other critics suggest that real reform will involve relevant and realistic inmate-service programs suggested by inmates and a policy that opens prisons to the media. From a feminist perspective, administrative and academic critics suggest that our human commonality with the prisoner needs to be recognized; that harmony rather than competition and conflict and zero-sum lifestyles should be emphasized; and that the empathy and compassion that we strive to emphasize in our personal lives should also dominate our political views.

While some of these proposals require fundamental change and others are less demanding, they all have in common the advisability of reducing inmate victimization by both other inmates and prison staff. They all see the appropriateness of maintaining the rule of law in prisons. In addition, all desire to provide inmates with activities that will occupy their time and provide opportunities for responsible behavior. Where they sometimes differ, however, is in the strategies they propose for getting from here to there.

STRATEGIES FOR GETTING
TO THE DESIRABLE FUTURE

"Back to the Future"

Some writers suggest using an essentially closed-system, mechanistic approach to correctional reform. Though noting the importance of supportive politicians, the media, and public opinion, the essential unit of analysis and attention is the prison itself. This view proposes that future prisons should contain order, the absence of prison violence in its myriad manifestations, amenity (e.g., food of appropriate quality and nutrition and clothing to keep out the elements), and service programs to support self-improvement. These elements are certainly worthwhile and reflect the goals of almost all reformers (at least partially). However, the techniques some writers propose to move from the present (a state characterized by increasing inmate–inmate victimization and a loss of staff control) to the future (where constitutional government controls both the keepers and the kept) imply a return to the "good old days" with a bureaucratically organized military regime for the keepers and the kept, charismatic leadership at the top, and supportive politicians, public opinion, and professors.

Unless we are entering a period in which increasingly docile inmates will be entering our correctional systems (and the available evidence suggests that we are not), then the "defects of total power" delineated by researchers forty years ago probably will emerge as they always have and abuses of power will occur as they always have. Future suggestions for improving the prison world by returning to the days when experienced wardens, supervisors, and correctional officers ran the prisons with paternalistic fairness seem to ignore the forces that shape the present and will shape the future.

This mechanistic view of organizations is a strength when (1) there is a straightforward task to perform, (2) the environment is stable enough to ensure that the products produced are appropriate, (3) one wishes to produce exactly the same product time and again, (4) precision is at a premium, and (5) the human "machine" parts are compliant and behave as they have been designed. Such organizations can function well when they are isolated from changing conditions. Such was the case to some extent with the "big house" prisons of the 1930s, '40s, and '50s and before the due-process and civil rights revolutions. When faced with change, however, mechanistic organizations either fail or become reactionary, living with the ritual present practice. They find it difficult to adapt.

If the above description and analysis of the current state of corrections and the historical forces and processes that go into the creation of prison life is at all relevant, then the mechanistic approach to prison change in moving to 2010 would seem to be fraught with problems.

As we have seen, mechanistic organizations respond to change in predictable ways: They have great difficulty adapting to changing circumstances; they result in mindless and unquestioning bureaucracy; they have unanticipated and undesirable consequences as the interests of those working in the organization take precedence over the goals the organization was designed to achieve; and they have dehumanizing effects on employees, especially those at the lower levels of the organizational hierarchy. All of these results have certainly occurred in relation to the substance and process of prison change during the past 200 years. And they were certainly evident during the turbulent years of the 1960s and 1970s as the previously isolated prisons were permeated by a wide variety of political and social forces.

If we assume that the nature and character of prison life at any one point in time are determined by more than management's ability and willingness to control inmates, the staff, and itself, then how can we think about moving from 1995 to 2010? What alternative processes are there for thinking about and managing the forces that shape the character of prison life?

Toward the Future:
A Proactive, Dynamic View

If we are to manage the next twenty years of change more successfully than we managed change during the 1960s and 1970s, then we need to think of prison organizations in more than mechanistic and militaristic ways. Morgan's description of organizations as brains and change as flux provides three concepts that we can apply to correctional change that may help us control and manage the changes of the next twenty years. By doing so, we might be able to avoid the reactionary and reactive approach that has led to so much conflict and suffering in the past.

Enfolding the Environment This view of the prison-change process recognizes that the factors and historical processes of prison change are interactive and dynamic. The environment in which prisons operate is shaped by what happens in prisons, and what happens in prisons is shaped by that environment.

From this perspective, the intervention of courts into the administrative activities of prisons would not be seen as something that must be resisted. Rather, court decisions become part of the environment that is expected to influence correctional behavior. The questions in moving toward the future thus become "How can we incorporate court mandates and still move toward the future state we desire? How can these decisions help us get there?" and not "How do they challenge and reduce correctional authority? How can we resist them?"

The same is true of demographic changes that will hit prisons and of the cultural, technological, and social changes that will come between the walls. If those who administer, manage, and live in correctional institutions can grasp and recognize the benefits of the new relationships with the environment implied by "enfolding," then correctional change as we move to the twenty-first century can be more proactive and positive.

Mutual Causality   Another concept for more successfully managing change is "mutual causality." That is, we need to think of the relationships between factors as mutually reinforcing. We gain the ability to move toward the desirable goals described above by identifying the many forces that shape prison life and how they interact with the prison environment. We identify those that help us reach our goals and reinforce them; we identify those that are keeping us from our goals and attempt to find appropriate ways to minimize their impact. Thus we return again to the idea that the prison environment is part of the wider society and its culture.

Using the relationships between courts and prison change as an example, we can see that viewing the courts as "causing" prison change through edict ignores the contribution of correctional administrators to "causing" the courts' intervention by administrative practices that increase court scrutiny.

Organizational Learning   Developing organizational learning capabilities is a third concept that will help us take a more proactive approach in reaching the year 2010. Organizations can learn to learn when they encourage and value openness and accept error and uncertainty as constants in a complex and changing environment; recognize the importance of exploring different viewpoints; avoid imposing structures of goals, objectives, and targets and allow intelligence and direction to emerge from ongoing organizational processes; and have organizational structures that encourage the above processes.

As applied to the life of correctional institutions, this means that administrators and policy makers need to be inquisitive about their success at achieving what they want to accomplish. If the goals set forth above become the goals for correctional administration, then it becomes necessary to monitor progress toward achieving these goals. It also means accepting the possibility that what we are doing and how we are doing it is not necessarily the "best way" to accomplish our tasks. Technological change and computerization of institutional data will certainly help facilitate this process. In addition, the recognition that there are valuable "data" resting in the individual and collective experience of correctional personnel will lead administrators to tap this data source in the development of policies and procedures designed to improve and successfully manage the quality of institutional life in the next century.

Examples of prisons where "learning" takes place can be found. In these organizations, employees are encouraged to learn from their (or the organization's) mistakes and to make adjustments in appropriate directions. Mechanisms that allow for this provide feedback loops, which characterize the brain.

For example, when courts mandate a new disciplinary procedure, they are acting as part of the environment that defines the boundaries of the prison. That is, courts are within the organizational boundaries of the prison. In implementing the changes, it is expected that mistakes will be made because of uncertainty. If the staff reviews disciplinary tickets that were not upheld with an eye to finding out what went wrong, then the action provides the feedback loop necessary for learning and adjustment to take place. When such learning processes become part of organizational culture, the likelihood of smoother organizational responses to changing conditions is enhanced.

INCARCERATION 2010: CONCLUSION

The only certainties I can offer as we move toward the year 2010 are (1) that the multilayered environment within which correctional facilities operate will not be the same as it is today, and (2) this new environment will have an impact on the character and quality of incarcerative life. I have tried to identify some of the processes and forces that I believe have shaped and will shape prison life as we move to the future. I described some "desirable" characteristics of prisons. Whether these environmental changes will have a positive or negative impact on the quality of institutional life is up to us. Though we may have to change our ways of thinking about change to achieve positive results, the tools and concepts needed to do so are now available. The future is up to us to create.

FOR FURTHER READING

John DiIulio. *Governing Prisons: A Comparative Study of Correctional Management.* New York: The Free Press, 1987.

This book compares three distinct prison systems across the country and offers three models of prison management: consensual, responsibility, and control. The author's policy prescriptions have far-reaching implications for the future management of prison facilities.

Robert Johnson. *Hard Time: Understanding and Reforming the Prison.* Pacific Grove, CA: Brooks/Cole, 1987.

Johnson traces the historical development of prisons predicated on the notion that they are painful places. He also compares and contrasts two divergent views of prisons: the private and public cultures of prisoners and correctional officers. He concludes by examining the elements of a "mature" coping strategy for prisoner adjustment.

Lucien Lombardo. *Guards Imprisoned: Correctional Officers at Work* (2nd ed.). Cincinnati, OH: Anderson, 1989.

This study of correctional officers' work setting stresses the dynamic and complex nature of their work. The author's research emphasizes the importance of viewing correctional officer work within the realm of human service delivery and beyond the incarcerative approach.

Gareth Morgan. *Images of Organization.* Beverly Hills, CA: Sage Publications, 1986.

Morgan's analysis uses metaphors in exploring organizations. From mechanistic models to more sophisticated views, the author highlights the diversity of organizations and the necessity of viewing them in multiple ways.

Hans Toch. *Living in Prison: The Ecology of Survival.* New York: The Free Press, 1977.

In this groundbreaking work, Toch describes the multiple needs and adjustment strategies found among prisoners. He shows how prisoners individually and collectively develop "niches" within the prison environment. He concludes with the importance of niche development in the adjustment of prisoners and the management of prisons.

DISCUSSION QUESTIONS

1. Lombardo argues that change in prisons has been additive. New things are added and nothing truly disappears. How is the past interest in treatment and rehabilitation still evident in today's prisons? How significant is the treatment role in modern prisons?

2. How do the tendencies to be humane and the "principle of lesser eligibility" relate to one another? Do you think a balance of these ideas can be sustained?

3. How will social concerns with poverty, employment, and education shape prison goals in the future? Can you imagine a scenario in which the same concerns can trigger opposite goals?

4. If, as Lombardo suggests, the ambiguous legal authority and power of correctional officers is clarified in the future, what will be the impact on the types of relationships between officers and inmates?

5. Lombardo emphasizes a future that can be shaped by proactive leadership in criminal justice. How can goals be set? What factors must be influenced in order to achieve those goals?

11

Ophelia the CCW:

May 11, 2010

TODD R. CLEAR
Rutgers University

Ophelia Edison awakened gently, brought slowly to awareness by the vibrations of her massage bed. She opened her eyes to look at the ceiling of her bedroom, where the tele-inform displayed the time: 5:45 A.M. As she got up from her bed, the vibrations abruptly ceased, turned off by the body sensor, which felt her weight leave the bed's surface.

Walking to the lavatory center adjacent to the bedroom, she said in a firm tone, "Shower." Automatically, at the sound of her voice, the shower came on and the cascading water began to heat to a predetermined temperature. Because she wore no clothing to bed, she could walk right into the washing compartment of the lavatory, and she installed the VOICE-START system as a convenience. She loved their advert slogan: "A minute saved is a dollar earned."

Glancing back at the massage bed, she smiled slightly to herself, thinking it was one of her favorite indulgences. Actually, though, it was not an indulgence at all. Her union, the Middlesex Association of Community Control Workers, had negotiated them as part of last year's contract with COMCON, the firm that has the probation contract in her county. The COMCON contract specified merit bonuses for all employees whose performance scores were above the office average. Ophelia, who qualified easily, chose the massage bed instead of cash—inflation being what it was, it seemed a better investment.

Ophelia was a Community Control Specialist II, what used to be called a "probation officer" in the old days. She earned the "specialist" grade because she worked only with child sex offenders—it was her area of expertise. She was designated as "II" because she had been doing the work for five years, and every year her work performance scored out as "satisfactory"—within two standard deviations of the mean for the office.

She might not have said it publicly, but she was really glad she joined the union back when it first started up. Ever since COMCON got the contract for probation supervision services, there had been tension between the workers and the firm. COMCON was a wholly owned subsidiary of IBM, and it was in the money-making business. One way to make money, of course, was to keep salaries and wages down. In fact, the financial pressure to find ways to cut costs was worse now than in the old days, when government managed probation.

So no one could blame the CCWs (Community Control Workers) when they formed a union to protect their interests. After all, their work was difficult and dangerous, and they deserved to be well paid. Too bad the relations between the union and COMCON had been so vitriolic—there had been two strikes and a work slowdown in the first six months of the union. If the government hadn't stepped in and forced a settlement (by threatening to cancel the COMCON contract), things never would have calmed down.

She understood COMCON's problem very well, of course. With liability costs soaring (fighting civil suits and paying damage for lost suits had been more than 20 percent of last year's COMCON budget), the firm was even more pressed than ever. But the CCWs had the bosses between a rock and a hard place on this one: Suits were caused by failures to follow legally approved procedures and policy, and the slow-downs and strikes guaranteed more such failures.

"Let the management and union go after each other tooth and nail," she thought. "It doesn't bother me."

These were the sorts of things Ophelia pondered as she first showered, then dressed for work. She liked her job overall, and in the mornings it was good to reflect on that. The thoughts sort of warmed her up for the day ahead of her.

While drying her hair and dressing for the day, she turned on the audio news. "Good Morning America" was on, that old-time standard. The big news was the progress on talks of Ukraine and Mexico joining the United States, following Puerto Rico's lead. But this story interested her very little. She was waiting to hear about road conditions along the Eastern Seaboard, because today was a field day.

She chose her green flak-blouse for the day. It was hard to believe this stylishly cut material, which weighed only 2 pounds, could stop a bullet fired at point-blank range. All CCWs were required to wear flak-tops, ever since the massacre three years ago during a routine arrest, and she certainly felt safer with one on. Typically, COMCON had resisted the policy, citing "absurd costs" of providing flak-clothes for everyone. In the end, the union won out by threatening to stop all arrests.

Strapped inside her field boots were a stun gun and an electric revolver. She checked to see that each was working. After finishing dressing, she pulled a breakfast tube from her pantry and microtoasted it. With coffee and orange juice it was a perfect 320 calories, just right to start the day but not too much for her exercise–health program guidelines.

When she walked out the door, the tele-inform said 6:05.

Ophelia needed to start early on field days. Policy standards required home contacts at certain intervals for offenders whose profiles fit the complicated criteria. It was good to start out early so she could catch as many as possible before they reported to work (or to their "service post" if they didn't have a job). On the normal working day—there were only five randomly scheduled field days a month—she would awaken at 8:30 A.M. and be at the office by 9:30. But the days when she was to be "in the field" were determined by the office computer in a random basis. Randomness prevented the offenders from being able to pick up a "routine" field time and arrange to be "out" when she came by. It also kept the bosses in charge of things, at least so she thought.

The way everything worked now, her entire daily schedule was handled by computer. This was a good thing, she felt, since she couldn't make heads or tails out of the supervision policies.

The whole thing ran on "profiles." Profiles were really a complicated, interlocking pattern of criteria that were applied to offenders to determine how they should be supervised. Some offenders were seen as often as daily in the field; these cases were handled by Community Control Specialist IIIs, who carried only the "intensive" cases. Since

Ophelia's cases were sex offenders, she averaged seeing them fairly frequently, sometimes even twice weekly, depending on their profile.

According to what she had been told in her orientation training, the profiles were all determined by scientific research approaches called "actuarial tables" that predicted how offenders having certain backgrounds would behave and specified the best way to deal with them in order to prevent problems. She found the whole thing a bit confusing and a bit far-fetched, but the computer system made it all easy anyway, so she didn't mind. And they said it was based on literally thousands of case histories.

Stepping out into the sidewalk in front of her apartment building, Ophelia took a deep breath and looked around for the car she would be using. It was a company car and was in use nearly twenty-four hours a day. The carpool service would have delivered it to her street sometime in the night, after a night shift of CCWs had finished with it. It was never hard to find, since it was easily identifiable: military green, nondescript, and one of the few American-made cars on her street. She just looked around for a car nobody wanted to own. There it was, right across the street.

Getting into the car, she did a voice-start, saying simply, "Start." The engine softly hummed on, and the computer sitting under the dashboard engaged.

"Good morning," said the gender-neutral voice inside the machine. "Please identify yourself."

"Kiss my butt," said Ophelia with a sneer, as she punched in her ID. She knew this machine was deaf, and it amused her to be insolent to it.

"Good morning, Ophelia," the machine voice said. Ophelia winced and hit the function key that turned off the sound. The computer voice really annoyed her, and she preferred to read the instructions on the monitor rather than hear them.

On the monitor, the message appeared:

FIRST STOP: WALTER WILSON,
2721 LAKELAND BLVD., APT. 10G.

Ophelia remembered Wilson very well: He was on probation after being convicted of child sex abuse—fondling a neighbor's son. It was his first offense, but the profile indicated a "likelihood" of prior, unreported offenses. After meeting him, she thought the profile was dead-on.

These days he lived in an "iffy" neighborhood, and it made her uncomfortable to visit him there. He was a co-share case, and so she had only been out to see him a half-dozen times or so in the two years he had been on probation. A co-share case was one seen by more than a single CCW. Apparently, research had demonstrated that with certain cases, a joint-supervision approach was more effective, because one CCW might pick up on cues that another missed. She co-shared with Andy Rajandra, and about once a month or so the computer would set up a co-share conference between them to discuss this and other jointly supervised cases.

Ophelia liked sharing cases and she had a lot of respect for Andy's expertise. In the old days, a person had a caseload and was pretty much completely in charge of it. But this meant that offenders could learn officers' weaknesses and figure out ways to manipulate them—often with tragic consequences. Under joint supervision, she was paired with the other CCWs who specialized in sex offenders, and they reinforced each other's strengths while canceling out the weaknesses. She had grown so used to co-sharing her work that she didn't even think of herself as having a "caseload" anymore. She just had work assignments.

Today she was lucky. The first visit scheduled by the accountability system was along an "electric commuter" path from her apartment. She could let the transportation macrosystem drive the car for most of the way, and that would give her time to read the paper while in transit.

She used the computer to contact Transit and punched in her location and destination. Transit "accepted" her request (it almost always did, since government workers on duty had priority) and eased her into the morning traffic. She reached into the glovebox and pulled out the newspaper that was automatically printed there every morning. The front-page story made her chuckle: Congress had started the investigation of the report that thirty years ago three actors had impersonated Ronald Reagan during his presidency, because he had actually been secreted away in a coma off in some CIA basement room.

Twenty minutes later, she was across town and within a few blocks of Wilson's apartment. She reached down to the computer and hit the function key for "instructions." The monitor printed back:

> WALTER WILSON, AGE: 53, ETHNICITY: WHITE.
> PROFILE: SEX OFFENDER, TYPE A-2.
> DURING MOST RECENT CONTACT BY CCW
>   RAJANDRA (MAY 3) SUSPICION OF ALCOHOL
>   USE, BUT SKIN SCRATCH WAS NEGATIVE. PLEASE
>   OBSERVE THE FOLLOWING PROTOCOL:

1. TAKE SKIN SCRATCH.
2. DISCUSS JOB SITUATION—SUPERVISOR RELA-
   TIONS.
3. CHECK ANGELA (DAUGHTER, AGE 9) FOR MARKS.
4. TALK TO MYRA (CO-INHABITANT, AGE 47).
   CCW VIOLENCE RISK PROFILE, NEAR ZERO.

Ophelia made a mental note of the instructions, then took manual control of the car to drive up to Wilson's apartment. Moments later, she was facing him in his doorway.

"Good morning, Mr. Wilson," she began, "I hope I didn't awaken you."

"That's all right," he responded groggily. "Come on in."

Inside, they sat across from each other in the living room. Ophelia glanced about her, quickly taking in her whole surroundings. This was her habit, to see if anything struck her as amiss. It was a sixth sense she had developed about things and honed over her years on the job. This time her invisible antenna picked up nothing out of the ordinary.

Looking back at Wilson, she began. "I'd like to start with a skin scratch."

It was an abrupt way to start, she knew, and it made them both momentarily uncomfortable. But the computer system had been plain that this was the thing she would have to do, and if she deviated from specific instructions she would have to have a good reason, one her supervisor would accept. Her own preference would be to chat awhile before doing the test, but experience had taught her that a mere personal "preference" would not be enough to override "instructions," and then she would be liable for whatever happened.

And liability was a very big deal at COMCON. Workers who deviated from "instructions" too often or who did so without good, tangible reasons did not last long.

Wilson rolled up his sleeve. "Sure thing," he said. She pulled a styletometer from her bag and took a scratch. Three seconds later, the light on the styletometer showed green. A red or yellow reading would have required Wilson to give a full urine sample—a part of the job Ophelia disliked—and if that was positive, he would be arrested on the spot, since his violence profile was so low. The green reading meant he was clear.

"Good," said Ophelia, replacing the styletometer. "Let's talk about how you are doing."

They spent about 15 minutes talking about his comings and goings. Her aim was to help him relax and to gain a little rapport before getting on with the "instructions." This was one of Ophelia's skills—getting clients to relax in her presence—and she enjoyed being in control of her interaction style. All the while, she was watching him, looking for any cues that something might be wrong, that he might be trying to hide something.

Then she asked about his job, testing out how well he was doing with his supervisor. His answer was hesitant, and she realized this was an area to probe further.

With a bit of relief, he told her that his boss at the supermarket where he worked was giving him a hard time about his conviction. He wanted to quit. They talked about it for awhile, and she convinced him to stick it out for awhile longer. Mentally, she made a note to report the problem, knowing that a community relations specialist would follow up with the supervisor to try to head off any trouble. Wilson's job was a good one, and if he quit he would have trouble finding something in its place. Better to get the supervisor to stop the harassment.

After they had talked about the job for awhile, and Wilson seemed a bit more settled about it, Ophelia changed the subject.

"How's Angela? Could I talk to her?"

Wilson said he would have to wake her up, and when Ophelia said "Thanks," he realized that she intended to talk to his daughter anyway. So he went to get her.

A few minutes later, Angela walked out yawning and wearing her nightgown. She was a cutie—a redhead with big freckles.

Ophelia broke into a big smile and reached out, taking Angela's little hands into her own.

"Angela, how are you?" she asked sweetly. She and Angela had talked several times before, and she sensed that Angela liked her. By holding her hand, Ophelia would be able to talk to Angela for awhile and, without being obvious, check her arms for marks.

They talked about Angela's schoolwork and the play she was going to be in this term. Satisfied that there was no evidence of physical abuse, Ophelia gave Angela a hug and sent her back to bed.

It was routine to check for any evidence of violence for all child sex offenders who lived with children. Ophelia was very good at it—children seldom realized what she was doing. This was just another of the many ways that Ophelia had talents that justified being a specialist.

Being a specialist was very important, of course. Regular CCWs had a hard job. They got routine cases with mediocre profiles of risk and problems—and they got lots of them. It was not unusual for them to have as many as 300 cases to keep track of, and the compuwork, videophoning, and coordinations were a huge headache. And all they ever seemed to do was monitor payments of fines and performance of community service. No wonder turnover was so high for these jobs.

The specialists got better pay and better benefits and had much more interesting work organized into more reasonable workloads. There were three child–sex offender specialists in Middlesex County, and they co-shared a total of about seventy cases. Ophelia loved her work—and she was known to be good at it.

After Angela left the room, Ophelia complemented Wilson on how lovely a child she was. Then she asked to talk with Myra. Alone.

Her conversations with Myra were always a little strained, for Myra had never gotten over her partner's arrest and conviction. But her willingness to stand behind him—that and the lack of evidence that sexual misconduct had occurred with Angela—persuaded the judge to put Wilson on Special Probation rather than sentence him to three years in prison. He would be on probation for a full decade, according to his profile. Myra would have plenty of time to get used to supervision, which would grow gradually less frequent as Wilson continued to show no new misconduct and continued to respond well to therapy.

The most discomfort between Ophelia and Myra came when she asked about Wilson's sexuality with her. Even though Ophelia was very good at handling this sensitive area, Myra was embarrassed to discuss it. But according to his profile, his heterosexual adjustment was a key indicator of his overall adjustment.

An hour after arriving, Ophelia left Wilson's apartment. She was satisfied that all was well there, and she felt good about it. Wilson, she thought, had a great chance to make it.

Back in the company car, she entered the data about her visit. It took just a minute or two because the accountability system was designed to record what were called "key indicators" very efficiently. While Ophelia was free to add anything she wished, her experience was that the system usually asked everything that was important. Profiles again!

Once done with the Wilson report, she again asked for "instructions." The computer routed her to her next case, one Florence Trueblood.

But halfway to the Trueblood house, the computer voice abruptly chimed out the words, "Override. Override. Override." Ophelia took manual control of the car and pulled over. The computer screen gave her information that one of her cases—a Vernon Granger—was being questioned by police about his daughter's accusation that he had beaten her up. The instruction was to go immediately to Granger's house to investigate and—according to office policies—consider making an arrest. She put on her siren and sped away to Granger's.

The override was itself office policy. Specialists took pride in making their own arrests; the saying was, "The specialists clean up after themselves." By making their own arrests, specialists reinforced the importance of their work and kept their credibility high with courts and the police. It was a matter of pride.

When Ophelia arrived at Granger's, the police were about to handcuff him. She recognized one of the officers and went to him to learn what had happened. She learned that the daughter had been reported missing by Mrs. Granger, and that an hour or so ago the girl had been found hiding in some bushes near the edge of the city's main park. She told the police she had run away because she was afraid of her dad. There were ugly bruises on her head and arms. Granger denied everything, but they decided to make an arrest anyway.

Ophelia asked permission to take over on the arrest, and the police agreed to let her. They had learned that the specialists handled these situations very well, and they could save a lot of police time by letting CCWs do the dirty work. She went over to Granger, read him his rights, handcuffed him, and put him in the back of her car.

The whole arrest process—taking him to the precinct, booking him, and filing the appropriate information with headquarters—took nearly two hours. By the time she was done, she was tired, hungry—and a bit angry. After talking to Granger's daughter, Ophelia had decided to ask for a semen exam. The results weren't in, but she was pretty sure they would be positive. If so, Granger was looking at a long sentence: He was already on parole for assaulting a daughter from a prior marriage. The shame of it was that the whole family—Granger, his wife, and the three daughters—had been watched closely and in continual therapy ever since the wedding—as a condition of parole. How did people get themselves into these problems?

Back in her car, she asked again for "instructions." The computer said mutely, "Well done, Ms. Edison." Ophelia answered back absently, "Kiss my butt" and requested her lunch break. It was approved.

Lunch improved her mood a little, and the next three hours went fairly smoothly. She made four routine home visits—unusually, all without a hitch. By 3 P.M., it was time for "group."

One of the job satisfactions for specialists was participation in treatment. It was an area where she was able to use her skills and knowledge regarding sex offenders to best effect. It was also one of the few areas left where the accountability system allowed her free rein. By office policy, she was left completely on her own during the hour and a half of group. She wasn't even interrupted for an arrest.

Her co-therapist was Dana Richardson, a clinical social worker who was experienced with sex offenders. They conducted a weekly group therapy program for eight probationers or parolees convicted of child sex offenses. During group, they discussed a wide range of feelings and reactions the offenders had, and they confronted the offenders about the rationalizations they used to excuse their behavior.

The groups were one of the main reasons Ophelia liked the job. Much of her work involved monitoring offenders, and sometimes this work could get oppressive and heavy-handed. The group was a way to humanize her work, dealing with the lives of her clients and helping them work through their adjustment problems. It was also a great way for her to grow professionally. In addition to her contact with Dana, a man with whom she shared mutual respect, she had monthly meetings with a psychologist who consulted with Dana and her about the group's progress.

Today's particular group session was exhilarating. One of the members had made a new friendship with a divorcee who had a young son. The group spent a lot of its time focusing on the issues surrounding disclosure of his past to the woman. By the time group was over at 4:30, Ophelia had overcome her anger about the Granger episode and accepted it as a part of the job.

Learning to live with failure—not internalizing it when it happened—was probably the most difficult aspect of the job for Ophelia. When her sex offenders failed, it was almost always a tragedy that damaged a child's life. That made it hard to get over the feeling that "she could have done something to prevent it," a common feeling among her peers.

That was why she felt compassion without sympathy when she arrested someone for violating the rules. On the regular probation caseloads, people were almost never revoked from probation for mere rules violations. There had to be a new arrest to force the system to take action. But for the specialists, the stakes were too high. The first indication that a person was sliding into misconduct was always met with swift and stern action. There could be no other way.

Sometimes, though, after she arrested one of her clients for a new offense, she was tempted to leave the job. After all, there were plenty of correctional businesses out there she could work for: electronic monitoring, drug-control systems, work camps, and so on. In the last twenty years there had been a proliferation of nonprison programs for criminals, and they were all grouped together and called "intermediate sanctions." More than 40 percent of offenders were sent to one or another of these private programs. Only a handful were put on probation or parole and thereby assigned to community control.

By the end of her group session, she was pretty drained, which was typical. She and Dana talked for awhile about the clients in the group, after which she spent twenty minutes recording information about the session into the accountability system. It was important to record everything, because at the end of the year she would be evaluated. Her performance—arrests, groups, client progress, policy adherence, and so forth, all added together in a master formula—would be computed. Based on her score, and based on how the score compared to everyone else, she would receive a raise and a bonus. Ophelia was proud that she scored in the top 20 percent of staff every year on the job.

Her day had lasted nearly twelve hours, and she felt it was high time she left the office. On her way out the door, she inserted her index finger into the bioreader machine that stood at the end of the office hallway. The bioreader was a combined drug-testing device and physical checkup machine. It took her blood pressure, tested for illegal substances, and checked for developing infections. The machine, which helped prevent employee stress and work-related maladies, was another accomplishment of the work of the union.

The light burned green—"no problem"—and she unconsciously nodded a "thanks" to the inert device and headed out the door. Machines seemed to get better treatment than people these days.

She would make a stop at the health club; regular visits there reduced her health insurance costs and resulted in another work bonus. Then she would get a bite to eat on her way home. By now, the office car was in use by another CCW, so she would have to walk home from the health club. It was only a few blocks, and she didn't mind the stroll. The spring air smelled unusually clean, and she felt good about herself. She broke into a whistle.

EXPLANATION

Only people stupid enough to bet on the Baltimore Colts to defeat the New York Jets in the 1968 Super Bowl would try to predict the nature of community corrections in 2010. I did the former, and so I did the latter.

But the reader should be advised that it not only is hazardous to one's intellectual health to believe that one can foresee the future, but also a proven idiocy. In 1967, when the presidential commission ushered in an era called "reintegration," everyone foresaw the coming of a decade of community corrections. The prison was seen as an outdated and proven failure. Treatment methods in the community were seen as the only truly effective methods for dealing with crime as well as the certain wave of the future. Experts geared up for a generation of prison reform and community programming.

What then happened? During the 1970s and 1980s, America's prison population experienced a growth unprecedented in American history. The number of citizens locked up in prisons quadrupled, from fewer than 200,000 in 1967 to more than three-quarters of a million in 1990. The imprisonment rate per 100,000 citizens tripled from 97 in 1967 to 293 in 1990. Every failure should be so successful.

The point is that, however confident one might feel that the future is clearly laid out before one's eyes, the future that eventually occurs is bound to disappoint. Bearing this in mind, I offer the above speculative leap to the year 2010. It was based on a few ideas about some things that I think are likely to happen over the next twenty years.

Before getting into the predictions, I need to clarify a couple of terms used throughout. Sometimes, I will use the term *traditional* probation or parole supervision. By this, I mean the regular agencies' practices, which have remained fairly stable over the last century. In the case of probation, this means offenders who are assigned to the oversight of an officer in lieu of a prison sentence. For parole, "traditional" programs are those where an offender is released by a parole board and is placed under the supervision of a parole officer. My use of the term "traditional" means that there are "nontraditional" versions of these programs: Intensive probation, electronically monitored supervision, and special early release programs are illustrations.

This distinction is important because, as my predictions make clear, community supervision is increasingly splitting into two, sometimes quite different versions. The traditional versions remain funded and respected about as much they always have: not very well. The "new" versions are high-profile, ambitious attempts to be responsive to the main complaints people have lodged about traditional methods.

There is also one dominant force that will shape every aspect of the next two decades in corrections: The capacity of the prison system is finite. The rest of the criminal justice system can produce as many offenders as it can—and the capacity of law enforcement and the courts to produce them has accelerated—but prisons can absorb only so many offenders. The rest have to go to other correctional assignments.

Because of this, there will always be a powerful need for nonprison correctional alternatives. It is not merely a matter of justice—although for many, perhaps most, offenders a prison sentence is not just a punishment—it's a matter of economics.

With these points in mind, let us proceed to the predictions.

TEN PREDICTIONS

1. Specialized nontraditional supervision services will predominate in field services. In the 1980s, research and programming have both documented the complexity of criminality, from the general idea of criminal careers to the specific examples of drug-using offenders, sex offenders, and violent criminals. There is no way that a single person, carrying a heterogeneous caseload comprised of all types of felons, can be a fully capable "expert" in how to deal with all of them. Specializing caseloads into subgroups of more homogenous types of problems is an idea that simply makes sense.

2. Intermediate sanctions options will grow in number and size. Intermediate sanctions are types of punishment that fall in severity between traditional probation and traditional parole. Since the mid–1980s, there has been a proliferation of correctional programs that are not as lenient as probation but not as severe as prison. Besides being politically popular, these programs are a public-relations godsend to community corrections. They advertise themselves as "tough," they cost far less than prison, and many have been shown to have very low recidivism. With a good "rep," a real demand, and a history of delivery on its promises, it is hard to see how intermediate sanctions are not the correctional growth industry of the future.

3. Traditional probation and parole supervision will handle a decreasing share of the offender population. It follows from the first two predictions that the future of the traditional supervision methods is not a bright one. This does not mean that community-based sanctions will be unimportant by 2010. Frankly, there is no way that corrections can survive without a strong, healthy nonprison component. Yet there is also no way that full funding of nonprison alternatives is feasible.

The likely scenario is that traditional types of community supervision—which have not enjoyed strong support in criminal justice since the 1960s—will languish. Instead, growing emphasis will be given to correctional approaches that are not as expensive as prison, but which do not align themselves with traditional techniques.

4. *Private-sector involvement in community corrections will have grown to become a powerful factor in policy and program development.* We already have seen a growth of privatization in community corrections. The profits have apparently been enough that new businesses are starting in many areas of the country. The conditions for new businesses are ideal. Correctional crowding guarantees a large pool of potential "customers." Disquiet about traditional methods guarantees a business environment sympathetic to new ideas and new businesses.

5. *A probation office will lose a civil liability suit for $5 million.* The liability of probation and parole officers has grown dramatically in recent years. Some agencies now calculate liability settlements into their annual budgetary projections.

Civil liability occurs when a probation or parole officer fails to supervise a client according to established policies and procedures, enabling the client to commit a new crime. Already, there have been suits that resulted in awards to victims of more than $1 million. The only thing that will stop an eye-popping, multimillion-dollar award against a probation agency is a legislative cap on the size of allowable civil damages.

6. *Accountability-oriented systems will dominate new technologies.* In the last decade, the story about community corrections has been its growing reliance on systems of accountability. The most obvious example is the National Institute of Correction's Model Case Management System. This approach sets specific standards for supervision contracts and bases the distribution of cases among officers on time-study data about prior performance. There has also been an emphasis placed on managerial supervision of the work of line officers, especially as it relates to conformity with policy and procedure.

Two forces have spawned this wave of accountability measures: (1) the powerful threat of agency liability and (2) the fact that funding is increasingly dependent on showing that programs are effective. These forces will continue to grow in importance over the next twenty years, and so agencies will be even more inclined to remedy them by developing techniques of improved accountability.

7. *The amount of "formal" discretion exercised by line workers in community corrections will diminish.* Accountability systems, when they work well, have one main result: They reduce the range of decisions officers can make regarding their clients. They do so by reducing the amount of discretion that officers have concerning how to manage their cases.

The loss of discretion is an important change in the nature of the job for the officer. For many officers, what makes the job interesting and challenging is the chance to "work with people." The phrase, as they use it, connotes the ability to be creative in case management, to respond to cases with gut feelings and seat-of-the-pants decisions. It makes the officer feel like something of an artist—or maybe more like a cowboy or a "Lone Ranger"—in control of his or her own caseload as though it were a domain.

8. *Treatment programs will make a comeback in the field, especially those based on a "partnership" between corrections and a treatment provider.* Evidence is growing that treatment is one of the best ways to control clients' criminal behavior. It is a surprising circumstance, after all the criticism that has been applied to the concept, to find that in the mid-1990s, treatment programs appear to be more important than ever as a part of the correctional arsenal.

The nature of the treatments have changed, of course. They are no longer the general "counseling" approaches designed to generate "insight" into the causes of criminal behavior. They are much more structured interventions—treatment systems—that combine behavior monitoring and control with cognitive counseling. They presume a depth of knowledge about particular patterns of criminal behavior, so they are often done collaboratively with "experts."

9. *The importance of information technologies will overwhelm traditional practices in virtually every way.* It would be remarkable if the computer age, which has transformed the world of work, did not also change the nature of probation and parole work. The only real question is, "How will the work change?"

The description of the need for accountability systems has already shown how important information will be for parole and probation agencies. Critical to accountability is the ability to demonstrate what has been done about cases, and this requires recording information about actions. Moreover, it is information about offenders that provides treatment profiles, classification scores, and instructions for supervision from case-management systems. It is impossible to think of the future of community supervision without also thinking about information.

10. Labor–management relations in probation and parole will be increasingly vitriolic. If earlier predictions are correct, then the job will change a great deal in the coming years. Officers' discretion will be essentially eradicated, at least formally. All actions will be sifted through the "opinion" of a computerized prepackaged set of policies and procedures. Liability for failures to follow the procedures will be higher than ever.

In the face of these pressures, local professional organizations will be more and more inclined to focus on bread-and-butter labor issues instead of problems of the profession. Salaries, wages, benefits, and working conditions will be the area of contention between government and workers. Probation and parole organizations will become increasingly antagonistic about these issues.

FIVE MORE TENTATIVE PREDICTIONS

1. Caseloads will not be the only way in which probation and parole caseloads are organized. The caseload is an administrative convenience; it allows the "boss" to decide how to hand cases out and how to hold officers accountable. When there are new accountability systems available, the caseload will be valuable only to the degree that it manages cases well.

2. Revocation of community supervision status will become dual track: Regular cases will be revoked only for new arrests, and specialized cases will be revoked for rules violations. Already it is difficult to get a case revoked from traditional community supervision without evidence of a new crime. This has not been the case for the special programs, however: These normally have very high "technical" failure rates. There is no obvious reason why this trend would stop.

3. A completely private community corrections system will be tried somewhere on an experimental basis. Depending on how the privatization experiments turn out, this is a likely scenario. After all, private vendors provide medical services to government on a contractual basis. Why not extend this to community corrections? The promise will be pretty tempting: better service at less cost. Some jurisdiction somewhere is bound to try it. The only thing that would interfere would be a resounding failure of correctional privatization in other spheres. This seems unlikely.

4. Fines and community service will replace traditional probation for nonserious, low-risk offenders. These are cheap, effective, and popular sanctions.

5. Supervision role conflict will be considered unimportant. Evidence is mounting that far too much has been made of the "conflict" between law enforcement and social work in community supervision. Increasingly, it will be recognized that the role is not a duality of two ideas, but an integration of two themes: control and change.

FIVE DEFINITE PREDICTIONS (PROBABLY)

1. Risk prediction will not be more accurate. There are a few ways to improve profiling systems to increase prediction accuracy. But in the long run, prediction will not become more refined until people become more predictable. This is a problem of evolution and is not going to be resolved in two decades.

2. Every state will experience a "Willie Horton" case—a situation in which a serious offender who is released into the community commits a heinous crime. Failure—and its effects on the system—will continue to be uniform experience in community corrections. Nothing will eradicate it—the only solution is to prepare for it.

3. The probation or parole officer's task uncertainty will not diminish. All of the above means that the work of the probation officer will still contain a great deal of subtlety. Seeing how offenders act, making interpretations of their behavior, managing the interaction of supervision—this will be the main content of the job. No amount of performance structuring can eliminate it.

4. The use of "electronic monitoring" will have topped out. Such use is limited to only certain kinds of cases—those whose effective management is augmented by making sure they are home at certain times. The number of cases fitting this profile will be finite and will not feed an ever-expanding industry.

5. One or more of my predictions will not pan out. No comment.

FOR FURTHER READING

Todd R. Clear and Vincent O'Leary. *Controlling the Offender in the Community: Reforming the Community Supervision Function.* Lexington, MA: Lexington Books, 1983.

This book focuses on the important role of reducing risk to the public through probation supervision. Attention is given to the role of the probation officer in reducing recidivism and protecting the public. Arguments are made for focusing on risk reduction as the traditional treatment role.

Todd R. Clear. *Offender Assessment and Evaluation: The Presentence Investigation Report.* Cincinnati, OH: Anderson, 1989.

The presentence investigation is a key document in criminal justice, influencing decisions from sentencing through parole release. This book examines the role of the presentence investigation, how reports are constructed, and how they are used.

John Irwin. *The Felon.* Berkeley: University of California Press, 1987.

This classic study examines the life of the felon from criminal history and identity through prison and supervision in the community. The book examines issues of adjustment in the community and recidivism. The research is based on offender interviews and describes the many obstacles to reintegration into society.

Joan Petersilia, Susan Turner, James Cahan, and Joyce Peterson. *Granting Felons Probation: Public Risks and Alternatives.* Santa Monica, CA: RAND Corporation, 1985.

This important study of the use of probation for felons in two California counties examines adjustment on probation and makes significant argument for intensive supervision. This involves supervision based on risk criteria and the provision of services.

Elliot Studt. *Surveillance and Service in Parole: A Report of the Parole Action Study.* Los Angeles: Institute of Government and Public Affairs, 1972.

This is the classic study of probation and parole supervision. It focuses on the task of supervision and the competing demands put on probation and parole officers and how they cope with them.

DISCUSSION QUESTIONS

1. How does the "community control agent" of the future differ from the tradition probation officer of today?

2. Comment on the role of computer-assisted technology in the provision of probation services. Will such technology enhance the supervision roles or dehumanize the probation profession?

3. Discuss the relationship between growing prison populations and the structure of probation services in the year 2010.

4. What is the role of "accountability-oriented systems" in the future of probation services? Are there any inherent dangers and concerns with such a system?

5. How will alternatives to traditional probation affect the future of the organization of probation systems?

☆

PART III

Other Crime and Justice Issues in the Year 2010

What are some of the concerns that will face the criminal justice system in 2010? The authors of this final section address significant issues that will continue to be of importance to society and affect the way the criminal justice system will function in the next millennium. Issues such as drugs and crime, the role of the death penalty in deterring crime, juvenile crime and society's response to it, and conceptualization of crime and justice in the next century are all important topics that citizens of the future will have to confront. Today's criminal justice student will be forced to deal with these issues as both citizen and member of the criminal justice profession.

In Chapter 12, Ralph A. Weisheit begins this section by exploring a serious issue. He examines the complexities of drugs and crime. Both the advocates of drug decriminalization and critics of such an approach have their rationales as to why their views are the most appropriate in dealing with the drug problem. Whether you are a supporter or critic of the government's role in handling the drug problem, Weisheit provides an insightful analysis of how the issue of drug legalization raises central questions about the efficacy of the law in handling the drug problem.

Weisheit suggests that before legalization can be seriously considered, there must be an examination of several factors relevant to the
debate. Professor Weisheit is interested in exploring the drugs and crime
connection. His analysis highlights how this relationship must be understood within the context of many social, economic, and technological factors. He provides neither easy answers as to whether drugs and
crime are related nor ready-made prescriptions for the future. Instead,
he leaves us with more questions about the drugs and crime connection
and asks us to consider the complexity of the issue.

The notion that the criminal justice system is complex is not a new
one. Proponents and critics of the death penalty, for example, have often
used technical, moral, and scientific arguments for their various positions. In Chapter 13, Gennaro F. Vito adds to this debate by exploring
the complexities associated with the imposition of the death penalty
into the next century. In particular, he examines the evolving case law
and how it is making the imposition of the death penalty much easier
for criminal prosecutors. In addition, Vito argues that the issue of
deterrence and the death penalty must be examined within the context
of much uncertainty. His review of available evidence suggests that we
simply do not know whether the death penalty deters criminal offenders. He proposes that this uncertainty will not diminish by 2010 and
that there will still be many supporters of the death penalty. We are
offered no reason to believe that there will be a changing attitude in
society or in the courts to restrict the application of the death penalty.
Vito, in fact, sees the death penalty as being more generously used by
2010.

For critics of the death penalty, such a projection is disconcerting
and troublesome. For death penalty advocates, this general societal
acceptance of its usage in the criminal justice system is viewed as a
reaffirmation of core values. Most notable is the value position that
justice demands extreme forms of punishment in cases in which the
crimes are so serious that they threaten the very fabric of social order.
It is the idea that there are primary values in society and that the
criminal justice system must respond to protect such values that makes
the death penalty, in part, such a volatile issue in contemporary society.

Differing values have always been a part of American society. One of
the noticeable differences between our society and others has been the
willingness of groups of people to live in harmony even with intense

divisions among them. These divisions are usually over competing values and ideas on how a particular issue should be addressed by society. In Chapter 14, Carl E. Pope examines the issue of values when he speculates on the future workings of the juvenile justice system. He introduces several concerns that can be construed as value positions on how juvenile offenders should be treated and processed in the criminal justice system.

One value position is that our society generally has viewed children as different from adults; as a result, we have treated children differently in the juvenile justice system than we have adults in the criminal justice system. This general sentiment has been criticized as too soft on both crime and youthful offenders. Critics have argued that many juvenile offenders have committed serious, often violent, crimes, and that "getting tough" with such offenders is an appropriate response. Such a position reflects a set of values that says societal protection is more important over the welfare of the child and that the delinquent today is not the same as the offender of the past. Pope examines the historical distinction between the juvenile justice system and the adult criminal justice system, which is blurred now and may be lost in the next millennium. Examining trends found across the country, Pope concludes that in many cases the juvenile justice system is becoming similar to the adult system in some dimensions while remaining different in others. As such, it is not clear that the juvenile justice system of the future will mirror its adult counterpart, although evidence clearly suggests that the traditional distinction will continue to be blurred as we move into the twenty-first century.

12

Drugs and Crime:

What If . . .

RALPH A. WEISHEIT
Illinois State University

I n the 1980s and early 1990s, the criminal justice system has been
overwhelmed by an unprecedented number of offenders. The "assembly line" of justice has been speeded up by expanding police
efforts, augmenting the courts, building new prisons, and seeking alternative sanctions that allow some offenders to bypass several stages of the
process. Some observers have predicted that if the number of offenders
continues to increase, the system will break down completely.

Many problems now facing the criminal justice system have been
attributed, either directly or indirectly, to drugs. In a direct sense, the
criminal justice system has given an increased emphasis to making drug
arrests and extending the penalties for drug offenses. At the same time,
there is evidence that even these expanded efforts have had only a
minimal impact on the number of users in society. Nationally, drug use
is declining, but people are more likely to avoid drugs or to quit using
them because of health concerns rather than from fear of criminal
prosecution. Further, these declines may be primarily among casual
users, leaving a core of heavy drug users who may account for more
than their share of crime and drug use.

Drugs have also had an indirect effect on the system. Drug users place greater demands on services than do other offenders because drug use is often only one of a constellation of health, social, and economic problems facing these offenders. Prisons, for example, face dramatically escalating costs in caring for offenders who contract AIDS from intravenous drug use. Their own problems with drugs also can have an impact on addicts' immediate families. The children of drug users are of particular concern because of the role models drug users provide, because of the inability of some users to care adequately for their children, and because of exposure to drugs during neonatal development. Further, the impact of drugs on the system extends beyond those arrested for drug offenses. Studies show that the majority of people in prison have a substance-abuse problem, whether or not they were arrested for a drug or alcohol offense.

Some theorists believe that responding to the drug problem has also involved adopting practices and laws that may undermine basic principles of fairness and justice. Among these practices are lengthy court delays and concomitant pressure on defense attorneys to enter guilty pleas, which has the effect of denying offenders their day in court or which may require them to spend a year or more in jail awaiting trial. At the other end of the process, prison crowding has forced the early release of inmates. In some jurisdictions, convicted offenders serve only one month in prison for each year of their sentence. Justice has been undermined not only by a system that some observers fear is nearing collapse, but also by changes in the law that, for drug offenses, suspend otherwise important constitutional and procedural protections. For example, as many as 80 percent of those whose homes, cars, boats, or other property has been forfeited under drug laws are never charged with a criminal offense, and many are completely innocent citizens. Even if their property (such as the truck of the professional truck driver) is eventually returned, they may be bankrupted by the lack of income during the months that might take.

It is not only that forfeiture laws are sometimes applied overzealously, but also that they are applied in drug cases but not in other serious crimes. For example, an individual who has a marijuana cigarette in his car risks losing the car to authorities, while a similar response would be considered brutish and uncivilized for most other crimes, such as driving under the influence of alcohol (DUI). It has been noted that only a few states allow forfeiture of cars used in DUI, and even in those states forfeiture may be avoided by showing that the family would be inconvenienced by the action. Imagine seizing the cars and houses of corrupt savings-and-loans executives because they used the cars to take them to work, and their home was sometimes used for meetings with clients. Before his retirement, Justice Thurgood Marshall, easily the most liberal justice on the Supreme Court in the 1980s and early 1990s, was quoted as saying that he would not even consider the appeals of drug offenders, because he would not wish to help them in any way. In short, we have tolerated laws and practices in drug cases that are not allowed for other crimes and that strain the very notion of justice.

The number of cases that must be processed reflects the magnitude of the problem, and the willingness to surrender basic principles of fairness and justice shows the emotional response created by the issue of drugs. Both factors make long-term predictions even more tenuous than is true for other kinds of projections. Even short-term (i.e., within a year) guesses about the nature of the drug problem have persistently been incorrect. Predictions in the 1980s that crack cocaine would become commonplace throughout small cities and rural areas within a year did not materialize. Similarly, predictions that methamphetamines would replace cocaine as the drug of choice and would sweep the nation within a year or two of their discovery in several urban areas were not proven true. Even worse is the inability to agree on how the nature and extent of the problem might be measured. Some measures of the drug problem (e.g., arrest rates) suggest that it has increased dramatically, while other measures (e.g., household surveys) suggest that it has been declining for some time. Further, there is no measure that appears more than modestly accurate as a gauge of the overall problem.

Predicting the nature of the drug problem and its impact on the criminal justice system in the year 2010 is important for planners and for those preparing to work in the criminal justice system. Given its current impact, the nature and extent of the drug problem in the year 2010 might well determine the character of law and criminal justice, and it will shape the nature of work in the system.

Before making guesses about how the problem might look and how policies might shape the problem, it is necessary to consider the factors relevant to the nature and extent of drug use. There are great variations in patterns of drug use over time, from one country to the next and even within an individual country. Understanding the factors that account for these variations is an important step in the formulation of successful drug policies. These variations also warn against the utility of a single policy over time and warn against the development of a global drug policy. Although some theorists have suggested that a single drug policy is appropriate for all nations, even a cursory glance at cultural variations in drug use make it clear that what works in one country may not work in another.

Finally, it must be cautioned that predicting the rise or fall in popularity of a particular drug or of a particular means of ingestion is as difficult as predicting fashion trends. And, like fashion trends, no single factor satisfactorily accounts for changing patterns. With this caveat in mind, the focus now shifts to factors that shape the patterns of drug use.

UNDERSTANDING
PATTERNS OF DRUG USE

Predicting the impact of various policy alternatives regarding drugs requires understanding the factors that shape the nature and extent of the drug problem. These factors can be broadly placed in four categories: the social context of drug use, economic factors, the political context of drug policies, and technological developments relevant to drugs and the drug business.

The Social Context of Drug Use

History shows that patterns of drug use can only be partially attributed to characteristics of a drug itself. What may seem to be clear connections between the pharmacological action of a drug and subsequent behavior are anything but clear. The way a drug is used and the perceived effects are also determined by custom and culture. The following examples will make the point.

Alcohol Although heavy alcohol use is associated with aggression and expressions of bravado in this country, there are cultures in which alcohol does not lead to such behaviors. In fact, in the early United States, there was no connection between alcohol and crime, although heavy alcohol use was common and there were few rules regulating alcohol. In contrast, current per capita alcohol use is lower, but alcohol is now strongly linked to aggression and crime, with at least half of prison inmates reporting they used alcohol at the time of the offense and a high percentage reporting a history of alcohol problems. Such physical reactions as delirium tremens (the DTs or "shakes") are common features of withdrawal from alcohol by full-blown alcoholics, although not in early America and apparently not in all societies that use alcohol. Similarly, heavy drinking is commonly followed by hangovers in this country, but that is not true in all societies.

Marijuana In the United States, marijuana is thought to make the user passive, calm, and peaceful. But in the early 1900s in Mexico, marijuana was believed to lead users to acts of violence and aggression (similar to the association we now believe exists between alcohol and aggression). Further, although marijuana is defined as a mind-altering recreational drug today, early Americans used it extensively in medicines without seeing it as a recreational drug and, apparently, without reported problems of psychological dependency or abuse.

Heroin Although heroin use is associated with increased criminality and street addicts are thought to be willing to do just about anything to get their fix, researchers have found that heroin sold on the streets is often several times weaker than the concentration required for subjects to recognize its presence in blind tests. Similarly, I have been told by jail officials that withdrawal from heroin is no problem for most new inmates because the purity of street heroin is so low. How can someone be driven to crime and be obsessed with obtaining a drug that is so diluted that they cannot detect its presence and whose "addiction" is not even accompanied by withdrawal? Clearly, the "effects" we associate with heroin are shaped by more than the chemical reaction of the drug.

Aspirin Routinely taken by millions of Americans, aspirin is thought of by few in this country as an addictive drug. This was not the case in the 1950s, however, when aspirin "addicts" were considered a problem. Perhaps the most celebrated case is that reported by Truman Capote in his book *In Cold Blood,* in which one of the killers was routinely feeding his addiction to aspirin.

Although the biochemical action of a drug is relevant to addiction and the drugs–crime connection, it is only one part of the issue and perhaps a minor part at that. More important may be the social context in which drugs are used and the expectations users have about the impact of the drug. Prediction about coming "drug crises" are so often wrong because policy makers focus on the biochemical action of the drug and ignore the social contexts.

Economic Factors

The most disturbing effects of drugs are most concentrated in the most impoverished sections of our country. Drug dealing can provide income when few legitimate opportunities exist. It can also supply dealers with a sense of purpose and achievement when there are few other opportunities for success. Gangs are increasingly described as businesses rather than as purely social groups, and drugs are usually their main business.

It would be a mistake, however, to view the drug business as only tied to the impoverished. During much of the early 1980s, banks routinely ignored laws requiring them to report large cash transactions, and several U.S. banks not only facilitated laundering drug money but also found the practice highly lucrative. During the early 1990s, in the largest banking scandal in history, the Bank of Credit and Commerce International (BCCI) was shown to have built its operations on, among other things, the laundering of drug money. Similarly, sellers of luxury cars, boats, and homes have directly profited by helping drug dealers conceal the source of their illegal income.

Although the ties between poverty and drugs may seem obvious, it is also true that the drug trade is facilitated by economic development. It has been suggested, for example, that the flood of cocaine from South America to the United States would never have been possible without the construction of the Pan-American highway in Peru—a country that is perhaps the largest single producer of coca in the world. The same highway that fueled economic development by making it easier to move products over land also facilitated moving cocaine from remote areas to seaports and airfields.

Similarly, as we move toward a world economy, the sheer volume of people and products that cross national borders make it necessary for governments seeking economic development to make such travel as fast and simple as possible. Knocking down international barriers to legitimate trade also makes it easier to smuggle drugs undetected. Improvements in air, sea, and land transportation help drug traffickers as much as legitimate businesspeople. The same technologies of communication and transportation that have made international corporations flourish have also facilitated the rise of international drug operations.

Economic development is not only directly related to the production and use of drugs but also has an impact on drug-related activities, such as money laundering and the transshipment of drugs. It is ironic, for example, that the bank secrecy laws of Panama, which allow traffickers to secretly launder drug money, were initially encouraged by the

United States as a way for Panama to become a major center of international finance—drawing investors through bank secrecy laws that facilitated tax evasion. Similarly, developing a thriving tourist industry can make a country an attractive transshipment point. Developing tourism requires laws that allow people to easily move in and out of a country, and it also means that strangers with large amounts of cash arouse little suspicion.

The link between economic development and drugs is clearly illustrated by one of the most shameful events in the history of drugs, the Opium Wars between Great Britain and China from 1840 to 1842. In the early 1800s, the Chinese government, with strong public support, sought to control opium within its borders by strictly prohibiting it and by banning opium ships from its ports. These ships were controlled by British and U.S. companies, who first responded by arming their merchant ships and firing on Chinese patrols. Then, in 1840, the British declared war, the result of which was a victory for the British and the forced opening of Chinese ports to the opium trade.

Though on a much smaller scale, the United States is currently involved in a contemporary version of the Opium Wars. Several Asian countries have adopted restrictions on the use and availability of tobacco, parallel to developments in the United States. The United States, concerned about the impact of slumping cigarette sales on domestic tobacco manufacturers, has threatened harsh economic sanctions against Asian countries that do not increase their purchase of U.S.-made cigarettes.

The Political Context of Drug Policies

Unfortunately for the war on drugs, drug policies are created and enforced in a highly charged political climate. Within this climate, drugs are only one among many problems that must compete for resources and attention. Quite often, other considerations are given a higher priority than combating drugs. For example, between the 1960s and the 1980s, Great Britain adopted increasingly restrictive policies to curb access to narcotic drugs (which previously could be dispensed by a licensed physician). In the late 1980s, however, this trend was halted by the concern with AIDS. Needle-exchange programs were established, and educational programs shifted from a focus on abstinence to a focus on using drugs safely (i.e., not sharing used needles). The nature of drug policies and practices in Great Britain in the 1980s has been contrary to the trend it was following and could not have been predicted before the rise of AIDS.

Similarly, although the United States has a long history of opposing drugs, it has frequently given a higher priority to international relations and fighting communism. As a result, drug trafficking in other countries has been overlooked, tolerated, or in some cases facilitated by the United States. Although dozens of examples are available, only a few will be given here to illustrate the point.

Panama In 1989, the United States invaded Panama and arrested its military leader, Manuel Noriega. The invasion and arrest were to carry out an arrest warrant against Noriega for drug trafficking. It was the first time a foreign head of state had ever been arrested in his own country to carry out a U.S. arrest warrant. While many applauded the arrest, there was considerable evidence that the United States had known about his drug activities for some time, even while he was receiving commendations from the United States for his antidrug activities and while he was on the payroll of the CIA. There is also evidence that the United States moved against him only after he had outlived his usefulness in supporting other political objectives for the United States in South America. As an ironic aside, it has been reported that following the removal of Noriega, the drug trade is more active than ever in Panama, and Panamanian resources for fighting drugs have been sharply reduced.

Mexico In 1985, a U.S. Drug Enforcement Administration agent, Kiki Camerena, was seized, tortured, and killed by Mexican police officers because he was coming too close to interfering with their drug activities. There is substantial evidence that the United States helped to delay investigations into the murder because there was concern that Mexico might not sign a trade agreement if the integrity of its government were called into question. It has also been charged that the United States went forward with an investigation only after the evidence tying the murder to high-ranking officials had disappeared, leaving a few low-level Mexican police officers to take the blame for the killing.

Afghanistan During the Russian invasion of Afghanistan in the 1980s, rebels in that country took up the fight with covert assistance from the United States. Afghanistan also happens to be among the largest producers of opium in the world, and it was through the heroin trade that rebels were able to generate additional funds to support their resistance movement. While the United States was cracking down on heroin dealers within its own borders, it apparently tolerated the production and sale of opium by rebels in Afghanistan.

El Salvador There is some support for allegations that in their passion to help the rebels in El Salvador (against the wishes of the U.S. Congress), several members of the Reagan Administration not only provided secret money to the rebels, but also used military aircraft to facilitate drug shipments into the United States. Allowing these drug shipments was part of an agreement from which the United States gained access to secret airfields that it could use to supply arms to the rebels.

The above illustrations are only a few of many. The purpose in presenting them is not to pass judgment on the wisdom of those policies, but to demonstrate how policies that focus on the control of drugs are sometimes subverted in favor of other objectives. These are examples of conscious decisions to undercut drug policies. Perhaps more common are drug policies that are well intentioned but have unintended consequences that may make the problem worse. A few examples will make the point more clear.

Scotland and AIDS Within the British Isles are variations in handling the drug problem. In Scotland, for example, police have been relatively less tolerant of drug paraphernalia such as needles and syringes. They have discouraged their sale within cities and confiscated them from people's possession. Although such policies are undoubtedly intended to curb intravenous drug use, one consequence has been a shortage of clean needles. As a result, the incidence of seropositivity for AIDS among drug users in Edinburgh is nearly five times that of users in London, where clean needles are more readily available.

Marijuana and the Military Another example of well-intentioned policy with harmful unintended consequences is the U.S. military's response to marijuana use by soldiers during the Vietnam War. To curb marijuana use, strict regulations against it were put in place and enforcement was stepped up. Although some marijuana users did quit, others simply switched to heroin, which was relatively cheap, easier to hide, and harder for enforcers to detect. It is not clear that a policy that reduces marijuana use is a good bargain if it increases heroin use. More recently, a similar phenomenon was reported in Wisconsin, where it was speculated that a crackdown on marijuana among high school students did make the drug harder to get and did drive up the price, but that students were simply switching to LSD as an alternative drug.

Turning Kids into Dealers In 1973, Governor Nelson Rockefeller of New York signed legislation that dramatically increased the penalties for selling even small amounts of drugs. Although those convicted faced a minimum of fifteen years and a maximum of life imprisonment for selling as little as one ounce of heroin, the tough sanctions did not make an appreciable dent in drug trafficking. In fact, drug use and drug-related crimes actually rose under these laws. Instead, dealers simply recruited as sellers kids who were too young to be included within the law's harsh sentencing requirements. Thus, the law had the unintended consequence of introducing an entire generation of young people to the business of dealing on the street, a condition that has been repeated in cities across the country.

Technology

Anticipating drug patterns and their relationship to criminal justice also requires forecasting technological changes. Over the years, technology has shaped drug production, drug smuggling, drug dealing, the means by which drugs are administered, the ability to detect drugs, and drug treatment. The focus now shifts to brief illustrations of technology's role in each of these aspects of the drug issue.

Production Although a few illegal drugs occur in nature (e.g., marijuana, mushrooms, and opium), many are either chemically altered versions of natural drugs (e.g., opium is made into morphine or heroin) or entirely synthetic (e.g., LSD and methamphetamines). It should be obvious that LSD could not exist until the technology was in place to produce it. It should also be obvious that the number of synthetic drugs that may be created in the future is almost unlimited. Further, synthetic drugs can be hundreds or even thousands of times more potent that the natural derivatives they simulate. This is a problem for the midlevel and street-level dealer because it is more difficult to dilute such chemicals into small batches of consistent potency. It is a great boon, however, for the trafficker trying to move drugs across the country or across national borders. More important, the ability to synthesize drugs in the laboratory precludes the need for open land for growing crops, special climatic conditions, or elaborate international smuggling networks. It is no longer necessary to enter the jungles of Peru to obtain the raw materials needed for cocaine or to travel to Pakistan to obtain the raw opium for heroin.

In addition to replacing existing drugs (and generating entirely new ones), technology can also enhance the production of naturally occurring drugs such as marijuana. Today, hydroponics and special lighting systems make it possible to grow marijuana virtually anyplace on the globe and also make detection significantly more difficult.

Finally, technology may lead to the development of entirely new techniques for altering consciousness, techniques that are already being referred to as "electronic drugs." One category of electronic drug is produced by what the magazine *High Times* refers to as "brain machines." These devices use special goggles and headphones to send images and sounds that alter mood and can induce particular emotional responses. Another form of electronic drug is *virtual reality,* a computer simulation in which the user wears goggles and special gloves to create and move around in completely artificial "worlds." In virtual reality, the user and the simulation become one (or so it seems to the user). Dr. Timothy Leary, the former Harvard psychologist who urged students of the 1960s to use LSD, now rejects chemical drugs and argues that virtual reality will be the drug of the 1990s. One thing is certain: Electronic drugs will require us to rethink what we mean by addiction and drug use.

Drug Smuggling Smugglers have benefited greatly from sophisticated radar and communication systems. Further, the development of electronic money transfer has greatly assisted in international money-laundering operations. Smugglers have also used technology to help hide their supplies. One particularly innovative strategy involved putting cocaine into molded vinyl, such as that found in the soles of tennis shoes. The vinyl objects were then brought into the United States, where the cocaine was extracted. It has also been suggested that in the future smugglers might utilize such things as remote-controlled aircraft to transport drugs over the borders at altitudes below radar detection, with little risk of arrest should the plane be detected by officials or even shot down.

Drug Dealing Drug dealers have a variety of technological innovations at their fingertips. Telephone pagers and the wide availability of mobile telephones have made it possible for dealers to conduct a high-volume business while having no more than a small amount of drugs on their person at any given moment. Improvements in transportation and communication have also made it possible for dealers to expand their operations into other cities and states, in some cases using overnight express-mail services to ship drugs from city to city. Dealers (and smugglers) also have access to sophisticated weapons with laser-guided sighting systems and ammunition that is capable of piercing bulletproof vests.

Using Drugs Perhaps the single most significant technological development regarding the use of drugs was the development of the hypodermic needle in the mid-1800s, making intravenous drug use possible. In an effort to boost heroin consumption in the era of AIDS and a shortage of clean needles, heroin suppliers in the early 1990s began shipping heroin in smokable crystalline form. Of all the issues relating to drugs, it is consumption that remains the most technologically primitive. There is no reason why this should continue to be true, however.

Developments in medicine suggest one way in which the administration of drugs may change in the future. The nicotine patch, for example, slowly administers a steady dose of nicotine through the skin without puncturing it. A similar patch has been used with highly concentrated morphine. The high concentrations of drugs required for these patches to work would be a problem for many drugs now available on the street, but patches would be ideally suited for administering the extremely potent synthetic drugs discussed above.

Detecting Drugs Those in the drug business are not alone in benefiting from technology. Enforcement and prevention efforts have also utilized technology not available even two decades ago. To counter drug production, authorities have at their disposal satellite information and an improved communications network to coordinate eradication activities. It has also been suggested that by examining pollen grains in drug shipments, authorities can determine the source of a drug shipment. In addition, eradication efforts have relied heavily on technologies for producing herbicides, helicopters, and cameras for recording evidence. Technology has also been utilized to determine drug use. Widespread drug testing, for example, is a relatively recent phenomenon made possible by improved tests and reduced costs for testing. Although nothing as portable and accurate as the breathalyzer now exists for detecting drugs, the development of such instruments is likely by the year 2010, making laws against driving under the influence of drugs enforceable—provided that new drugs are not developed that are not easily tested for or that mask the presence of existing drugs.

Drug Treatment Technology also has an emerging role in drug-treatment programs. Drug testing can ensure that participants in drug treatment remain drug-free during their treatment, and electronic monitors can track their behavior to keep them from high-drug areas. Biofeedback has been tried with drug users, as has a device that when attached to cigarettes gradually weans the user from nicotine. Several treatment programs have experimented with computers programmed to provide self-directed diagnosis of drug problems and, on the basis of this diagnosis, assist in the selection of treatment strategies.

Technology may also have a role in developing drugs for the treatment of drug dependency, though its record in this regard has been mixed to date. Antabuse, for example, causes the user to have a violent physical reaction to the presence of alcohol in the body, and it has been used to treat alcoholics. It has not, however, proven to be a magical cure for the problem. Some tobacco smokers have reported success using nicotine gum to withdraw from cigarettes, though the long-term effectiveness of this approach is not yet clear. Similarly, it was once thought that methadone would block the effects of heroin and thus prove successful in treating heroin addicts. Although initial reports were positive and it may have worked for some, other addicts simply added methadone dependence to their other drug problems, and a black market in methadone quickly developed.

It is unlikely that technology will ever solve the problem of addiction, but it is certain that new technologies will be applied to drug treatment and that some of these may speed the process of recovery. It is also possible that, as in the case of nicotine gum, technology will provide safer ways to use existing illegal drugs.

For both sides in the drug war, technology has proven a two-edged sword. Although producers can duplicate cocaine or heroin in the laboratory, some of their mixtures have proven poisonous and crippling. And although technology has made marijuana eradication easier, it may also have contributed to the problem. For example, vigorous enforcement efforts in California may have hastened the development of marijuana growing in other states and encouraged the development of indoor growing. Similarly, drug tests currently focus on a limited number of drugs, making other drugs (such as hallucinogenic mushrooms and LSD) attractive alternatives for users who risk being tested.

In this section, some of the factors that shape patterns of drug use have been discussed. Many of these factors are difficult to predict, and the particular combination of outcomes by the year 2010 is impossible to know. In addition to formal legal proceedings, the drug problem is shaped by a combination of the social context of drug use, economic factors, the political context, and technology.

Our knowledge about the drug problem does make two points very clear. First, drugs will never be stopped by legal sanctions alone. No drug policy can solve the problem unless other influencing factors work in conjunction with the law. Second, although the law cannot stop drug use, legal policies do influence such things as the types of drugs used, methods for ingestion, means of transporting drugs, and the techniques for distribution to users.

FUTURE POLICIES
AND FUTURE PATTERNS

So many factors shape the availability and use of drugs that it is impossible to know precisely the nature of the drug problem in the year 2010. It is possible, however, to use the experiences of the past to suggest how various policies might shape the future. Many policy options are available, but much can be learned by focusing on two extreme (and opposite) responses: (1) enacting even tougher penalties and providing more resources for enforcement and (2) legalizing most drugs and emphasizing treatment and prevention rather than enforcement.

The discussion of each policy option is presented within the context of two important assumptions. First, we assume that some drug use will persist under any legal policy. Tobacco, for example, has never been successfully banned from any country to which it has been introduced, even though some societies have freely applied the death penalty for its use while others have made it completely legal. The problem is to find the policy that will lead to the smallest number of users and the fewest harmful side effects (e.g., crime and AIDS) among those users.

The second assumption is that the drug-using population really consists of two very different groups—casual users and heavy users. Popular images of drug users frequently equate use and addiction (heavy, uncontrolled use). In reality, it is estimated that between 80 and 90 percent of those who use heroin or cocaine do not become addicted. Although most drug users are not addicts, it is true that addicts account for a disproportionate share of the drugs consumed each year and for more than their share of crime and violence associated with drugs. The situation is similar to that of alcohol. One-third of Americans do not drink, but of those who do, 10 percent account for more than half of the alcohol consumed each year. This same heavy-drinking group is more likely to engage in crime, violence, and such offenses as DUI. The distinction between drug users and drug addicts is important because these groups respond differently to formal legal policies designed to control drugs.

Policy Option 1: Cracking Down on Drugs

Some theorists have argued that although increased drug enforcement has placed a burden on the criminal justice system, the problem of drugs has not diminished because formal control efforts have not gone far enough. The logic of their argument rests on both deterrence and incapacitation. Harsh, swift, and certain punishments will deter casual users and those with the will to stop. For those who are not deterred by harsh punishments, spending time in prison will effectively quarantine them from the rest of society and keep them from harming others.

This policy option has the effect of keeping the total number of users down, because people with little commitment to drug use and only a casual interest in it are likely to weigh the risks and decide against using. At the same time, this approach makes the life of the addict miserable and probably much shorter. It feeds a lucrative black market where addicts buy drugs at exorbitant prices, increasing the pressure to steal to support their habit and requiring money that might otherwise be spent for food, health care, and basic hygiene. There are already reports of AIDS-infected addicts selling blood and engaging in prostitution to support their habit. Beyond the bounds of regulation, black market drugs are of questionable quality and may even be cut with poison. Further, strict legal regulations and the need to keep their activities secret from authorities places pressure on addicts to use contaminated needles (increasing their risk of AIDS) and discourages them from seeking professional help.

It is possible that, given even greater increases in funding for drug enforcement, this policy option could substantially reduce the drug problem. It is an extremely unlikely outcome, however. Government expenditures to fight the war on drugs have skyrocketed in recent years. In 1981, the federal government was spending more than $1 billion in the war on drugs. By 1990, federal expenditures had risen to almost $10 billion. These expenditures proceeded without the desired reduction in drug-related problems. It might even be argued that drug-related problems actually increased during this time. It is unlikely that a country whose economic stability is threatened by the interest from a growing national debt will be in a position to expand funding and resources dramatically to combat drugs, particularly considering the long list of other social programs that need additional funding (e.g., Medicaid, highway repair, AIDS research, and education). Further, as concern with AIDS continues, policies that spur the spread of AIDS and discourage HIV-positive addicts from seeking help are unlikely to meet with continued public support. We have already seen the primary method for transmitting AIDS shift from homosexual activities to intravenous drug use, and harsh criminal penalties for drugs will likely only accelerate this trend.

Finally, it is unclear why harsh penalties should suddenly be effective when we remember that criminal penalties have been used to deal with the problem in the United States since 1914. If anything, drug problems have escalated since then. Further, harsh criminal penalties for marijuana possession were in place in the early 1960s, when marijuana use skyrocketed in the United States. It can be argued that frequent use *followed* harsh penalties, as did a public tolerance for marijuana use.

It is also likely that by continuing to arrest upper-level dealers and disrupting drug markets, law enforcement promotes instability in these markets. One by-product of this instability is increased competition among remaining dealers, a competition that too often results in violence since there are no formal mechanisms for dispute resolution for this group.

What would the future look like under a policy of escalated enforcement and punishment? We can speculate on the following points.

1. Even with some deterrent effect, the criminal justice system will continue to handle large numbers of drug offenders, ensuring that the United States will continue to have one of the highest imprisonment rates in the world.

2. The number of addicts will go down, but for those who remain, living conditions will further deteriorate. Addict crime will go up, as will disease and illness among addicts, and these problems will directly affect the nonaddict population through such things as criminal victimization and the spread of such illnesses as AIDS.

3. Harsher penalties will mean longer prison terms for addicts, making the transition to legitimate employment and away from drugs even more difficult on release—further reducing the quality of their lives and increasing their cost to society.

4. The number of people in the drug business will either go down or remain stable (as dealers and smugglers are taken off the street), but for those who remain, dealing in drugs will become even more lucrative. This will provide strong incentives for people who face desperate economic conditions or who find risk behavior challenging.

5. The same disruptions in drug markets that make dealing more risky and drugs more scarce will also mean that the higher prices for drugs will compel addicts to engage in even more crime to support their habits.

6. Increased enforcement will draw people into the drug business who are willing to take increased risks and also anxious to take advantage of higher profits. These same people, however, will be much more willing to use violence to protect their business, and the higher profits give them more to protect. Thus, violence associated with the drug business will probably increase.

7. Higher profits will also increase the ability of traffickers to bribe officials. Consequently, we can expect that official corruption will be more prevalent under a policy of stricter enforcement.

8. There will be strong incentives to develop new drugs. First, there will be considerable pressure to stay ahead of drug tests by developing new mind-altering substances. Second, increased enforcement will make international smuggling more risky, generating pressure to develop drugs that can be easily and cheaply manufactured in the United States.

Policy Option 2: Legalizing Drugs

At the opposite extreme from further cracking down is the strategy of reducing or eliminating criminal penalties for drug use and emphasizing treatment and prevention. The logic of this argument is that laws have not stopped the drug problem thus far and have done much to make the plight of the addict more miserable than necessary. It is also reasoned (with some support) that few people who stop doing drugs do so because of fear of legal punishment. Instead, people are more likely to give up drugs because of health concerns, because their friends stop using, or because they wish to restore some order to their chaotic lives. Further, to the extent that addicts recover by getting their lives in order, harsh legal intervention only makes the addicts' lives more chaotic by costing them their jobs, closing future job prospects, and disrupting their relationships with their families. In short, criminalizing drug use only serves to make the life of the addict more desperate and the addict more socially isolated, making the cycle of addiction even harder to break.

Legalizers argue that by eliminating criminal penalties addicts will be free to come forward for help, the money saved by reducing enforcement can be used to further treatment and education, revenue for treatment and prevention programs can be raised by taxing drugs, drug-related crime will go down because it will cost much less to support a drug habit, and the health of addicts will be much improved, reducing the spread of AIDS and other diseases.

A policy of legalization would open the way for dramatically improving the life situation of addicts. It would also, however, lead to a dramatic increase in the number of casual users. Dropping legal sanctions against drugs would provide an important symbolic statement that drugs are no longer "officially" considered harmful or dangerous. Further, although legalization would undercut some aspects of the black market, it would not eliminate black market activities. Even today, as many as one-third of the drugs sold on the street are illegally obtained prescription drugs. These drugs are legally manufactured, but their distribution is controlled by law.

Just as prescription drugs and alcohol are controlled, nearly all suggestions for legalization include provisions to regulate the manufacture of drugs and to prevent sales to minors. Legalizing drugs for adults but maintaining prohibition for children would still make drugs more available to children than they are now. This is illustrated with the regulation of alcohol, where 17-year-olds were found to have more access to alcohol when the drinking age was lowered from 21 to 18.

Although some types of crime would go down, legalization would not end the link between drugs and crime. The fact that alcohol is legally (and freely) available has not meant that alcohol use and crime are unrelated. What has been undercut (but not eliminated) is the illegal business of selling alcohol.

There is also no reason to believe that legalizing drugs will remove organized crime from the drug business. Legalizing gambling did not end organized crime's involvement in gambling. Instead, it simply has benefited from being involved in both legal and illegal gambling activities. The same would likely be true for drugs.

There is an additional practical problem with legalizing drugs. In the wake of an ever-growing environmental movement and a concern with health, legalization seems unlikely to garner much public support. At a time when the use of tobacco is being restricted and the public is very concerned about food additives and chemical pesticides, it seems unlikely that it would rally around proposals to legalize drugs. Even within the legalization movement there are sharp disagreements about which drugs should be legalized and how far legalization should go in making drugs available.

What would the world look like under a policy of legalization? We can speculate on the following possibilities.

1. The number of drug users will increase dramatically, although the number of addicts will increase at a much smaller rate.

2. The prices of drugs will drop somewhat, but not dramatically. Although the actual costs of production will be low, manufacturers will undoubtedly pay exorbitant fees for liability insurance. After all, the government has spent nearly a century amassing information to show the harmfulness of these drugs, information that would provide a strong basis for civil suits by users who claimed injury or addiction.

3. Tax revenues from drug sales will be substantial, perhaps rivaling those from alcohol and tobacco. These revenues will, in turn, make possible the funding of expanded treatment programs.

4. Crimes related to the drug business will be reduced considerably, but interpersonal crimes such as assault will increase as drug users consume drugs in more open social contexts (such as bars).

5. A black market in drugs will exist, as it does now for prescription drugs, but be much less powerful than today.

6. The problem of contaminated drugs will go down dramatically, but such problems as accidental overdose, driving while intoxicated, and reduced productivity among users will increase.

7. Drugs will be more available to young people.

8. Drug-related corruption will go down, but drug abuse by criminal justice officials will go up.

Neither legalization nor increased criminal enforcement are panaceas for the drug problem, and each creates problems of its own that are relevant to criminal justice. Of course, these represent the most extreme responses, but the United States has a history of excess in both the consumption of drugs and in formal reactions to them—including alcohol. In the 1820s, drunkenness was a common feature of American life, and per capita alcohol consumption was about triple current levels. A century later, the United States reacted not only by banning alcohol, but also by doing so with an amendment to the Constitution, the country's highest form of law.

Even today's debates about long-term drug policies are often reduced to comparing these extremes. The fact that these polar views each have a strong following tells us little about their practical utility. In reality, practical considerations will make neither extreme response likely by the year 2010. Further cracking down on drugs is simply too expensive, and neither state nor federal governments are in a position to dramatically increase antidrug budgets. If anything, antidrug budgets (in constant dollars) are likely to shrink by the year 2010. Conversely, practical problems of manufacturer liability and regulating distribution make legalization unlikely. A concern with health issues will also undercut public support for this option, though many of today's illegal drugs will be allowed for specific medical treatment under the strict supervision of doctors.

The precise look of drug policies in the year 2010 cannot be known but will probably be a mixture of these extreme policy alternatives rather than the wholesale adoption of either. This will happen for two reasons. First, there are the practical limits discussed above. Second, the same forces that are creating a world economy will also encourage U.S. policy makers to examine the wide variety of strategies adopted in other countries and to select the best elements of each.

SUMMARY

The problem of drugs will persist through the year 2010 and continue to place demands on the criminal justice system. Patterns of drug use and the problems associated with drugs are shaped by a variety of factors, only one of which is the law. It is clear that by itself the law can do little to stop the drug problem and by itself creates problems of its own. Questions of effectiveness aside, Americans are fond of using the law as a first line of response to a variety of social problems, including prostitution, domestic violence, drug use, and gambling. There is little reason to believe this will change in regard to drugs by the year 2010.

Equally popular are cost–benefit analyses that calculate the costs and benefits of various drug policies. Such analyses are based on the assumption that the public and policy makers are careful, rational "shoppers" for good policies. In practice, however, policies regarding drugs are as likely to arise out of emotion, moral indignation, and a sense (perhaps false) that something must be done about the problem.

Finally, running through all of the preceding discussion is the reality that what we "know" about drugs changes over time. What appear to be indisputable "facts" one day are shown to be myths the next. James Inciardi, for example, has noted that at one time or another marijuana, LSD, cocaine, and heroin have each been designated as "the most dangerous drug on earth." Similarly, in the 1980s, physicians and drug-abuse experts were absolutely certain that women who used cocaine during pregnancy produced "cocaine babies" who suffered withdrawal symptoms at birth, were slow to develop, and would be plagued by learning disabilities and attention disorders for much of their lives. Policies arose to take children from these mothers and, in some cases, to imprison pregnant cocaine users for the protection of the fetus. In the early 1990s, however, doctors who followed cocaine babies over time found that the long-term effects of the drug on the infants had been greatly exaggerated. Some of the most serious damage to these infants came not from cocaine, but from such complicating factors as poor nutrition and inadequate prenatal care. This turnabout in what was believed to be true about cocaine and pregnancy mirrored what happened in the late 1960s and 1970s regarding "heroin babies."

Therefore, it is ironic that the "truth" about drugs is often elusive and constantly undergoing change. That many of today's policies will be seen as folly in the future also should be no surprise.

Understanding the past and the present is essential in making predictions about the future. This essay has attempted to show that the problem of drugs cannot be considered as a single issue apart from the social, economic, and political forces in which it exists. Those who shape criminal justice policy in the year 2010 will need knowledge from a variety of areas to understand the problem of drugs. This same knowledge is indispensable in understanding crime and criminal justice more equally.

FOR FURTHER READING

James A. Inciardi. *The War on Drugs, II*. Mountain View, CA: Mayfield Publishing, 1992.

This is perhaps the single best overview of the drug problem and easily the best introduction to historical developments, international trafficking, AIDS, crack cocaine, and legalization.

J. B. Jacobs. *Drunk Driving: An American Dilemma*. Chicago: University of Chicago Press, 1989.

Alcohol is by far the most abused and destructive drug in the United States, and drunk driving is one of the more visible manifestations of the problem. This is an excellent and highly readable overview of a well-studied arena.

Rensselaer W. Lee III. *The White Labyrinth: Cocaine and Political Power.* New Brunswick, NJ: Transaction Press, 1990.

This work describes the cultural, political, and economic factors that have made it so difficult to stop drug production in South American countries.

G. Pearson. "Drug Control Policies in Britain." In M. Tonry (ed.), *Crime and Justice: A Review of Research,* Vol. 14, pp. 167–228. Chicago: University of Chicago Press, 1991.

This is the best description of the so-called British system for handling the drug problem, which gives medical and law-enforcement considerations equal weight.

Ronald K. Siegel. *Intoxication: Life in Pursuit of Artificial Paradise.* New York: Dutton, 1989.

This is one of the most insightful books available on why people use drugs. The author persuasively argues that the drive for altered consciousness is universal.

Terry Williams. *The Cocaine Kids.* Reading, MA: Addison-Wesley, 1989.

This look at the lives of young people in the business of selling cocaine highlights the social and economic factors that make drug dealing a choice for some young people and how entering the business can shape their daily lives.

S. Wisotsky. *Breaking the Impasse in the War on Drugs.* Westport, CT: Greenwood Press, 1986.

This is an excellent statement of problems with current drug policies and an excellent source for those interested in the justifications used by those who would decriminalize drugs.

DISCUSSION QUESTIONS

1. According to Weisheit, many factors influence the nature and extent of drug use. Which factors will be the most critical by the year 2010?

2. Discuss both direct and indirect links between economic development patterns and drug usage. Do economic realities overshadow law-enforcement attempts to curb the sale and distribution of illegal drugs?

3. What role will technology play in halting growing drug trafficking in the United States? What legal and ethical questions will future law enforcement need to address?

4. If future law enforcement were to adopt a policy of "cracking down" on drugs, what impact would this policy have on both drug usage and criminal justice operations?

5. How would the legalization of drugs in the next century alter the directions and purposes of the criminal justice system?

13

The Penalty of Death
in the Next Century

GENNARO F. VITO
University of Louisville

According to the NAACP Legal Defense and Educational Fund, 2,802 prisoners nationwide were held under a sentence of death on December 31, 1993. To use a Ronald Reagan style of analogy, the national death row is approximately 3.2 miles long (cell after six-foot-wide cell placed end-to-end). If we began executions immediately and put one inmate to death each day, we would need almost seven-and-one-half years to clear this strip. This rate of bloodletting assumes that death sentences would cease.

It would also represent a tremendous acceleration in the present pace of execution. Figure 13.1 presents the actual rate of execution. Currently, the average time from sentencing to execution is seven years and eleven months. If this figure is accurate, the number of executions required to clear death row (without replacement) would extend far into the twenty-first century. The purpose of this essay is to consider the future of the death penalty in the year 2010. What are the repercussions of continuing to execute convicted killers? What are the probable consequences? What choices are available?

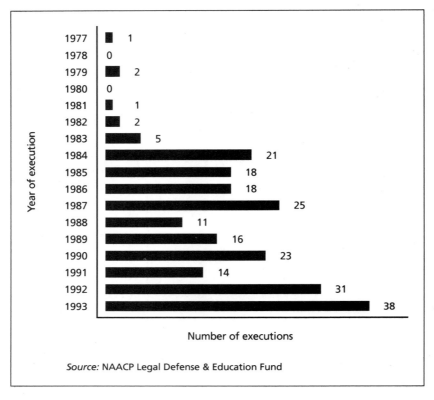

Year of execution	Number of executions
1977	1
1978	0
1979	2
1980	0
1981	1
1982	2
1983	5
1984	21
1985	18
1986	18
1987	25
1988	11
1989	16
1990	23
1991	14
1992	31
1993	38

Number of executions

Source: NAACP Legal Defense & Education Fund

Figure 13.1   Executions from January 1, 1977, to December 31, 1993

Zimring and Hawkins (1986) have predicted that abolition of capital punishment is inevitable. They believe that the elimination of the death penalty is a part of the evolutionary process of civilization in the West. However, they are uncertain when abolition will occur:

> Notably, we lack a timetable, but if conjecture is in order, we would surmise that the last execution in the United States is more likely to take place in fifteen years than in fifty years; and it is not beyond possibility that executions will cease in the near future. (p. 157)

My prediction is that the death penalty will not be abolished by the year 2010—although there are a number of sound reasons why it should be. However, nothing is inevitable.

Predicting the future is a precarious business. How many criminologists in the late 1960s would have predicted the current size of our burgeoning prison population? If we could accurately gaze into the future, we could actually solve the crime problem. The methodological problem here is that we must guard against our own beliefs and biases. No doubt, the selection of arguments and issues presented here is subjective, yet I have attempted to buttress my conclusions in typical social science fashion with data or supportive material taken from other studies.

REASONS FOR ABOLITION

The Failure of Deterrence

A tremendous volume of literature has addressed the deterrent effect of the death penalty. There is no question that the death penalty is an effective special deterrent or incapacitative punishment. The issue is whether it inhibits the crime of others and prevents homicide—that is, whether it provides general deterrence. We can only estimate the deterrent effect of any penalty. People do not report crimes that they were tempted to commit but decided not to because of the threat of punishment. Studies of the deterrent effect of the death penalty typically make two comparisons of homicide rates: (1) between states that have the death penalty and those that do not, and (2) before and after an execution.

Among the studies of the first type, Sellin used a matching technique to compare the murder rates of death penalty states with abolitionist states for the years 1920–1955 and 1920–1962. He found that the number of murders was not substantially different between the two. His conclusion was that executions have no effect on homicide rates.

On the other hand, Ehrlich examined the national data on the relationship between the homicide rate and executions for 1933–1969. In particular, he studied the "execution risk": the ratio of the number of executions compared to the number of homicides. His hypothesis was that the higher the execution rate, the lower the homicide rate. Using multiple regression to account for other factors, he found that a 1 percent increase in the execution rate accounted for a 6 percent decrease in the homicide rate. Although his analysis and the results have been severely criticized, it is still cited by supporters of capital punishment (see van den Haag in his text with Conrad, 1983). Another study by Layson suggested that each execution deters eighteen murders. This debate will no doubt continue.

If the death penalty is a general deterrent, then the number of murders following executions should decline. Research on this subject has yielded conflicting results. For example, Bowers and Pierce examined this relationship in New York state for 1907–1963 and found that an average of two additional homicides were committed in the month following an execution. Executions have a "brutalization" effect. The authors suggested that some persons may seek vengeance against their enemies, as the state did, as a result of execution. On the other hand, McFarland examined the pattern of homicide rates in the United States following the first four executions after the death penalty was reinstated in 1976. He failed to find a significant deterrent or brutalizing effect (nationally or locally) for executions.[1]

There is also no evidence that the rate of execution enhances the deterrent effect of capital punishment. Decker and Kohfeld examined the effect of the death penalty on the homicide rate over a fifty-year period (1930–1980) in the five states with the highest number of executions (Georgia, New York, Texas, California, and North Carolina). Using lag correlations, their "inescapable" conclusion was that "executions have failed to exert a consistent deterrent impact on homicides in the five states most likely to execute."

In sum, the various types of studies concerning deterrent effect of the death penalty fail to consistently demonstrate evidence of effectiveness. The death penalty does not appear to consistently deter homicide.

---

1. On the subject of deterrence, Brown (1989, p. 157) offers the following anecdote:

A convicted robber at the state prison there [in Ohio], assigned to maintenance duty in the room that housed the electric chair, decided that it was a most inefficient instrument of death. Because the condemned prisoner was not bound tightly in the chair, sometimes the electrodes did not make perfect contact with the skin, so the massive charge of electricity hopping between the electrodes and the body would produce burns and an odor that witnesses found distasteful. This convict-inventor designed a set of iron clamps to hold the legs of the condemned solidly against the electrodes, and the problem was instantly solved.

The robber got time off his sentence for his ingenious service to the state. Out on the street again, he quickly added first-degree murder to his list of crimes, and he wound up dying in the Ohio electric chair—his legs securely clamped to avoid embarrassment.

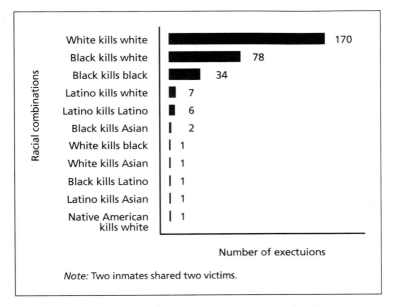

FIGURE 13.2   Executions, 1977 through 1993, by race of victim and offender

Race and the Death Penalty

Figure 13.2 presents execution data on the race of the victim and the offender since reinstatement of capital punishment in 1977. Victims of color are remarkably absent from these statistics. A recent 1991 execution was the first national instance since 1944 when a white died for killing a black (more than 1,000 executions later). Donald (Peewee) Gaskins was executed in South Carolina for the 1982 killing for hire of a fellow black inmate. Gaskins had been previously convicted of nine murders and was serving consecutive life sentences. Apparently, only the combination of a heinous crime and a serious offender could ensure the execution of a white for killing a black.

Recent U.S. Supreme Court decisions have attempted to provide a constitutionally acceptable framework for capital sentencing. For example, in the *Furman* v. *Georgia* (1972) decision, several justices cited racial discrimination and the arbitrary use of capital punishment as reasons to (temporarily) outlaw executions. In *Furman*, Justice Douglas noted that the death penalty was "cruel and unusual" and "pregnant with discrimination" because of its selective application to minorities.

The Court ruled that this situation was remedied by the new Georgia statute. In the *Gregg* v. *Georgia* decision, the court approved Georgia's system of "guided discretion," which outlined several procedures designed to correct and prevent arbitrary and discriminatory sentencing.[2] It was hoped that these requirements would eliminate and prevent racial bias in capital sentencing.

Despite procedural efforts to prevent it, capital sentencing in the United States since 1976 has been plagued by discrimination. For example, studies of the capital-sentencing process in Florida reveal that blacks who kill whites have the greatest probability of receiving the death penalty. Research has also demonstrated similar results in Arkansas, Florida, Georgia, Illinois, Kentucky, Mississippi, New Jersey, North Carolina, Ohio, Oklahoma, South Carolina, Texas, and Virginia. This pattern of discrimination by race of the victim holds true despite the severity of the homicide.

This research evidence was reviewed by the U.S. General Accounting Office (GAO). This evaluation synthesis was required by law. The Anti–Drug Abuse Act of 1988 requires a study of capital-sentencing procedures to determine if the race of either the victim or the defendant influences the likelihood of a death sentence. The GAO uncovered fifty-three studies of capital sentencing and then excluded those that did not contain empirical data or were duplicative. This review produced twenty-eight methodologically sound studies. Based on their review, the GAO concluded the following:

- In 82 percent of the studies, race of the victim influenced the likelihood of a defendant being charged with capital murder and receiving the death penalty (especially those who murdered whites).

- The influence of the victim's race existed at all stages of the criminal justice process. This evidence was stronger at the earlier stages of this process (e.g., prosecutorial decision to seek death penalty or to proceed to trial rather than plea bargain) than in the later stages.

---

2. The Georgia system subsequently became the model for other states. This system features a bifurcated trial (a guilt and then a penalty phase), consideration of aggravating and mitigating circumstances in the case during the penalty phase of the trial (an aggravating circumstance must be present before the prosecution can seek the death penalty), a proportionality review of similar cases by the state supreme court to determine if the sentencing process was being fairly applied, and the automatic appeal of all death sentences to the state supreme court.

- "Aggravating circumstances" (e.g., prior record, culpability level, heinousness of the crime, and number of victims) were influential but did not fully explain the reason for racial disparity in capital sentencing.

- The evidence for the influence of the race of the defendant was equivocal. The race of the defendant interacted with another factor (e.g., rural versus urban areas and blacks who killed whites).

- More than three-fourths of the studies that identified a race-of-the-defendant effect found that black defendants were more likely to receive the death penalty.

The synthesis demonstrated a strong race-of-victim influence on capital sentencing.

Yet the U.S. Supreme Court had already ruled favorably on the constitutionality of a capital-sentencing system that produced evidence of racial discrimination. In *McCleskey* v. *Kemp*, the Court stated that the research on the new Georgia capital-sentencing system revealed that only "a discrepancy . . . correlated with race." This study found that blacks who killed whites were nearly three times more likely to be sentenced to death than were whites who killed whites. A cited study by Baldus, Woodworth, and Pulaski did not focus on McCleskey's case (a black charged with the killing of a white police officer during an armed robbery). Therefore, the Court found that the study did not demonstrate that race was a factor in his death sentence. Rather than demonstrating a pattern of discrimination in sentencing, the *McCleskey* decision requires defendants complaining about discrimination to prove directly that it existed in their individual case.

Recent legislation attempted to address this crucial defect in capital sentencing: In 1991, for example, the Fairness in Death Sentencing Act (H.R. 2851) was proposed in the House of Representatives, but it failed passage. The bill called for research to determine whether racial discrimination is a factor in capital punishment. The act made it unlawful to execute a defendant whose death sentence was the product of racial discrimination (by race of the defendant or the victim). The defendant must provide proof that his or her death sentence is a product of racial bias. The prosecution can challenge the evidence or demonstrate that legitimate factors (such as prior record) account for racial differentials in capital sentencing. If the defendant prevails, the death sentence, but not the conviction, is set aside. In sum, the act offered a possible means of identifying and substantially eliminating the influence of race in capital sentencing.[3]

It is also unlikely that the changing racial composition of the country will change this pattern of discrimination. In some states, such as California, "minorities" are becoming the largest population groups. Yet this demographic shift will not alter capital sentencing. Traditionally, persons of color have had the highest probability of being a murder victim. For example, in 1985, the U.S. Department of Justice reported that the lifetime risks of becoming a homicide victim were 1 in 179 for white males, 1 in 30 for black males, 1 in 495 for white females, and 1 in 132 for black females. Offenders who kill persons of color should be on death row in great numbers. If the death row population does not reflect this imbalance now, then it never will. Instead, killers of whites are most likely to attract a capital sentence.

Executing the Innocent

In his classic work opposing the death penalty, Black (1981) contends that mistake within the process of selecting the offender is inevitable. Bedau and Radelet studied defendants convicted of capital (or potential capital) crimes in the twentieth century. They uncovered 350 cases in which the guilt of the defendants was at issue. Twenty-seven of these cases occurred after the reinstitution of capital punishment and the safeguards endorsed in the *Gregg* decision (Bedau & Radelet, 1987, pp. 178–179).

Recent calls to accelerate executions enhances the probability of executing an innocent person. For example, in *McCleskey* v. *Zant,* the Supreme Court placed stricter limits on the filing of writs of habeas corpus by convicted persons. In this case, McCleskey attempted to file a habeas corpus writ to decide the admissibility of evidence obtained against him by a jailhouse informant. His attorneys did not file on this issue in an earlier writ because prosecutors withheld documents demonstrating that the informant was illegally planted by the police. Justice

---

3. The legislative route was suggested by the Court. In *McCleskey* v. *Kemp,* Justice Powell's majority decision noted that:

McCleskey's arguments are best presented to the legislative bodies. It is not the responsibility—or indeed even the right—of this court to determine the appropriate punishment for particular crimes. . . . Legislatures . . . are better qualified to weigh . . . and evaluate the results of statistical studies in terms of their own local conditions and with a flexibility of approach that is not available to the courts.

Thus, the Fairness in Death Sentencing Act places statistical evaluations of capital sentencing systems in the proper arena.

Kennedy ruled that this action by the state did not represent sufficient cause for failing to raise a more timely defense. The standard established by the Court is that defendants must show cause for not bringing up a claim sooner. They must also demonstrate that this factor greatly prejudiced their case.

Streamlining the capital punishment process enhances the likelihood of the wrongful conviction and execution of an innocent person. If the speed of execution continues to quicken, this unfortunate event can occur by the year 2010.[4]

The Alternative to Capital Punishment

One of the major obstacles to death penalty abolition is the absence of a clear alternative. This policy thicket represents the criminal justice equivalent of the "winnable nuclear war." If a mandatory sentence of life without parole becomes the replacement, what will inmates have to lose by killing another inmate or institutional staffmember? If such an inmate escapes, how many people would die in the attempt at recapture? These questions assume that convicted murderers are an extremely dangerous segment of the prison population.

Several recent studies have followed the recidivism rates of former death row inmates who had their sentences commuted to life in prison as a result of the *Furman* decision. They test the argument that the death penalty protects the public from repeat murders. Marquart and Sorensen followed the entire cohort (243 of 558 inmates were paroled) and determined that only one committed murder following release. Individual studies of *Furman* inmates in Kentucky and Texas revealed a similar pattern. Another study found that two Ohio inmates murdered two correctional officials after their sentences were commuted. Collectively, these findings indicate that the death penalty is no more inhibiting than imprisonment. Public and institutional safety can be accomplished in some other manner.[5]

Life without parole looms as the obvious alternative. Cheatwood identified twenty-seven states with life-without-parole statutes in force. Yet these statutes may not actually represent "life without release," depending on the jurisdiction. The only way that life without parole could replace the death penalty as a sanction would be if it represented

---

4. In fact, a noted conservative criminologist Richard R. E. Kania of Guilford College, has stated that the execution of an innocent is bound to occur. When it does, Kania predicts that executions will come (temporarily) to a halt.

5. Since this research was conducted, a Texas *Furman* inmate, Kenneth McDuff, was paroled, convicted of murder, and returned to death row.

lifetime imprisonment. However, this conversion does not answer all policy issues. It would still be necessary to increase security levels and operate a system of one person per cell—that is, solitary confinement.

This system is not an uncommon measure in institutions. "Lockdowns" can stave off altercations and riots in prison. In fact, the lockdown method is standard operating procedure at the maximum security prison in the federal penitentiary at Marion, Illinois. Two inmates who murdered guards on the same day in a sadistic, "copy cat" manner serve time in separate three-room cells. At that time, the federal sentencing procedures did not include the death penalty.

This system could become the national norm for death row inmates. Regional facilities could be structured under the old Pennsylvania model of incarceration, featuring one person per cell. Few states would have enough inmates to bear the cost of constructing or renovating space for such an institution. The institution would have to be secure enough to protect the public from escapes, as well as to protect those individuals who live and work inside its walls.[6]

In terms of retribution, life without parole in solitary confinement could represent a fate worse than death. After all, we do not know what death holds for us. The loss of time, cut off from the world, from all friends, family, and creature comforts, is an explicit and hence more disturbing proposition. When the death penalty was reinstated in 1977, several inmates declared that they would rather die than spend the rest of their life in prison.[7] For these reasons, the goals of incapacitation, social defense, and retribution could all be carried out by penalty other than death.

---

6. The commonly held presumption is that life imprisonment is far more costly than the death penalty. Cost studies have not supported this assumption. For example, the state of Kansas estimated that death penalty prosecution would cost $10 million with an additional $2 million necessary to fund the mandatory appeals process. A cost analysis by Duke University researchers estimated that it costs $329,000 more on average to try, convict, and execute a murderer than it does to gain a first-degree murder conviction with a twenty-year prison term. There is little reason to believe that the proposed system of life without parole could be any more costly than a capital-punishment system. It is clearly the most expensive program in the entire panoply of punishment.

7. The last words of the first inmate executed in 1977, Gary Gilmore (Utah), were "Let's do it." Others in the first group—including Jesse Bishop (third, Nevada, 1979), Steven Judy (fourth, Indiana, 1981), Frank J. Coppola (fifth, 1982, Virginia), and John Louis Evans (seventh, 1983, Alabama)—either asked that their appeals be stopped and the sentence carried out or expressed a preference for execution over life in prison. When an Oklahoma death row inmate (Thomas Grosso) was sentenced to life in prison for a previous crime in New York state, he expressed a preference to return to Oklahoma for execution. Governor Cuomo quipped that the inmate was naturally interested in the "lesser sentence."

REASONS FOR RETENTION

The Increasing Homicide Rate

The average American is now twice as likely to be a homicide victim as in 1960. This surge in violence, coupled with the capture of serial murderers such as Jeffrey Dahmer, can only increase the public demand for the ultimate panacea, the death penalty.[8]

Former President Bush and Republicans in the Senate capitalized on this sentiment by introducing the 1991 Omnibus Anticrime Bill. The bill extends the death penalty into the federal system for fifty-one crimes, including the killing of a meat inspector, a mail carrier, or an astronaut. Other details of the bill include the following:

- Both the length of time allowed to file for habeas corpus and the number of times a defendant can apply are limited.
- The "full and fair" proposition: A judge can deny an appeal if the defendant received a "full and fair" trial at the state level.
- Any homicide committed with a gun that either crossed state lines or was used in the commission of a federal crime could be under the federal jurisdiction.
- The death penalty was extended to the District of Columbia.
- Mentally disabled individuals who cannot assist in the preparation of their defense are not excluded from the death penalty.
- The minimum age for execution was lowered to 17.

Debate on this bill was summarized by Senator Moynihan (D–NY) as "Throw the switch and watch them twitch." In fact, the death penalty was offered as a recommendation to combat violent crime and strengthen criminal justice in a report by then-U.S. Attorney General William Barr. Here, an "effective death penalty" is touted as a way to deter and punish "the most heinous violent crimes." "It reaffirms society's moral outrage at the wanton destruction of innocent human life and assures the family and other survivors of murder victims that society takes their loss seriously." It recommends capital punishment (1) when a law enforcement officer is killed, (2) for those who kill in the course of serious felonies, and (3) for killing in prison. Thus, political sentiment, plus the fact that the current conservative majority on the

---

8. The ultimate irony is that Dahmer will never even face the death penalty because Wisconsin does not have a capital punishment statute.

U.S. Supreme Court will probably still be on the bench in 2010, ensures that the death penalty will remain with us.

The Death Penalty and Public Opinion

In the past fifteen years, American attitudes toward the death penalty have dramatically shifted toward support of the most extreme of all criminal penalties. For example, a 1991 Gallup poll reported that 76 percent of American adults endorsed capital punishment for murder. Yet recent research has shown that the purported overwhelming national consensus on capital punishment may not be as solid as public opinion polls suggest. In his review of fifty years of Gallup death penalty polls (1936–1986), Bohm reported that whites, wealthier people, males, Republicans, and Westerners supported capital punishment more than did blacks, poorer people, females, Democrats, and Southerners.

Abolition of capital punishment will no doubt require immense political pressure. A recent survey of Kentuckians' attitudes toward capital punishment shows why it may be difficult to gain passage of abolition legislation. Blacks, women, and the poor were the strongest opponents of capital punishment in Kentucky. Unfortunately, these groups have the fewest political resources to bring to bear on such an issue and have other matters that they may perceive as more pressing than the issue of capital punishment. It would be difficult to organize these groups around the issue of capital punishment. Their opinions run contrary to those of more powerful groups in this state. If this pattern is present across the nation, then the potential for abolition is weak and bleak. The weakness of the opposition and the absence of political will ensures that the death penalty will not be abolished by the year 2010.

The Death Penalty: A Potential Political Symbol

A politician's position on capital punishment has become the definitive litmus test of his or her crime platform. An opponent of capital punishment gives its political challenger a potent campaign issue. For example, former California Governor Edmund Brown, who commuted twenty-three of sixty-nine death sentences while in office, gives the following example of the political pressures he faced:

> In spite of the continuing executions, and the fact that I was denying about half again as many requests for clemency as I was approving, in 1962, Richard Nixon attacked my perceived anticapital punishment stance when he ran against me; and

Ronald Reagan made it a major issue in his 1966 campaign. I knew that I was a better governor for California than either one of them, and I also knew that if I soft-pedaled the death penalty issue I'd have a better chance of being reelected; the polls over the years showed the people of California in favor of the death penalty by a margin of at least 60 percent and sometimes as high as 70 percent. And yet I continued to go against public opinion in my search for reasons to commute death sentences. (Brown with Adler, 1989, p. 121)

Although supporting the death penalty does not necessarily ensure victory, opposing it is tantamount to political suicide. The only major political figure who has managed to survive while maintaining an abolitionist stance is New York Governor Mario Cuomo.

Another example of the political potency of the death penalty was revealed by the actions of then–presidential candidate Bill Clinton during the 1992 campaign. Clinton returned to his home state to be present for the execution of a brain-damaged inmate, Rickey Ray Rector, who had killed a police officer and then attempted suicide. The suicide attempt resulted in the equivalent of a prefrontal lobotomy. Clinton's role in the execution was raised as a political issue by Jerry Brown (Edmund's son and a well-known maverick) but largely ignored by the press.[9] Instead, Clinton's sex life was examined thoroughly and helped to topple him from his standing as the leading candidate before the New Hampshire primary.

CONCLUSION

The death penalty will be with us in the next century—for all the wrong reasons. It fails to deter murderers. There is strong evidence of racial discrimination in capital sentencing. It is only a matter of time before we rush to execute an innocent person. Life without parole could become a strong incapacitative, retributive punishment.

But the death penalty will remain and perhaps even flourish because it represents the supreme quick fix for the violent crime rate. Public opinion, although not unanimous, supports executions. Politicians use the issue to play on the fear of crime. The abolitionists do not have the

---

9. In fact, the decision to execute Rector is related to the *Ford* v. *Wainwright* decision (1986). In *Ford,* the court stated that the Eighth Amendment bars the execution of the insane. Rector was clearly incompetent at the time of his execution.

political strength to overcome such conservative opinions. It is difficult to mobilize political support for convicted murderers. Perhaps groups such as Amnesty International and the NAACP Legal Defense and Education Fund can meet this challenge, but it will be an uphill battle.

Unfortunately, education offers no concrete guarantee out of this dilemma. Bohm, Clark, and Aveni have demonstrated that education on the death penalty failed to significantly affect opinions on capital punishment (including retributive reasons). Clearly, the electric chair, the gas chamber, and the lethal needle will be in full operation in 2010.

FOR FURTHER READING

D. Baldus, G. Woodworth, and C. Pulaski. *Equal Justice and the Death Penalty: A Legal and Empirical Analysis.* Boston: Northeastern University Press, 1990.

This is a comprehensive analysis of Georgia's capital-sentencing process. This research also formed the basis of the *McCleskey* v. *Kemp* decision.

H. A. Bedau and M. L. Radelet. "Miscarriages of Justice in Potentially Capital Cases." *Stanford Law Review, 40,* 21–179, 1987.

This offers a detailed examination of capital cases in which the guilt of the defendant was at issue.

C. Black. *Capital Punishment: The Inevitability of Caprice and Mistake.* New York: Cambridge University Press, 1981.

This classic work presents strong arguments against the retention of the death penalty.

E. G. Brown with D. Adler. *Public Justice, Private Mercy: A Governor's Education on Death Row.* New York: Weidenfeld and Nicolson, 1989.

This unique memoir provides a view of the capital-sentencing process at the final stage. Brown provides a chilling look at life-and-death decisions by an elected government official.

E. van den Haag and J. P. Conrad. *The Death Penalty: A Debate.* New York: Plenum, 1983.

Clearly, this is the best debate on the subject in print between two intellectually powerful adversaries. Van den Haag is one of the strongest proponents of capital punishment, and Conrad's background in corrections gives him firm grounding in this subject.

F. E. Zimring and G. Hawkins. *Capital Punishment and the American Agenda.* New York: Cambridge University Press, 1986.

This work is a cogently argued case for the abolition of capital punishment; it makes detailed use of international data.

DISCUSSION QUESTIONS

1. Vito disagrees with scholars who predict that the death penalty will be abolished in the not-too-distant future. It has, however, been abolished in most Western countries. What forces make its continuation likely in the United States?

2. Racial discrimination has been a central issue in debates over the death penalty. How have the courts addressed this issue? How will the increasing heterogeneity of the U.S. population affect this concern?

3. What arguments are there for and against "life without parole" as an alternative to the death penalty?

4. How does the distribution of political power in this country contribute to the retention of the death penalty? What groups oppose the death penalty? How likely are they to succeed in abolishing it?

5. Consider the scientific evidence on the value of the death penalty. What role is there for research and education in the continuing debate over this sanction?

14

☆

Juvenile Justice in the Next Millennium

CARL E. POPE

University of Wisconsin, Milwaukee

Futures are always uncertain, and attempts to predict them are even more so. Without the advantage of a "crystal ball" or some accurate method of "stargazing," no one can be, or has been, very successful in charting future courses. Whether one is dealing with long-term fluctuations in the stock market, political upheavals and revolutions, global war, urban unrest, or the nature of crime and responses to it, there is great potential for error. For example, more than four decades of attempts to predict success and failure (by both simple and complex mechanisms) in probation, parole, pretrial release, recidivism, and so on have been pretty dismal. Such attempts have frequently been plagued by errors of "false negatives" (those who should not do it but do it anyway) and "false positives" (those who should do it but for some unknown reason do not). In other words, we have not been very successful in predicting individual behavior (or group behavior, for that matter) or other social processes and events. We look back at the past with knowledge and understanding and perhaps should have seen it coming, but, more often than not, we did not. Does this mean that we should abandon or limit attempts to see into the future or speculate about what might be? Probably not.

If nothing else, gazing into the future and the unknown is fun. The scientific, the not-so-scientific, and the just plain curious have been doing it for centuries. It sparks imagination, which is the foundation for new discoveries. It provides a forum for debate and discussion and delimits new scenarios, some of which may be uplifting, while others are frightening. Even given a potentially large margin of error, predicting the future can still provide us with a vision to contemplate. And who knows? We may get it right.

Having said all this, during the course of this chapter we will attempt to look at the juvenile justice system in the next millennium. In doing so, we will focus on three major issues: (1) whether there will be a separate juvenile justice system in 2010; (2) if so, the form it will take; and (3) the probable composition of the system. In attempting to make these assessments, we will use the past and present as a guide to the future. Without our proverbial crystal ball, we cannot do otherwise. We do not know, for example, what new political agendas will appear, how public opinion may shift, what major economic cataclysms, if any, lie ahead, and similar factors, all of which may shape the future of crime control and the juvenile justice system. On the other hand, two decades is not a long period of time when considering the potential for change within the justice system. Therefore, the past and present may be a fairly reliable guide into the future. The shorter the interval, the more likely we are to guess within some known limits of accuracy. We would be on much shakier ground if we were trying to chart the course of juvenile justice in 2110; moreover, all of us will be dead then, anyway.

WILL THERE BE A JUVENILE JUSTICE SYSTEM IN 2010?

Perhaps the major consideration as we move into the twenty-first century is whether there will, in fact, be a separate system of juvenile justice. Some theorists have argued that over the past few decades the adult and juvenile justice systems have moved closer together and that the lines separating them are blurry at best. There is also concern that the current operation of the juvenile court results in greater injustices than are found in the adult criminal justice system. For example, one juvenile justice scholar has argued that:

> [a]bolishing the juvenile court is desirable both for youths and
> society. After more than two decades of constitutional and legis-

lative reform, juvenile courts continue to deflect, co-opt, ignore, or absorb ameliorative tinkering with minimal institutional change. Despite its transformation from a welfare agency to a criminal court, the juvenile court remains essentially unreformed. The quality of justice youths receive would be intolerable if it were adults facing incarceration.

The history of the juvenile court began in Illinois in 1899 with the passage of the Juvenile Court Act, which provided separate proceedings for the handling of juvenile offenders. Originally, the court had jurisdiction over dependent and neglected youth, so-called status offenders (including such acts as truancy and incorrigibility) and those youth committing criminal offenses. The overall goal was the removal of stigma and the provision of treatment alternatives rather than punishment as provided in the adult system. The philosophical underpinning was derived from the concept of *parens patriae,* in which the state functions as a surrogate parent and in the best interests of children. Since a social welfare and treatment perspective was the benchmark of the juvenile justice system, it was not concerned with various constitutional rights and due-process provisions found within the adult system. Therefore, the operation of the juvenile justice system tended to be informal in nature and concerned with expediency.

Major Supreme Court decisions of the 1960s and early 1970s began to reshape the juvenile justice system toward a more formal and legalistic operation with a variety of procedural safeguards. In perhaps the most famous of these cases, *In re Gault,* the Supreme Court held that juveniles facing the possibility of confinement have certain constitutional rights, such as the right to be notified of the charges, to confront and cross-examine witnesses, and to have counsel present. While recognizing the *parens patriae* model of the juvenile court, the Supreme Court also noted that juveniles faced confinement (punishment) without constitutional safeguards. As Justice Fortas stated:

> Ultimately, however, we confront the reality of that portion of the juvenile court process with which we deal in this case. A boy is charged with misconduct. The boy is committed to an institution in which he may be restrained of liberty for years. It is of no constitutional consequence—and of limited practical meaning—that the institution to which he is committed is called an Industrial School. The fact of the matter is that, however euphemistic the title, a "receiving home" or "industrial

school" for juveniles is an institution of confinement in which the child is incarcerated for a greater or lesser time.

The net effect of case law was to move the juvenile justice system closer to the adult system. While not guaranteeing juveniles all rights found in the adult system, case law did move the juvenile court from a more traditional and informal pre-*Gault* model toward a more formalized and procedurally correct court, at least in urban areas.

Aside from these legal changes, there were also marked changes in the nature of crime. Over the past few decades (especially during the 1980s and into the 1990s), the types of crimes typically committed by youthful offenders became more serious and more violent. For example, in 1989, 15.8 percent of those charged with violent index offenses (murder, forcible rape, robbery, and aggravated assault) and 30.7 percent of those charged with property index crimes (burglary, larceny and theft, motor vehicle theft, and arson) were under age 18. Furthermore, data also suggest that involvement in violent crime is increasingly becoming the prerogative of the young. Thus, as one commentator noted:

> a greater percentage of young people are getting arrested for violent crimes today than thirty years ago and adolescents 15 years old and younger are more involved in violent behavior than ever before. The fact that kids are committing violent acts at an earlier age may help account for the growth in the nation's violent-crime rate.

With regard to the nature and type of offenses, the juvenile court began to resemble the adult court and was less likely to be construed as a "kiddie" court. An increase in the nature of gang and drug activity greatly contributed to this change.

Perhaps as a response to these events, the juvenile court began to take on a more retributive posture that is similar to that of the adult criminal justice system. While still concerned with rehabilitation, diversion, and "less restrictive" alternatives, the ideology and operation of the juvenile system became much more punitive in nature. This was witnessed by an increase in the use of short-term detention as well as the use of longer-term secure lockup. Another example is seen in the use and nature of waiver decisions that transfer custody of youth to the adult court. While at one time adult waiver was a minuscule part of the system in that proportionately few youth were waived, this is not the case today. The system is now characterized by increased use of waiver to adult court and the lowering of the age at which waiver is permissible (down to 14 years of age in many states). These trends lend some support to the argument that juvenile justice is archaic and therefore a relic of the past.

Will there be a separate juvenile system in the year 2010? Probably so. As noted previously, the juvenile justice system dates back to 1899 with the founding of the first juvenile court in Cook County, Illinois. Thus, it has a strong legacy and tradition within the justice system. History and tradition are hard to overcome. It was spawned in the wake of the child saver movement with its larger concern with the protection of children (from sweatshops, compulsory labor, lack of educational opportunities, etc.). Removal from the adult system was seen as in the best interest of children; it served to provide treatment and remove stigma. These are worthy goals (although the system often failed to live up to them) and are not likely to be completely abandoned. Further, there is a large investment of personnel and resources supporting a separate juvenile justice system (e.g., probation officers, judges, courts, and facilities). Just as adult prisons are rarely abandoned (or turned into museums), it is unlikely that the juvenile system will suffer this fate.

WHAT WILL
THE JUVENILE JUSTICE
SYSTEM LOOK LIKE IN 2010?

If the juvenile justice system does survive to the year 2010, will it be similar to its current form? The answer is likely to be both yes and no. It will be similar in that it will continue to provide separate services for youthful offenders. It will be different in that it may relinquish more authority to the adult criminal justice system. This could take one or a combination of directions. First, it is likely that increased use of waiver to adult court will be utilized for those who commit the more serious and more violent offenses. Second, the juvenile court may automatically release jurisdiction for older youth committing specific violent crimes such as gang- or drug-related homicides. A third possibility (although less likely than the first two) would be to lower the age of jurisdiction, for example to less than 16, as is now the case in a few states. Regardless of these possible options, in all likelihood the juvenile justice system will move into the twenty-first century as a more retribution-oriented system. While not abandoning diversionary and other rehabilitative efforts, the juvenile justice system of the future will most likely place more emphasis on secure confinement for longer periods of time. With a heightened concern about crime, politicians are unlikely to want to appear soft on this issue, especially with the public clamoring for "get-tough" policies. The net result is likely to be more youth confined in secure facilities, most of whom, unfortunately, are likely to be minority.

WHAT WILL THE FUTURE COMPOSITION OF THE JUVENILE COURT BE?

If conditions continue on their current course, we will probably see more minority youth (especially black youth) confined in secure public facilities with more white youth moving into diversion programs and private facilities. Recent data have already documented this trend over the past ten years, and there is little evidence to indicate any changes in the near future. Increasing gang violence coupled with drug use and trafficking will serve to exacerbate the problem. These activities tend to be most prevalent in low-income inner-city areas. Indeed, recent data underscore the fact that alcohol abuse is most prevalent among white youth, with drugs being the choice of black youth. Drug arrests account for the largest number of youth held in secure facilities and, hence, differentially impact black youth.

Demographic shifts will also play a role. While the live birthrate for whites has been steadily decreasing over the last few decades, this is not the case for minorities, especially blacks. For them, the live birthrate has been climbing, especially among single females. Thus, by the year 2010 there will be a larger pool of minority youth from which to draw.

Economic conditions are also likely to play a major role in shaping the composition of the juvenile justice system in the years to come. While all societies face economic fluctuations over time, some major changes occurring within the United States may have a profound effect. For example, the last decade has witnessed the erosion of many industrial jobs and entry-level positions. In essence, we are rapidly moving into a service-based economy with lower wages and unskilled labor. Those industrial and manufacturing jobs that do remain not only have been sharply curtailed but also have tended to follow the population shifts to the suburbs. Moreover, many industries and factories have migrated from the northern "rust-belt" cities to the sunbelt states, leaving in their aftermath a hopelessly sagging economy. Thus, we are rapidly moving from a postindustrial society to one marked on one end of the scale by "high-tech" positions and on the other end by low-wage service positions. These economic shifts have differentially affected large segments of the U.S. population.

Many scholars have documented the plight of the so-called ghetto underclass, sometimes referred to as the "urban poor." In every major city across the country there exists a large segment of the population trapped within the inner cities. More often than not, this population segment is characterized by family disruption, poor school systems, segmented communities, visible gang activity, and a high incidence of drug abuse, violence, and the like. Moreover, for most of these residents (who are mostly minority and mostly black) there is little chance of escaping these conditions or of meaningfully participating in the labor force. In studying Chicago's low poverty and inner-city areas, researchers note that problems associated with joblessness and economic exclusion have triggered a process that they have termed *hyperghettoization*. Under such conditions, the stabilizing forces of the inner city have deteriorated:

> Social ills that have long been associated with segregated poverty—violent crime, drugs, housing deterioration, family disruption, commercial blight, and educational failure—have reached qualitatively different proportions and have become articulated into a new configuration that endows each with a more deadly impact than before.

The decline of business and industry, the reduction in service entry positions, and the like have created stagnant pockets of the city that breed despair and hopelessness. While such conditions affect all members of the underclass, they are more pronounced and have more serious implications for black adolescents.

Changing structural and economic conditions have isolated the "underclass" in a rather hopeless position. If such a large segment of the population is confined to exist under conditions so vastly different from those of the mainstream population, one could logically expect differences in behavior and outcome, and so it is. Youth residing in these areas and growing up under such conditions have few opportunities to improve their lot and are preoccupied with survival. Unfortunately, there is little evidence that these conditions will improve in the near future; rather, the evidence suggests that they will worsen. Given these trends, it is quite likely that these youth will increasingly become the fodder that fills both the adult and juvenile justice system.

There is also evidence to suggest that the juvenile justice system itself may not be "just." Recent data underscore the increasing rate at which minority youth are housed in secure detention facilities in both the adult and juvenile justice systems. There is also reason to believe that race itself may directly or indirectly play a role in processing decisions, including the decision to confine. A recent review, for example, examined previous studies exploring the relationship between race and juvenile processing. The results of that analysis found that approximately two-thirds of the research conducted over the past two decades did find a race effect. In other words, minority youth (specifically, black youth) were more at risk than majority youth of receiving the most severe outcomes at various stages of juvenile processing. Such disparities occurred at numerous decision points even when legal factors and other case characteristics were controlled.

More recent research conducted in three states (Georgia, Florida, and Missouri) support these findings. All three studies are consistent in showing that minorities are at risk with regard to processing within the juvenile justice system. This was especially true in Missouri with regard to short-term detention decisions in urban areas. Black youth were significantly more likely to be held in detention compared with their white counterparts. Research suggests that detention decisions have major implications for later outcomes. Typically, those youth held in detention are more likely to be adjudicated delinquent and placed in secure confinement facilities.

The above studies also lent support to findings in Minnesota of "justice by geography" in that there are distinctly different juvenile justice systems that vary across counties. For example, urban areas tend to have a more bureaucratic and legally oriented system compared with a more traditional pre-*Gault* model found in rural areas. Unfortunately, both systems frequently work to the disadvantage of minority youth. In addition, these studies underscore the role of family situation in outcome decisions. In those cases in which families were willing or less able to provide support, the youth tended to receive the more severe dispositions, which, in turn, had a differential impact on minority youth. Indeed, recent data portray a trend in which minority youth are more likely to be housed in public facilities while white youth are housed in more treatment-oriented private facilities. Given these data, one could reasonably predict that, by the year 2010, secure juvenile facilities will disproportionately become the residence of minority youth unless something is done to reverse this trend.

There are, however, several federal and state efforts now underway to reduce the proportion of minority youth within the juvenile justice system and in secure facilities. In 1988, Congress amended the Juvenile Justice and Delinquency Prevention Act to require states to address the issue of minority overrepresentation. Under Phase I, as part of the formula grant-funding process, participating states were asked to determine whether or not minority youth were overrepresented with regard to their population base in secure facilities. If so, states were required under Phase II to examine their respective juvenile justice systems in order to account for such overrepresentation and then develop strategies to reduce it. Phase II efforts were completed in Georgia, Florida, and Missouri and are continuing in about a dozen other states. In addition, the Office of Juvenile Justice and Delinquency Prevention has recently awarded a grant to assist five states (Oregon, Arizona, Iowa, North Carolina, and Florida) in meeting Phase II goals. Here the objective will be to collect data and analyze each state's juvenile justice system with regard to the processing of majority and minority youth. Based upon that analysis, prototypes, manuals, and training packages will be developed to serve as national models to reduce the presence of minority youth in the juvenile justice system. If successful, these efforts will, it is hoped, result in a more equitable juvenile justice system as we move into the next century.

While the attempt to ensure equity within the juvenile justice system is in itself a worthy goal, it is not likely to have a major impact on minority overrepresentation. While slight reductions are likely, conditions still existing in the urban ghettos will continue to serve as a driving force, funneling more and more of the minority poor into the juvenile justice system. Only by attending to substandard structural (i.e., inner-city schools) and economic (i.e., lack of meaningful employment) conditions will any substantive changes come about. The structural and economic realities of the urban ghettos are the forces behind entry into the justice system. Thus, policy decisions must address not only problems in the case processing of juvenile offenders, but also preexisting social conditions. Only by such a two-pronged attack is there any viable chance of reducing youth crime generally and the disproportionate overrepresentation of minority youth within the juvenile justice system. Unfortunately, there is little evidence that such an attack will be forthcoming.

CONCLUSION

What is the prognosis for the juvenile justice system in the year 2010? First, there is little doubt that it will still exist in some form. More than 100 years of history and tradition are hard to abandon, and the ideology on which the system is based makes intuitive sense. On the other hand, we might expect the system to relinquish more of its jurisdiction to its adult counterpart. This may occur through the increased use of waiver or by statutorily limiting its jurisdiction (e.g., lowering the age of accountability). Second, given present trends, the juvenile justice system in the year 2010 will probably be based on a "just desserts" model. While not completely abandoning the goals of rehabilitation, diversion, and the like, we might expect a tougher system in which punishment becomes the overriding concern. Third, with regard to the composition of the system and its secure facilities, we might expect an increase in the proportion of minority youth. Unfortunately, given the present structural and economic factors coupled with past research on race effects within the system, we could hardly expect otherwise.

FOR FURTHER READING

J. Whitehead and S. Lab. *Juvenile Justice: An Introduction.* Cincinnati, OH: Anderson, 1990.

In Chapter 13, the authors identify several issues not dealt with in this chapter. For example, they discuss arguments for ending and continuing jurisdiction over status offenders, chronic violent juvenile offenders, and the movement toward privatization of juvenile facilities.

E. F. McGarrell. *Juvenile Correctional Reform: Two Decades of Policy and Procedural Change.* Albany: State University of New York Press, 1988.

This book is essentially a case study of changing directions within New York's juvenile justice system. Examples are also drawn from other states, such as Massachusetts, and the implications of the changes are discussed. By examining the past, this book lays a foundation for what the future might be.

W. Wilson. *The Truly Disadvantaged: The Inner City, the Underclass and Public Policy.* Chicago: University of Chicago Press, 1987.

Although not directly related to juvenile justice, this book paints a bleak picture of the economic deprivation of the "ghetto poor" and their children. As noted in this important work, unless steps are taken to reverse current trends, ever-increasing numbers of minority youth will be funneled into the juvenile justice system.

C. E. Pope and F. Feyerherm. "Minority Status and Juvenile Justice," *Criminal Justice Abstracts, 22*(2), 327–336 (Part I); *22*(3), 527–542 (Part II). 1990.

This article reviews and analyzes more than three decades of research examining the effects of race within the juvenile justice system. The authors conclude that the majority of research shows that race does make a difference: Minority youth receive more severe outcomes than do white youth.

B. Feld. "The Transformation of the Juvenile Court," *Minnesota Law Review, 75*(3) 691–725.

This article examines various changes occurring within juvenile courts with regard to such issues as diversion, deinstitutionalization, decriminalization, sentencing, and the like. Feld makes a convincing argument for the abolition of the juvenile court system.

DISCUSSION QUESTIONS

1. Pope suggests that, in the future, the juvenile justice system will become similar to the adult system of justice. What factors will facilitate this transition?

2. One suggestion for dealing with violent juvenile crime is lowering the age for waiver to adult court. What would be the impact of such an action on juvenile crime?

3. Discuss the relevance of the disproportional representation of minority youths within the juvenile justice system.

4. Describe the importance of economic and social conditions on the nature of juvenile crime. Which of these factors do you think is the most important and should be addressed by future criminal justice policy makers?

5. What policy initiatives would you advocate in dealing with juvenile crime and the disproportional representation of minority youth in the juvenile justice system?

PART IV

Criminal Justice in 2010: A Final Look

In this final section, we conclude by examining the themes addressed by our contributors. In Chapter 15, we suggest possible issues that will directly affect the future of crime and justice in 2010. Most important, we discuss the difficulty of projecting into the future given the many unpredictable influences that may shape crime and the criminal justice system. Nevertheless, we do suggest that some things are known to influence the future.

Social forces, for example, have always played a major role in shaping both the present and the future. More children within the crime-prone age group, greater racial diversity within the population, and limited financial resources will each have a direct influence on the nature of crime as well as how the criminal justice system responds to it. Moreover, communities will demand greater accountability of the system.

In addition to this greater accountability, criminal justice will incorporate evolving technologies to arrest, prosecute, adjudicate, and supervise criminal populations. In this way, the traditional roles of criminal justice workers will also change dramatically in the future. Increased specialization of work assignments will be likely, and the work itself will become more complex. This increased complexity and specialization will foster greater conservatism and increased reliance on the private sector to meet the challenge of crime.

What will the student of criminal justice need today to confront the realities of crime and justice in the year 2010? We conclude the book with both a statement of values and a discussion of a future curriculum for students. These views represent an amalgam of concerns, interests, and positions created by the contributors to this volume. For us, the future is understood by knowing both the past and the present; more important, the future is ours to create. We challenge students to become actively involved in their future. It is they who will ultimately affect the future of crime and criminal justice in the United States.

15

Preparing for the Year 2010

STAN STOJKOVIC

University of Wisconsin—Milwaukee

JOHN M. KLOFAS

Rochester Institute of Technology

How are we to prepare for the future? Even weather forecasters seem to be wrong as often as they are right. How can anyone be expected to predict something as complex as the future of crime and the mechanisms for controlling it? The answer is, of course, that one cannot be expected to make such predictions. Those who study the future—that is, futurists—do not try for the level of accuracy achieved by weather forecasters. While you may rely on the forecaster to help you decide to carry an umbrella, most futurists do not seek such a direct influence over your behavior. The role of most futurists, instead, is to describe possible alternative futures and to consider the ways they can be achieved or avoided.

To do that, those who study the future must first come to terms with three important issues. They must decide how they will understand the past and present. They must make judgments on how direct or how convoluted the path is from the present to the future. And they must decide what their role may be in altering that path.

UNDERSTANDING THE
PAST AND THE PRESENT

Everyone seems to agree that they key to understanding the future depends, to some degree, on our understanding of the past and of the present, but agreement may end there. Historians may interpret past events in vastly different ways. Is the origin of the juvenile court to be found in the benevolence of the upper classes in the nineteenth century or in their concern with controlling and Americanizing the new immigrant population? Likewise, there is disagreement over how to understand the present. Is urban unrest the result of decaying social values or the declining quality of city life? Differing interpretations of the present and the past cannot help but lead to different expectations of the future. Perhaps the most important consequence of considering the future, then, is that it forces us to question our understanding of the past and present. It forces us to identify important influences and events and to decide how we will interpret them. As Conley suggests in Chapter 2, the past is most certainly prologue, but little agreement may exist as to what the past exactly is and how it shapes both the present and the future. One thing is clear: You cannot look into a crystal ball without first seeing your own reflection.

PROJECTING FROM THE PRESENT

Even if we could agree on a common understanding of the past and present, however, their relevance to the future may not be obvious. The authors of these chapters, and anyone who would speculate about the future, cannot help but base their vision on some assumption about how much the future is determined by the past and present. How much will crime in the year 2010 be a function of the changing demographics of our population? On the other hand, are there ideas, events, or policies that may interrupt a straight-line march to the future? In the late 1970s, forecasters predicted that growth in the prison population would slow as baby boomers matured out of the crime-prone age group (16 to 24 years). The war on drugs, and an increasingly conservative political climate, however, intervened to continue an upward spiral in the prison population. Such a precipitous increase in the prison population cannot be explained solely by changing characteristics of the population. Rather, one must consider the influence of variables that are beyond the domain of demographers. The future, therefore, may be a product of influences that lay outside of a straightforward projection from the present.

Does this mean that the contributions of demographers are of little value or that prediction is impossible? Clearly not. It suggests only that we can also attempt to describe futures that are not necessarily a straight line path from the present. One model that may be helpful is offered by *chaos theory,* which was first applied in the field of physics. Unlike traditional linear models, chaos modeling seeks to explain the future by examining the uncertainty of influence created by a host of variables that may shape the future. This approach is significant in that, unlike the straight-line method, it not only assumes the relevance of multiple variables in forecasting the future, but also questions the relative importance of these variables and the degree to which random events have a direct impact on the future. It stresses the importance of "playfulness" among the variables. As a result, direct prediction is neither possible nor desirable. The language of chaos theory presupposes uncertainty as a general rule and proceeds based on possible outcomes of events.

The relevant question becomes not "What will follow?" but rather "What may happen if some event occurs?" Multiple contingencies exist. It is not that we cannot predict the future but rather that we must predict multiple futures. The present is relevant because it influences the probability of some event in the future, but those futurists who rely on chaos do not ask simply "What next?" but rather "What if . . . ?" For example, in Chapter 12, Weisheit considers the consequences of both continued criminalization of drugs and the possible effects of their legalization.

There is, however, disagreement over the usefulness of a theory developed in the hard sciences for social sciences such as criminal justice. One should ask, "What event could occur that may sharply alter the course of crime policy? Did the revolt at Attica prison lead to significant change? Will the videotaped beating of Rodney King bring lasting social reform?" Some theorists may be optimistic, but others— such as Vito in his discussion of the death penalty—see little likelihood of major change.

INFLUENCING THE FUTURE

The third issue confronted by those who would study the future involves the question of our own role in creating that future rather than passively accepting it. For some, the role is not one of forecaster but of engineer of the future, creating it by the way that we interact with the present. The question for these futurists is not "What will happen?" but "How well can we recognize the consequences of our actions and chart our course?"

Beginning in the 1950s, for example, we prepared for nuclear war. Our military and political leaders armed the nation. Students learned to hide under their desks at the first hint of a nearby nuclear explosion. Some parents added family-sized fallout shelters to their suburban dream houses. It did not take long, however, before some started to question whether such preparations made nuclear war all the more likely. Were we preparing for or taking the first step toward Armageddon with such concepts as a winnable nuclear war? By accepting such a concept, we were defining the parameters for the foreseeable future. In this way, the concept of a winnable nuclear war served the purpose not only of forecasting the future, but also of constraining thinking about what the likely futures would be with regard to nuclear policy. Such forecasting projects as well as defines the way we view and interact with our future. We are, in effect, active participants in the development of possible futures.

As with nuclear policy, the issues of crime and justice may be influenced by those who examine the contours of the future. The futurists in this book vary in their approaches. They may become direct actors in the development of what is likely as it relates to the future of crime and how it is dealt with by society, or they may deny such an active role. In Chapter 10, for example, Lombardo stresses the importance of viewing the organizations of criminal justice as being directed by conscious decision makers. In his worldview, the future is not directed by forces entirely beyond the control of those in positions of power. Rather, the future reflects choices made by those actors. His interpretation is grounded in the belief that criminal justice administrators have a role in constructing their future realities, and, as a result, they have not only the capability but also the obligation to shape the future in such a way that is conducive to long-term stability in society. This view of the future takes on a prescriptive quality and requires those who control our criminal justice system to be more active, rather than passive, in determining the future.

Such views of the future combine prescription with prediction of the future. Thus, prescriptive futurists seek to provide specific recommendations as to how the future should look. They have definite ideas, and these ideas become critical to the shaping of the future world. With regard to criminal justice, some authors also want to comment on what they believe to be an ill-advised construction of the future by policy makers. For example, in Chapter 4, Acker argues that much of the direction of judicial policy is influenced by a conservative ideology, one that has minimized the rights of the convicted. His projection of the future is a gloomy one; it is one of limited due-process protections for offenders. His position is one of disagreement with the dominant view put forward by the courts.

COMMON THEMES

Those who would face the future, then, must deal with these three questions:

1. What understanding of the past and present do you carry into the analysis?
2. How flexible are you going to be in exploring ideas and events that may alter the future?
3. How much responsibility are you willing to accept for shaping the future?

The authors of these chapters sometimes differ in their answers to these questions. At the same time, however, common themes do emerge. We can identify seven themes that run through many of the authors' visions of the future.

Predictable Influences

It is clear that some things can be identified that will have a definite effect on the shape of criminal justice in the year 2010. The most direct statement on this matter is offered in Chapter 5 by Britt, who focuses on the impact of demographic changes on crime rates. The age distribution of the population contributed to the increasing crime rate through the 1960s and early 1970s and to their subsequent leveling off. As the children of baby boomers mature, we can expect additional increases. In Chapter 1, Cole offers a more expansive view of the predictability of influences. He looks beyond demographics to include economic, technological, and legal changes as they will influence the courts. The influences include such factors as the federal deficit, the decline of heavy industry, and the rise of technology-based businesses.

The suggestion that runs through these and other chapters is that some influences are clear, that they must be taken into account, and that we can prepare to address them. The list of certainties may be small, but nonetheless there is evidence of common ground upon which to base visions of the future.

Unpredictable Influences

While there are some relevant and predictable concerns with regard to crime and criminal justice, there are also unpredictable events that may clearly impact on the operations of future criminal justice systems. In Chapter 3, for example, Wells highlights the importance of uncertainty in the development of models of crime causation. He describes the many uncertain and unpredictable ways in which we may come to understand future crime. Appealing to the idea that crime causation models have changed over time, he notes the importance of viewing crime in a number of different ways. Crime of the future is going to look much different than it does today. With changes in technology, we will see the advent of new definitions of crime, and the criminal justice system will be asked to respond to these new crimes. This will require innovative and imaginative responses on the part of workers in the future criminal justice system.

Imagination is at the cornerstone of what Weisheit in Chapter 12 projects as possible futures facing the criminal justice system. By focusing on the conditional nature of crime and the system's response to it, he stresses the importance of examining likely scenarios as they relate to criminal justice. He suggests that the world of criminal justice would be vastly different from today if we were to legalize certain drugs. By noting the conditional nature of drug legalization, Weisheit, on one hand, introduces the uncertain nature of the response by criminal justice officials. As a result, it will become increasingly difficult to predict what the future may look like with regard to criminal justice policy if drugs become legal. On the other hand, while the world may be uncertain, Lombardo suggests that this does not relieve criminal justice personnel from doing what is essentially correct based on a specified set of beliefs and values. He recognizes the importance of uncertainty concerning criminal justice policy; nonetheless, he feels that the future should be directed by those who are obligated to manage the system. In short, uncertainty should not produce inaction. Instead, uncertainty should foster a greater sense of awareness that multiple forces will affect the future and that managers should become active in shaping and influencing those forces toward socially productive ends.

The Relevance of Social Forces

Several chapters identify social factors as likely to have a significant impact on crime and the nature of the criminal justice system. Beyond demographics, these factors relate to increasing problems of poverty and the emergence of what has been referred to as a permanent underclass. The authors argue that the social structure of American society is inevitably reflected in its criminal justice system.

In one approach to this analysis, McCoy in Chapter 7 indicates that courts must be prepared to face an increasingly diverse clientele and increasingly difficult problems. Forces of immigration, race, and poverty will contribute to growing tensions in society, and it will fall on the court to address these issues. In a more pessimistic view, Kalinich and Embert (Chapter 9) focus on the effects of changes in urban communities and their surrounding suburbs. The resolution of geographically and socially based tensions may be the creation of dual systems of social control as illustrated by jails. Class-based tensions may be institutionalized in a dual system of confinement in which modern, state-of-the art jails serve a suburban population, and decaying urban facilities confine the underclass trapped in the cities.

In Chapter 14, Pope also finds social forces changing the nature of judicial administration. Once the most hopeful and optimistic part of the justice system, juvenile justice is becoming increasingly harsh and punitive in its orientation. Furthermore, orientation is having a differential effect on minority children. In his vision of the future, waivers to adult court will increase, and secure facilities will expand and house urban minority youth, while suburban white and middle-class youth will increasingly take advantage of diversion programs and alternative sanctions. Only through conscious changes in policy regarding the processing of youth in the juvenile justice system and accompanying changes in policy to address urban poverty will substantial change in this prediction be possible. Perhaps Pope's most optimistic note concerns the role of research in identifying and tracking these problems so that appropriate policy initiatives can be formulated.

Increasing Accountability

An important concern for the future will focus on the issue of accountability of criminal justice personnel. We have already seen growth in accountability across the criminal justice system. Issues of police corruption and abuse are at the forefront of discussion among police reformers. In Chapter 6, Crank attempts to address this issue by examining the evolving and changing nature of police work. Employing the concept of community policing, he discusses the many issues and problems that current police departments face, but, more important, he underscores the increasing demand for accountability among the public. What will be important for the future will be how this concept will be able to make police more accountable to their various communities while still being accepting of their mission as protectors of the citizenry and pivotal agents in the reduction of crime.

In Chapter 11, Clear examines the issue of accountability by focusing on the rapid technological and legal changes that will occur in the delivery of probation services. He suggests that such services will become more technologically driven and constrained by legal decisions. The probation officer of the future will become more accountable through technological innovations that will limit his or her discretionary authority. Such innovations will force a redefinition of the traditional probation officer's role and reconsideration of the tasks associated with probation work. It is clear from reading Clear's chapter that accountability and specialization will be the main features of the probation officer job in the year 2010.

Complexity and Specialization

Another common element across many of the authors' views of the future deals with the very structure of the criminal justice system. Not long ago, police could be divided into patrol and detective divisions, courts were easily divided into those that handled misdemeanors or felonies, and corrections was split into incarceration or probation. That simplicity is lost, and the complexity of the criminal justice system will continue to increase. Community policing involves new and complex organizational structures. Courts are becoming specialized to handle limited categories of offenses, and intermediate sanctions will continue the trend toward specialization in corrections.

In Chapter 11, Clear describes the day of a community control specialist. Classification systems aid decision making, and technology guides the worker's routine. Special services are provided based on offense and supervision requirements. Drug offenders, sex offenders, and violent criminals are each targeted by specialized resources. Specialization, however, is not just a function of corrections. Specialized police skills will be needed, and, as Goodstein and Hepburn point out in Chapter 8, specialized proceedings will exist for certain kinds of offenses, and judges will have at their disposal a wide variety of specialized sanctions.

A Concern with Political Conservatism

Another concern of several authors deals with the continuing influence of conservative ideology on criminal justice. This concern is most evident among those authors dealing with law-related topics. The life tenure of conservative Supreme Court justices may be the strongest indicator of the continuing relevance of political conservatism. That is clearly the perspective taken in Chapter 13 when Vito examines the future of the death penalty in the United States. He sees executions occurring at an increasing rate as few major challenges to the ultimate sanction now exist and as the justices' tolerance for delay wears even thinner. In his analysis of the law, Acker also points to the continued influence of conservatism. He anticipates a continued wearing away of constitutional protections from a court over which the decisions of its predecessors hold little sway.

The effects of conservatism can also be felt in less likely places, including academic criminology. In his analysis of changes in theoretical explanations of crime, Wells (Chapter 3) points to the increasing pressure to reject key assumptions of positivism such as behavioral determinism and a neutral stance on questions of morality. The chapter makes an important contribution in pointing out the pervasiveness of ideological influences and thus the likelihood that their influences may become quite deeply rooted in scientific approaches to crime and to the efforts to control it.

The Role of the Private Sector

With the increased growth in technology, we have seen the development of many innovative approaches to dealing with criminal offenders. Technological developments have fostered and been fostered by private companies that seek to profit from the criminal justice system. Privatization of some correctional services, for example, is nothing new, as Conley points out in Chapter 2. We have had private entrepreneurs involved with criminal justice for well over one hundred years. What is new today is the spread of privatization to many more areas within criminal justice and its accompanying technological advances.

Clear's Chapter 11 is the most compelling in examining the influence of these technologically based systems on probation work. His view of the future portrays how technology may influence probation work, but, more important, it stresses the role of private companies taking over much of probation work. This departure from tradition will have a significant impact on the operations of probation work into the future. But the spread of private interests to traditionally public-run institutions is not limited to probation. Kalinich and Embert (Chapter 9) express similar concerns in their chapter on the future jail. Their vision of the future is an ominous one.

They project that jails will become separated along the public–private dimension. Large urban jails will be the home of the traditional criminal "rabble," while the suburban jail will house the less serious offender who is better off socially and economically. Such a polarization of our communities suggests that criminal justice may be at the forefront of separating the haves from the have-nots. This gloomy picture does not sit well with many in society, and it is possible that the privatization movement may serve as the impetus for major social, political, and economic changes.

PREPARING FOR INDIVIDUAL FUTURES

The idea of the future may seem like an abstraction, and looking into it could seem little more than an intellectual exercise. But there are also more practical implications. In personal terms, we can talk about our individual futures or, more specifically, our careers in the field of criminal justice. From that perspective, predicting the future involves identifying the types of knowledge and skills that will be needed in fifteen or twenty years. That is, preparing for the future means acknowledging that the jobs available today may be very different tomorrow and that you must prepare not only for your first job in the field but also for leadership positions in the future.

As the authors in this book met to discuss their visions of the future, we also sought to glean from them what they felt was most important to individuals preparing for their own futures. We could have included a long list of skills and knowledge that might help one prepare for a career in the year 2010. We settled, however, for a short list of four basic ideas to which one should be committed and to four basic skill areas. Attention to these cannot guarantee any particular future and does not support any particular vision of the future. It can, however, give all of us confidence that tomorrow's leadership will be thoughtful and prepared to deal with the difficult issues facing criminal justice in the year 2010. Here are four basic value positions that may help guide criminal justice leaders in the future.

A Commitment to Democratic Principles

Criminal justice is a public enterprise. In its most basic form it involves the exercise of coercive powers on behalf of the people. Leaders of criminal justice organizations will have to commit themselves to the principles of democracy—that is, to openness and to debate over public policy. When police make arrests or when a state executes an offender, it is done on behalf of the citizenry. It is incumbent on those would lead the field to be certain that the citizenry is informed and thoughtful in its understanding and expectations of criminal justice policy. This means educating the public about criminal justice and being intolerant of those who would hide the business of justice from their community.

A Commitment to Research

The criminal justice system is heavily influenced by ideology and politics, but those influences can be tempered by data. The collection and analysis of information about crime and criminals and about the criminal justice process will play an increasingly important role in the future. Research, including evaluation studies, therefore becomes an essential component of providing services to the community. Such research serves as a foundation on which future policies and procedures can be evaluated and corrective measures taken to improve the delivery of services. In this way, research is more than heuristic; it is now an important ingredient in the process of completing the multiple tasks expected of criminal justice leaders.

A Commitment to Cultural Diversity

It is well known that the criminal justice system has a disproportionate effect on the poor and on minorities in the United States and that those in whom the coercive power of the state is vested are disproportionately white and middle-class. The integrity of this system of social control depends on its being fair and equitable. Where disparity exists, we must be certain that it is not the result of either deliberate or unintentional differences in the treatment of citizens. While the criminal justice system cannot be expected to address inequities that may exist in the larger society, neither should it contribute to them. Leaders of the field must take responsibility for safeguarding the integrity of the criminal justice system and for working toward a system whose employees are sensitive to the cultures of those caught up in it and served by it.

A Commitment to Exploring Basic Values

Much of what the criminal justice system does can be seen as settling conflicts among citizens. Basic values of justice and fairness are central to such a system of social control. Anyone working in the system has the obligation to explore such basic values to understand their importance in criminal justice and to understand their meaning and value to them as individuals. Those who work in the criminal justice system must be responsible for their part in that system. Lawyers must not tolerate injustice, the police must not accept brutality, and prison officials must be responsible for prison conditions. For that to be true, we cannot rely on citizens with video cameras to expose and correct the system. Everyone must appreciate the importance of values that make the criminal justice system credible.

DEVELOPING
SKILLS FOR THE FUTURE

The topics discussed above refer more to basic outlooks than to specific knowledge or abilities. Even as basic beliefs, however, they suggest four specific areas for study and training that will help to develop the knowledge and skills necessary for the future.

The Study of History

It should be clear that an appreciation of the past is an essential ingredient to preparation for the future. This means that criminal justice leaders will have to have more than a basic understanding of history. They will have to be able to interpret and analyze the past. This includes not only the history of criminal justice, such as the development of the police or the history of efforts to control drugs, but also larger social histories. For example, knowledge of the origins of democracy as well as of contemporary democratic revolutions can be important to understanding the role of social control in the United States. Understanding of the links between reforms such as asylums, almshouses, and prisons can provide a valuable context for understanding contemporary reforms. Studying the cultural histories of minority and immigrant populations can help us to understand current social issues. An understanding of the past enables the criminal justice worker to appreciate where he or she came from and to incorporate things learned over time so that future failures are minimized. One cannot know where to go unless one has a firm grasp of both the past and the present.

Engaging in Political Debate

It is without question that the criminal justice system operates in a political arena. Policies emerge from a political process, and criminal justice competes with other governmental functions for support. Strong capabilities in this area are needed if criminal justice is to succeed in capturing needed resources during times of fiscal austerity.

Politics is also relevant in a deeper sense. There remain fundamental disagreements over issues such as what behavior should be considered criminal and how it should be handled. Debates over drug legalization, treatment of white-collar criminals, and capital punishment are only a few examples of the lack of consensus. These and other issues dealing with fundamental issues of justice as well as the allocation of resources are addressed through political discussions. It is important that future leaders of the field are prepared to organize and present arguments on such issues and to engage in debate over them in a thoughtful and productive manner. Those skills are enhanced by training and practice.

Study of Research Methodology

The political abilities of leaders in the criminal justice field are strengthened by analytical abilities. Never before have these skills been as necessary as they are today and will continue to be, and never before has the capacity to develop these skills been so close at hand. The technological revolution of the 1980s and early 1990s has put computers in nearly every work setting. Today, cash registers in supermarkets control inventory and track customers' preferences. In industry, everything from quality control to personnel records is done with the aid of computers. No longer is the collection and analysis of data left to technicians and researchers. They have become common tasks for all levels of workers. In criminal justice, tomorrow's leaders will need the tools to define and study complex problems of resource allocation and evaluation. They will need skills in research design and statistical analysis. As technology improves and increasing demands are placed on public resources, demands for accountability will also increase. Tomorrow's leaders will need to defend their policy choices through sound research and quantitative analysis.

Study of Philosophy and Ethics

Along with the need for increased awareness and appreciation of analytical capabilities, there will also be a need for those in criminal justice to have a thorough understanding of the philosophical foundations of the criminal justice system. That includes an understanding of the philosophical positions regarding the roots of crime as well as ethical positions regarding justice and fairness in the behavior of individuals and in the process of criminal justice.

Contemporary views of criminality now stress the integration of both classically oriented assumptions about free will with more positivistic notions on the etiology of crime. This more modern view requires the acceptance of a new set of assumptions about the nature of crime, the role of the state in the definition of crime, and different implications for crime control. Now, more than ever in the past, research has forced the criminal justice system to examine the importance of both individual choice and deterministic influences on the cause of crime. Being aware of the importance of our assumptions about crime allows us to construct policies that are not only more effective, but also more equitable.

The concern for equity in criminal justice operations suggests the need for attention to the proper ethical behavior for criminal justice workers. Higher expectations from the community will demand greater accountability, including ethical accountability, among criminal justice personnel. Exposure to and education in philosophy and ethics will help them prepare for that role.

INTO THE FUTURE

In a recent popular book, *Megatrends 2000,* John Naisbitt begins with the ominous observation that "We stand at the dawn of a new era." For generations, the new millennium has symbolized the future. Perhaps it will be a future of tamed technology, as Walter Cronkite seemed to suggest through his narration of the popular 1970s television show, *The 21st Century,* or perhaps reality will match Stanley Kubrick's vision of a computer in revolt in the film *2001: A Space Odyssey*. In either case, the point of demarcation is now upon us, and we have the opportunity of peering into the next millennium armed with appropriate methodologies and an appreciation for the past and the present.

But even as these chapters have struggled to present a rational view of the future, one influenced by changing demographics, or policy choices or even unplanned events, there remains an element of fascination and anticipation, something beyond rational discourse that pulls us toward the future. Philosopher of science Karl Popper has described it as follows:

> [T]he open future is, almost as a promise, as a temptation, as a lure, present; indeed actively present at every moment. The old world picture that puts before us a mechanism operating with causes that are in the past—the past kicking and driving us with kicks into the future—the past that is gone, is no longer adequate to our indeterministic world. . . . It is not the kicks from the back, from the past, that impel us, but the attraction, the lure of the future and its attractive possibilities that entice us: this is what keeps life—and indeed, the world—unfolding.[1]

---

1. Speech at the World Congress of Philosophy, Brighton, UK; cited in Richard Slaughter, "Changing Images of Futures in the 20th Century," *Futures, 23*(5), 117]

DISCUSSION QUESTIONS

1. Describe different ways in which you may think of history as relevant to understanding the future in the field of criminal justice?

2. Which view of the future is the closest to the way you have thought about it: a future that develops from complicated and uncontrollable forces or a future that is the result of deliberate planning and decision making? What are the implications of these different views when examining the criminal justice system?

3. Seven factors are reported as reflecting common concerns among many of the authors of this book. Try to put these in order of importance based on what you think will exercise the greatest influence on the criminal justice system in the coming years.

4. Try to predict your own future. What kind of career do you expect for the year 2010? Try to write a scenario for one day on the job in some field of criminal justice.

5. Describe the experiences and skills, both academic and nonacademic, that will help you to prepare for that future.

☆

About the Contributors

James R. Acker is Associate Professor of Criminal Justice at the State University of New York at Albany. He earned a J.D. from Duke University and a Ph.D. in criminal justice from the State University of New York at Albany. He has published numerous articles on the relationship between law and social science. He currently is working on a series of articles addressing death penalty legislation. His publications have appeared in *Law and Society Review, Law and Human Behavior, Criminal Law Bulletin,* and *Vanderbilt Law Review.*

Chester L. Britt, III, received a Ph.D. in sociology from the University of Arizona and is currently Assistant Professor of Sociology at the University of Illinois. His research interests focus on the relationship between demographics and crime. He has recently finished a project examining the relationship between drug testing and offenders' pretrial release behaviors. His recent writings have appeared in the *Journal of Research in Crime* and *Delinquency and Quantitative Criminology.*

Todd R. Clear is Professor of Criminal Justice at Rutgers University's Graduate School of Criminal Justice. He received a Ph.D. in criminal justice from the State University of New York at Albany. He has been awarded numerous academic and professional distinctions, including the Cincinnati Award from the American Probation and Parole Association. Coauthor of *Controlling the Offender in the Community* (Lexington Books) and *American Corrections* (Brooks/Cole Publishing), he has written many articles on corrections and currently is examining the importance of religion among prisoners.

George F. Cole is Professor of Political Science at the University of Connecticut. He is editor of *Criminal Justice: Law & Politics* (Brooks/Cole Publishing), now in its sixth edition. In addition, he has written extensively on the courts and has been published in a broad range of academic journals.

John A. Conley is Professor and Chair of the Criminal Justice Department at the State University of New York College at Buffalo. He received a Ph.D. from Michigan State University. His principal research interests are in the history of criminal justice, penal history, and law enforcement. He is the editor of *The 1967 President's Crime Commission's Impact on Criminal Justice* (Anderson Publishing) and a recipient of the Founder's Award from the Academy of Criminal Justice Sciences.

John P. Crank, Boise State University, received a Ph.D. in sociology from the University of Colorado. His primary research interests focus on the organization and management of police systems. He has published many articles on the nature and functioning of policing in such criminal justice and criminology journals as the *Journal of Criminal Justice, Justice Quarterly, Journal of Criminal Law and Criminology,* and *Quantitative Criminology.* His current work examines the symbolic nature of policy reform as well as the attitudes of police chiefs.

Paul Embert was the training specialist for the School of Criminal Justice, Michigan State University. He received his M.S. degree from Michigan State University and had extensive correctional experience within the military system of justice. Before his death, he had written many articles on correctional law and jail management and had also provided many training seminars to jail personnel. He was coauthor of *Behind the Walls: Correctional Institutions and Facilities, A Many Faceted Phenomena* (Sheffield Publishing).

Lynne Goodstein received a Ph.D. in criminal justice from the City University of New York Graduate School. Currently, she is Director of the Women's Studies Program at Pennsylvania State University. She is coauthor of *Determinate Sentencing and Imprisonment: A Failure of Reform* (Anderson Publishing) and coeditor of *The American Prison: Issues in Research and Policy* (Plenum Publishing). In addition, her writings on inmate adjustment to prison have appeared in *Criminology, Criminal Justice and Behavior,* and the *Journal of Research in Crime and Delinquency.*

John R. Hepburn is Professor of Justice Studies at Arizona State University. He received a Ph.D. in sociology from the University of Iowa. His research focuses on prisoner adjustment to incarceration and attitudes of correctional workers. He is coauthor of *Determinate Sentencing and Imprisonment: A Failure of Reform* (Anderson Publishing) and has published articles in *Criminology, Journal of Criminal Justice,* and *Sociological Quarterly.*

David B. Kalinich earned a Ph.D. in social science with cognates in economics, public administration, and criminal justice from Michigan State University. He is currently Chair of the Criminal Justice Department at Northern Michigan University. His principal interests are in jail management and the prevention of jail suicides. He has published extensively on the treatment of the mentally ill in jail facilities. He is the author of *Sneaking Inmates Down the Alley: Problems and Prospects in Jail Management, Principles of County Jail Administration and Management,* and *Surviving in Corrections: A Guide for Corrections Professionals* (all with Charles Thomas Publishing), as well as many articles and books on criminal justice administration and management.

John M. Klofas holds a Ph.D. in criminal justice from the State University of New York at Albany. He is Professor of Criminal Justice at the Rochester Institute of Technology. His research interests include the attitudes of correctional officers, criminal justice management and administration, and the effects of drug enforcement on local systems of social control. He is coauthor of *Criminal Justice Organizations: Administration and Management* (Brooks/Cole Publishing) and coeditor of *The Administration and Management of Criminal Justice Organizations: A Book of Readings* (Waveland Publishing) and *Sneaking Inmates Down the Alley: Problems and Prospects in Jail Management* (Charles Thomas Publishing).

Lucien X. Lombardo is Professor of Criminal Justice and Sociology at Old Dominion University. He earned a Ph.D. in criminal justice from the State University of New York at Albany. He has published research on correctional officers, prisoners, and prison environments. He is author of *Guards Imprisoned: Correctional Officers at Work* (Pilgrimage Press) and is currently working on a book examining differing perspectives on prison. He also is coeditor of *Prison Violence in America* (2nd ed.) (Anderson Publishing).

Candace McCoy received a Ph.D. in jurisprudence and social policy from the University of California at Berkeley and a J.D. from the University of Cincinnati. She is Assistant Professor of Criminal Justice at Rutgers University's Graduate School of Criminal Justice. She has published extensively on the relationship between law and social control and currently is working on a project to assess the future of the criminal courts in California. Her forthcoming book is titled *The Politics of Plea Bargaining* (University of Pennsylvania Press).

Carl E. Pope received a Ph.D. in criminal justice from the State University of New York at Albany. He is Professor of Criminal Justice at the University of Wisconsin at Milwaukee. His principal research interests are race and crime and juvenile justice. He has worked on many projects assessing the disproportionality of minorities within the criminal justice system. He currently is working with the Office of Juvenile Justice and Delinquency Prevention on reducing overrepresentation of minority youths in secure-detention facilities and the National Institute of Justice's "weed and seed" efforts.

Stan Stojkovic received a Ph.D. in social science with cognates in criminal justice, public administration, and philosophy from Michigan State University. He is Associate Professor of Criminal Justice at the University of Wisconsin—Milwaukee. His primary research interests are in corrections and the management and administration of criminal justice organizations. He is coauthor of *Corrections: An Introduction* (Anderson Publishing) and *Criminal Justice Organizations: Administration and Management* (Brooks/Cole Publishing) and coeditor of *The Administration and Management of Criminal Justice Organizations: A Book of Readings* (Waveland Publishing). He also has served as a consultant and trainer to many correctional agencies and currently is working on the development of an index to aid jail administrators in managing their facilities.

Gennaro F. Vito holds a Ph.D. in public administration from Ohio State University and currently is Professor of Justice Administration at the University of Louisville. He has published widely in the areas of the death penalty and the evaluation of intermediate sanctions. His written work has appeared in such journals as *Justice Quarterly, Criminology,* and the *Journal of Criminal Justice.*

Ralph A. Weisheit received a Ph.D. in sociology from Washington State University and currently is Professor of Criminal Justice at Illinois State University. His research interests include drug usage and the criminal justice system, including the cultivation of marijuana in rural states. He has published many works on the issue, including *Domestic Marijuana: A Neglected Industry* (Greenwood Press). He is now examining rural policing and crime patterns.

L. Edward Wells is Associate Professor of Criminal Justice at Illinois State University. He holds a Ph.D. in sociology from the University of Wisconsin at Madison. His research interests are in theories of criminal behavior and rural crime and delinquency. His recent writings have appeared in *Criminology, Justice Quarterly, Journal of Research in Crime and Delinquency,* and *Social Problems.*